Teach Yourself UNIX® Shell Programming in 14 Days

Kamran Husain

SAMS PUBLISHING
201 West 103rd Street
Indianapolis, Indiana 46290

To my parents.

FIRST EDITION

International Standard Book Number: 0-672-30583-6

Library of Congress Catalog Number: 94-67087

97 96 95 94 4 3 2 1

Interpretation of the printing code: the rightmost double-digit number is the year of the book's printing; the rightmost single digit, the number of the book's printing. For example, a printing code of 94-1 shows that the first printing of the book occurred in 1994.

Composed in AGaramond and MCPdigital by Macmillan Computer Publishing

Printed in the United States of America

Trademarks

Publisher
Richard K. Swadley

Acquisitions Manager
Stacy Hiquet

Managing Editor
Cindy Morrow

Acquisitions Editor
Rosemarie Graham

Development Editor
Scott Parker

Production Editor
Mary Inderstrodt

Editors
Deborah Frisby
Ryan Rader
Tonya Simpson

Editorial Coordinator
Bill Whitmer

Editorial Assistants
Carol Ackerman
Sharon Cox
Lynette Quinn

Technical Editor
Hugo Toledo

Marketing Manager
Gregg Bushyeager

Cover Designer
Dan Armstrong

Book Designer
Alyssa Yesh

Director of Production and Manufacturing
Jeff Valler

Imprint Manager
Juli Cook

Manufacturing Coordinator
Paul Gilchrist

Production Analysts
Angela Bannon
Dennis Clay Hager
Mary Beth Wakefield

Graphics Image Specialists
Clint Lahen
Tim Montgomery
Dennis Sheehan
Greg Simsic
Jeff Yesh

Production
Georgianna Briggs
Elaine M. Brush
Michael Brumitt
Cheryl Cameron
Mary Ann Cosby
Rob Falco
Donna Harbin
Aleata Howard
Danny Kidd
Louisa Klucznik
Shawn MacDonald
Stephanie J. McComb
Wendy Ott
Kaylene Rieman
Kim Scott
Susan Shepard
Jackie Tompkins
Dennis J. Wesner
Holly Wittenberg

Indexer
Greg Eldred

Overview

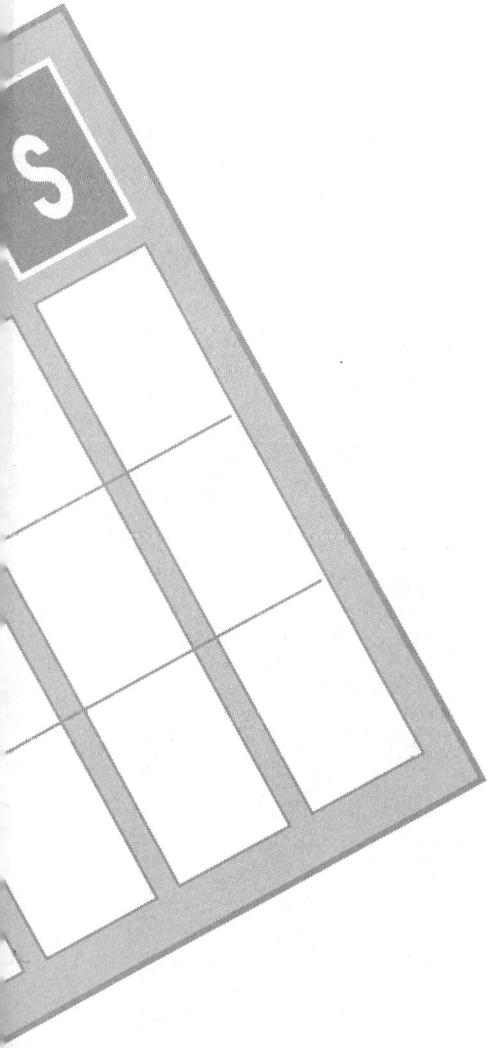
S

Contents

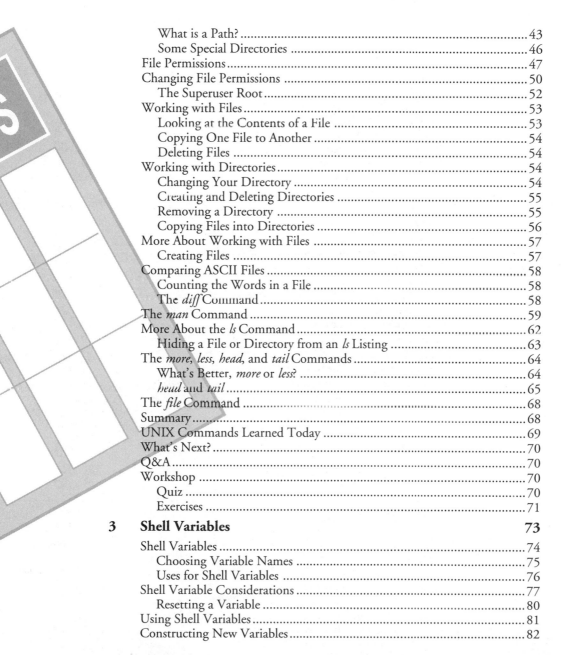

Acknowledgments

The first person to get credit for me being able to write *anything* belongs to my mother, Saleha Husain. Her own enthusiasm for writing and providing an education as a university professor has always been an inspiration to me. She instilled in me the desire to learn, and I cannot thank her enough for it.

I would also like to thank my wife for not deserting me while I spent long hours chained to the computers while writing this book. She took over a lot of worries and kept reminding me "work on your book." This book would not have made it to press without her persistence, patience, and proofreading, as well as the cooperation of my twin daughters, Haya and Hira.

Much credit also goes to Rosemarie Graham for keeping me on schedule, and ensuring that all changes were synchronized and that the process flowed smoothly. She put up with my last-minute changes and other assorted oddities. I would also like to thank Mary Inderstrodt for getting all the editorial changes through on time.

Thank you all very much!

About the Author

Kamran Husain is a software consultant with experience in UNIX systems programming. He has dabbled in all sorts of software for Real-Time systems applications, telecommunications, seismic data acquisition and navigation, X Windows/Motif, and Microsoft Windows applications. During his career, he has worked with assorted hardware, processors, and operating systems. Kamran offers consulting services and training classes in C, C++, and GUI development under UNIX through his company, MPS Inc., in Houston, Texas. He is an alumnus of the University of Texas at Austin.

Kamran also was a contributing author of *UNIX Unleashed* (by Sams Publishing). His next project, a follow-up to this book, is *Teach Yourself the Korn Shell in 14 Days*, also by Sams. He also has licensed his one-day course, "Introduction to UNIX," to training centers in Houston. He has written articles on programming issues for technical magazines such as *Dr. Dobbs*, *Embedded Systems Programming*, and *EDN*.

You can e-mail Kamran at `mpsi@aol`.

Introduction

Welcome to UNIX, the operating system that's been around "forever" and will be "forever." For UNIX programmers and users, once you fall in love with UNIX, it's hard to let go. The powerful tools, flexibility, and environment provide a healthy computing alternative. UNIX's wide assortment of standard tools (400+) is perhaps its strongest features. Added to that are the way the tools all work together to enable you to elegantly create more tools.

The shell is your interface to the heart of UNIX, its kernel. Once you master the shell, you will have the knowledge and tools to take better advantage of the features of UNIX. Once you learn its programming and data manipulation features, you will be able to see solutions to tasks by using the shell. The shell's programming features alone can get you by with a number of day-to-day tasks in UNIX.

The original shell distributed by AT&T was developed by Stephen Bourne at Bell Labs (hence, the name the Bourne shell). The Bourne shell is the standard shell covered in this book. Since the time it was introduced, more features have been added to it. Several other shells have been developed, each with its own way of doing things. One particular shell of interest is the Korn shell, which this book covers briefly. The Korn shell derives its features from the Bourne shell and then adds more features.

This book assumes that you have no prior working knowledge of UNIX and covers the basics of UNIX from the start. Even if you have some working knowledge of UNIX, you will learn from this book. On Day 2, you will learn about the file system and how to navigate directories. Experienced users may want to skip this. It is, however, the basis for the rest of the book.

The `awk` and Korn shell sections (Days 12 and 13) are included to provide a brief introduction only. These two days each deserve a book by themselves. However, you will learn enough from them to get a running start the first time you come across them.

As you work through the examples in this book, please improvise and learn from your mistakes. That is perhaps the only way to learn. After dealing with UNIX on a daily basis, I am constantly learning new ways to do things and about new tools.

I hope that you will learn enough from this book to understand UNIX and shell programming. This is only the beginning; the real fun starts in exploring UNIX yourself.

WEEK 1 AT A GLANCE

Prepare yourself for learning how to do shell programming in UNIX. This first week, you'll get your feet wet with the UNIX operating system and environment. The best way to learn about UNIX is to work with it. What you will require is an account on a UNIX system. Ask for the Bourne shell as your login shell. This will become meaningful to you after the first day is over.

Here are a few words of caution before you start: you will make a lot of mistakes as you go. Added to that, UNIX's cryptic command structure will not make life seem very easy. Expect problems, but do not get discouraged.

However, at the end of the week you will be familiar with the shell environment and some of the common UNIX tools. It will be the start to a long working relationship in the UNIX environment.

Week 1 at a Glance

Day 1 introduces you to the Bourne shell and shows you how to log into UNIX. Day 2 introduces the file and directory system that makes UNIX famous. On Day 3, you will work with shell variables, and on Day 4 you will work with metacharacters. Day 5 gives an introduction to the powerful feature called "Regular Expressions." Day 6 covers the user environment, which enables you to personalize your login session. On Day 7, you will learn about input/output redirection and pipes.

This first week will provide you with the foundation you'll need to develop your own shell scripts and programs. It will be a quick tutorial on UNIX, but if you learn one day at a time, you should not have any problems.

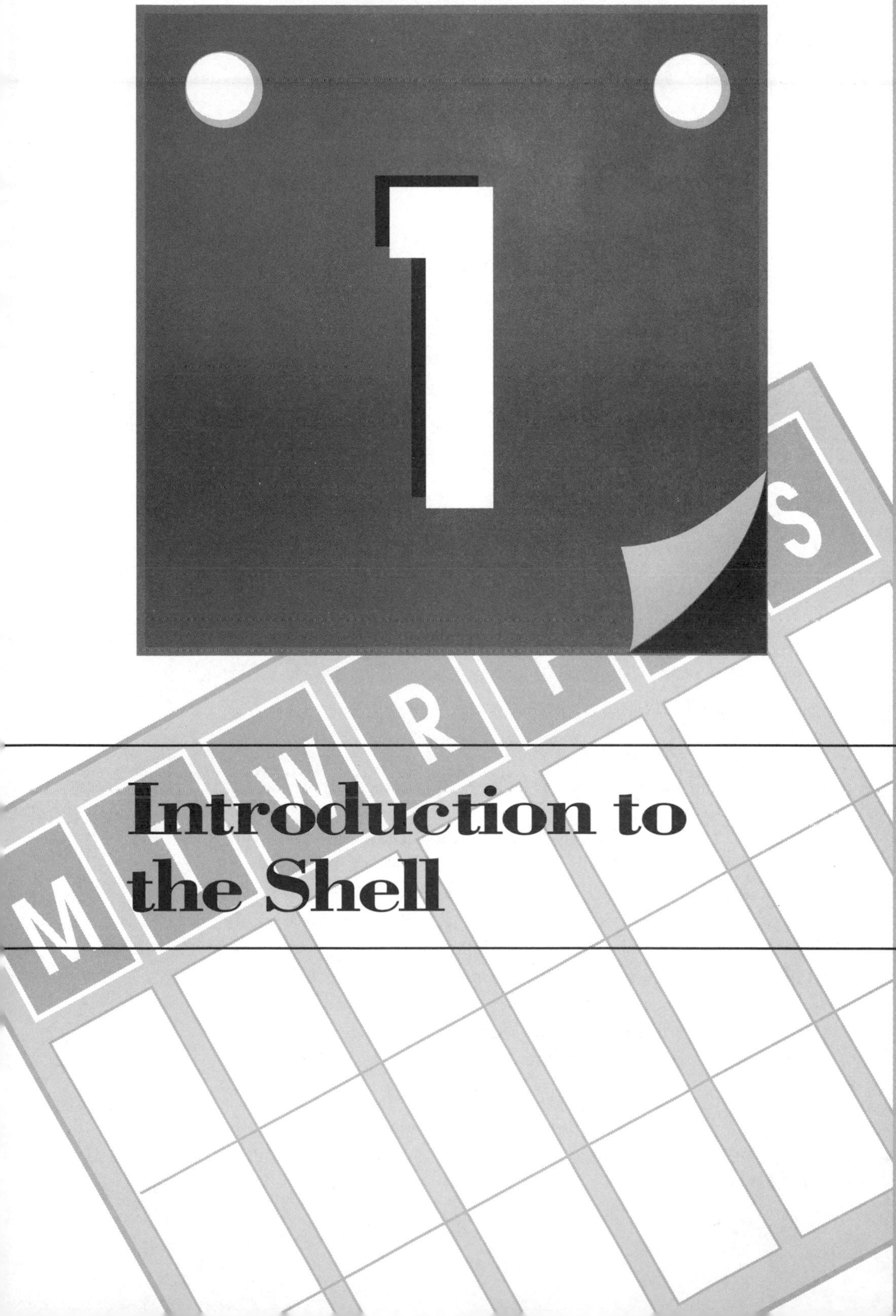

WEEK
1

Introduction to the Shell

You will learn about the following today:

- ☐ Introductory UNIX concepts
- ☐ How to log into UNIX
- ☐ How to differentiate between program and command
- ☐ What is a shell?
- ☐ Types of shells
- ☐ How to use a shell
- ☐ How to determine the type of shell
- ☐ How to use another shell
- ☐ How to recognize command-line arguments
- ☐ How to use more than one command per line
- ☐ UNIX desktop functions
- ☐ How to change your password
- ☐ How to stop long scrolling screen output
- ☐ How to log off UNIX

Introduction to UNIX

During the late 1960s, UNIX was developed at AT&T Bell Labs on a DEC PDP-7 computer. Until the early 1980s, UNIX was confined to university departments and laboratories connected with the Department of Defense. UNIX's popularity spread as machines became faster and more capable of handling complex tasks and as AT&T pushed into the commercial market. UNIX is a multitasking system, which means that a user can run more than one process at a time. UNIX is also a multiuser system. That is, it enables more than one user to be working on it at one time. It has the capability to distinguish between multiple users and can identify the data of one user from another. Therefore, many users can be working on the same thing at the same time.

UNIX is based on a few basic parts. Once you learn these parts, a lot of the mystery surrounding UNIX simply vanishes. In no time, you will be using UNIX comfortably. In fact, the simplicity of these concepts has enabled several versions of UNIX to be developed and customized.

The three major parts are

- *The kernel:* The part of the system that manages system resources, including all the hardware resources for a computer, such as its hard drive, memory, processing, and scheduling.
- *The file system:* The organizing structure for data in the system.
- *The shell:* The command interpreter and primary user interface to the kernel. Although the shell is a program, it's very closely tied to the kernel and will be the focus of this book.

Logging In

One of the first things you do when you work with UNIX is to log into UNIX and identify yourself. As stated earlier, UNIX is a multiuser system and can track many types of users.

When you first face UNIX, it asks for your user name with one word—`login`—which looks like this:

```
login: _
```

In fact, the exact text for the prompt could be completely different from the text shown here. Just look for the string `login:`. This is the UNIX way to request input. In some cases, you will see a welcome prompt in addition to the login prompt:

```
Welcome to Emu
mpsi login:
```

The login prompt is UNIX's way of asking you for your login name. For instance, my login name is `kbh`, so I would type **`kbh`** at the prompt. Generally, the login name (usually your initials) is assigned to you by your UNIX system administrator. There is nothing magical about a login name being your initials; it could your first name, the first two characters followed by your last name, or something else required by the policies at your UNIX site.

Tip: The login name is also referred to as the *user name.*

Type in your user name and press the Enter key. The Enter key is also called the Return key on some keyboards. After you type in your user name, you will be asked for a password. If you are not assigned a password by your UNIX system administrator, you may not be presented with this prompt.

Input Output

```
login: kbh <Enter>
password: _      (nothing will appear as you type; <Enter>
```

Analysis The text (`kbh`) after the login prompt is my user name. After typing this in, I pressed the Enter key (`<Enter>`). Remember that your user name may will be different.

At the next line, UNIX requests a password with the password key. Type in your password at this prompt and press the Enter key. The combination of login name and password serves the purpose of uniquely identifying you to UNIX as an known user. Do not type in the string `<ENTER>`, just press the Enter key.

Note: My password, for example, is `iamhere`. Nothing appears as you type in your password. This invisibility prevents others from looking over your shoulder as you type in your password. It also means, however, that you have to type your password without seeing what you type on the screen. Your password is your secret key word into UNIX.

If this is the first time you are logging in to UNIX, you will have been assigned a password. Your password is easy to change after you log in. Depending on your site's policies, you may actually be allowed to continue without a password.

Congratulations! You are logged into the UNIX operating system, and UNIX is ready to accept your commands The `$` sign (for the Bourne and Korn shells) is your prompt. If you are using another shell, your prompt could be the `%` character, the > character, or a combination of characters.

The exact text users see when logging in differs from system to system. Some systems give the time of day, the mail status, and so forth.

Press the Enter key a few times, and you should see the prompt displayed as many times as you press Enter. The following shows an example of this:

Input Output

```
$
$
$
```

By pressing the Enter key several times, you are presented with a prompt indicating that UNIX is ready for more commands. `$ _`. The prompt can be thought of as "What now, master?" for egocentric users, or "Well, now what do you want me to do?" for meeker users. The prompt will always reappear after you finish using a UNIX command.

Caution: Getting on a system with an account and password is perhaps the hardest thing for new users, and it might be the biggest hurdle you will face when you work with UNIX.

Note: UNIX distinguishes lower- and uppercase. For example, in UNIX, the string `EXIT` is different from `exit`.

Thus, if your password were `krlpt2` and you typed in `krlll2`, you would not be allowed access. Similarly, typing in an invalid user name would result in the same problem. See the following examples.

```
Welcome to Emu
mpsi login: hbg
password:
(as before, nothing is shown while you type your password)
Login Incorrect
mpsi login:
```

If you mistyped either your login name or password, you would not see the `$` sign. Instead, you would see the word `Sorry` or the string `Login Incorrect`, and would be asked for your login name again.

See the following for another example.

```
 Welcome to Emu
mpsi login: Login timeout after seconds.
```

Some systems have a *timeout* (a set time limit) for your to enter you user name after being presented with the login prompt. The timeout is generally set to 60 seconds but can be set to another time limit by your UNIX system administrator. If you see the timeout message, press Enter and you should be presented with a login name as before.

On some secure sites, especially using dialup lines, you will be allowed to log in three times before the system will disable logins on that particular terminal for a long time. Usually this is done on sites where security is an issue and the disable timeout is to prevent someone from trying to log in without having the proper authority. So, if you are particularly dyslexic one day and find the system not responding to your fourth attempt at logging in, contact your system administrator for help.

What Happens When You Are Logged In

When you type in your login name and password, UNIX looks at a file that lists authorized users, their respective passwords, and other information about their accounts. This file contains the passwords in an encrypted form to prevent others from finding out other users' passwords.

If UNIX found that your login name and password matched, it lets you log into the system. UNIX encrypts the password you typed in and compares it with the list of encrypted passwords it keeps on disk. The UNIX standard password scheme makes it very difficult to go from an encrypted password back to the original string. So it's faster and easier to compare the encrypted results of passwords.

UNIX then does some housekeeping and initializes your environment for you by starting up a shell for your login session. The shell provides a prompt and waits for your commands. Your *environment* includes your current directory and other variables about you as long as you're on UNIX. For more information, see Day 2, "UNIX Tools," and Day 3, "Shell Variables," respectively.

So, What is Your Shell?

The shell is in itself a program. It is loaded in memory when a user logs in and interacts with the user communicating with the kernel. The shell is also known as the command interpreter because it interprets the commands from the user and passes the commands on to the kernel. The shell is also responsible for returning the results of the commands to the terminal, a file, or another device such as a printer. See Figure 1.1.

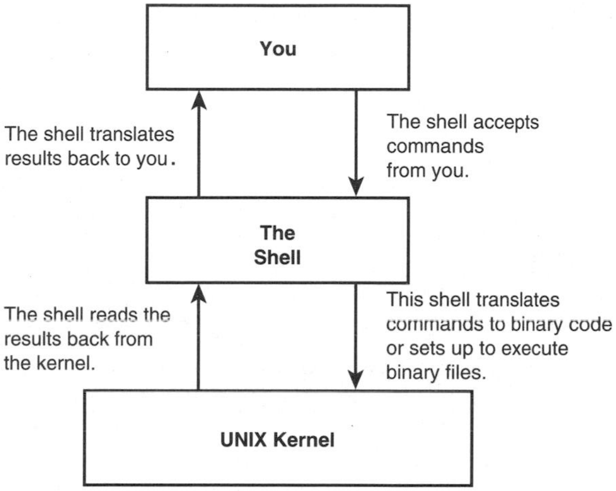

Figure 1.1. *Relationship of the shell to UNIX.*

Difference Between Program and Command

One of the key concepts of UNIX is that of command and program. A *command* is something that you request the UNIX system to do and is complete in itself. For example, `echo` is the command for UNIX to echo the arguments.

A sequence of commands is known as a *program.* A program can be a compiled binary code or a shell script. Compiled code is the output generated from a program (such as C, FORTRAN, Pascal, or another language) and is in a binary format. Binary format is intended to be read by machines only and is thus not readable by a text editor such as `vi`. Text files are those files that can be read by people and thus can be edited by a text editor such as `vi`.

Compiled code is generated in several stages, which includes creating the source file, compiling it with a compiler for language, and linking it with libraries of other code modules. The end product of these steps is a compiled binary file.

Shell scripts are text files with a set of UNIX commands that can be edited via a text editor and can be run without going through a compile cycle. Shell scripts are covered extensively in Days 8 through 14. The primary disadvantage of shell scripts (when compared with binary files) is that they run slower than a functionally equivalent, compiled program. Compiled code is better-suited for the kernel because it contains pre-translated read to run code. The shell script has to be interpreted by the shell during execution. UNIX shell scripts provide a flexible, fast way of hooking other scripts and programs together.

When using UNIX to perform a task, you have to decide how to proceed. Do you write a program, a shell script, or both? For example, to do a matrix inversion on a data file, you would be better off writing a compiled program. To do directory operations with types of files, you would write a shell script. In the latter case, your shell script will call other shell scripts, built-in commands, or programs on disk. For example, writing a shell script to do a sort is going to be much slower than writing a shell script that calls the UNIX compiled program "sort" on disk to do the task for you.

UNIX utilities (such as the shell, binary programs, and shell scripts) reside on disk and are loaded into memory by the kernel when required. When a program is loaded into memory, it is called a process. Naturally, all of the programs on disk cannot be loaded into memory at one time because memory is an expensive commodity and is generally much smaller than disk space. UNIX loads only the programs and data on an as-needed basis. If UNIX sees that there is not enough memory for a newly loaded program, it will make some room for the new program by taking processes from memory to a special area on disk called a *swap space.* This action is called *swapping.* When a program finishes running, it is marked as the first one to go when a new program is loaded.

> **Note:** All UNIX utilities do not necessarily have to reside on disk. They can exist on another disk, or even another machine. However, via a special program called `mount`, UNIX enables other machines to appear as though they are part of a machine. Using `mount` on disks is beyond the scope of this book. However, keep in mind that the next program you run may not really be on your disk.

Basic Features of a Shell

A shell provides the following features:

- Command execution
- Filename substitution
- I/O redirection
- Pipeline hookup

- Environment control
- Interpretive programming language

Don't worry if some of these terms and concepts are confusing now. This book explains all these items in great detail. By the time you are done with this book, these terms will all be meaningful to you.

Command Execution

This function of the shell is to find a command requested by the user and pass it on to the kernel for execution. The shell then passes the results of the command executed by the kernel back to the source that requested the command to be invoked. The source could be the user at the keyboard, in which case, the results are passed on to the terminal. The source could also be another program, another UNIX process or shell script, in which case the results are sent to the invoking program. See Figure 1.2 for the shell's execution process.

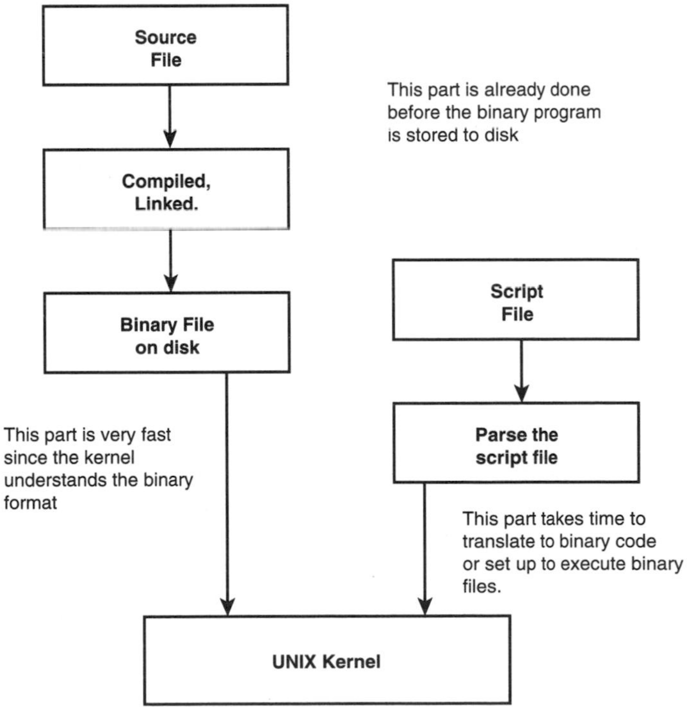

Figure 1.2. *The execution process in a shell.*

Filename Substitution

Shells recognize the `*`, `?`, or `[..]` as special characters when reading the arguments to a command line. Shells then perform filename expansion on this list before executing the requested program. This way, a program being executed does not have to worry about the expansions. See Day 4 for more information.

However, to get a feel for what this means, let's work with an example. Look at the results of the commands on a directory with the files `sams`, `sims`, `sane`, `sate`, `sage`, and `site`.

Input
Output

```
$ echo s*
sage
sams
sane
sate
sims
site
$
$ echo s?ms
sams
sims
$
$ echo sa?e
sane
sate
$
$ echo sa*
sage
sams
sane
sate
$
```

Analysis

The first command (`echo s*`) causes the asterisk (`*`) to be expanded into all the files in this directory. The second command (`echo s?ms`) causes the question mark to be replaced with one character of the alphabet in the second place of filenames. The third command (`echo sa?e`) causes the question mark to be replaced with one character of the alphabet in the third place of filenames. The fourth command (`echo sa*`) causes the `sa` and asterisk (`*`) to be expanded to all files in the directory that begin with the letters `sa`.

I/O Redirection and Pipeline Hookup

Input/output (I/O) redirection is a function of the shell that redirects the output from a program to a destination other than your screen. This way, you can save the output from a command into a file and redirect it to a printer, a serial port, or even another program. Similarly, the shell can make a program accept input from other than the keyboard by redirecting its input from another source. When you connect the output of one process into the input of another process, you have a pipeline hookup.

For example, the `who` command reads a list of the currently logged-in users and sends this list to your screen; the `wc` command prints out a count of the number of lines, characters, and words in its input. You can use pipeline hookup to count the number of logged-in users. Look at the following commands.

Input Output

```
$ who
kamran tty1 Jun 4 20:56
kamran tty2 Jun 4 21:03
ishee tty3 Jun 4 21:41
$
$ who ¦ wc
3 15 93
```

Analysis

The first command (`who`) gives the results of the `who` command. Currently, there are two users in this system, with user `kamran` logged in twice and user `ishee` logged in once.

The second command (`who ¦ wc`) redirects the output of the `who` command to the input of the `wc` command with the `¦` character. Day 4 covers this in greater detail. The `¦` character is known as the pipe because it pipes the output of the `who` command to the input of the `wc` command.

Environment Control

Your shell is fully customizable. You can specify all sorts of personal options. For example, you can display your current directory as part of your prompt or specify a special directory for all your files.

Although most of your environment is customizable, some values can either not be changed nor should be changed. These values include your home directory, user id, and login name. These values are required and managed by UNIX to maintain your user identity on the system.

Interpretive Programming Language

Shells enable you to assign values to variables. This is a basic feature of programming along with looping constructs, input, output, and testing conditions. The shell gives you a lot of power, which when combined with the UNIX kernel, can be an extremely powerful tool to work with. In fact, a lot of common tasks can be done with the shell and UNIX utilities, without writing a single line of compilable code.

Shell variables are commonly used as placeholders for arguments whenever long pathnames are too laborious to type. You can create a shell variable and assign it a value that is not so laborious to remember and type. Days 4 and 5 cover the components of the following example in greater detail.

Input Output

```
1. $ cd /usr/lib/X11/xdm
2. $ x=`pwd`
3. $ pwd
/usr/lib/X11/xdm
4. $ ch $HOME
5. $ pwd
/home/kamran
6. $ cd $x
7. $ pwd
/usr/lib/X11/xdm
```

Analysis

For this particular example and for other special examples, I'll number the lines for later reference. Line 1 requests a change of directory:

```
/(cd) to /usr/lib/X11/xdm
```

Line 2 forces the output from the print working directory command (`pwd`) into the variable `x`. Note the backward quotes used to take the result of the `pwd` command as the input into variable `x`. Day 4 covers this character.

Line 3 represents the request to execute the `pwd` command, and the following line shows the result from the `pwd` command.

Line 4 shows how you can get back to your login directory called `$HOME`. This is the directory you are assigned when you first log into UNIX. Day 3 discusses using the `HOME` variable.

Line 5 represents the request to execute the `pwd` command; the next line shows the result from the `pwd` command. This confirms that you are no longer in the `/usr/bin/X11/xdm` directory. Line 6 causes the variable in `x` to be expanded to the value of `/usr/bin/X11/xdm`. Thus, line 7 shows that the location of the directory was changed to `/usr/bin/X11/xdm`.

Remember that the "real" reason UNIX has cryptic commands is that sometimes programmers get lazy typing the same command over and over. The shorter the command, the less likely you are to mistype it. Of course, the fewer the keystrokes, the better. Reducing long pathnames, options, and command names to two-letter combinations is helpful. Only a programmer can really gloat in the feeling of running a four-hour job with the a program called `r`.

In addition to variable assignment, you also can have loops and tests for conditions. Day 9 covers these in greater detail.

Types of Shells

Shells are independent of the underlying UNIX kernel. This fact has allowed the development of several shells for UNIX systems. Each type of shell has features that enable you to have a choice. There are several versions of the shell available on UNIX systems. A partial list of shell types follows.

The Bourne Shell

This is the most common shell on UNIX systems and was the first major shell. The Bourne shell was released about 1979 and was called `sh`. If you learn this shell, you will probably be able to work with just about any UNIX system. This shell is distributed as the standard shell on almost all UNIX systems. This shell is named after its author, Stephen Bourne.

The C Shell

This is also called the programmer's shell and exists as `csh`. It was developed by Bill Joy at the University of California at Berkeley as part of the BSD release. The C shell got its name because its syntax and usage is very similar to the C programming language. Therefore, it's welcomed by C programming aficionados. Unfortunately, the C shell is not always available on all machines. Secondly, shell scripts written in the C shell are not compatible with the Bourne shell. Such scripts have to be modified for working with the Bourne shell. One of the major advantages of the C shell (over the Bourne shell) is its capability to execute processes in the background.

The Korn Shell

The Korn shell was developed by David Korn of AT&T Bell Labs. It's built on the Bourne shell. The most stable version was released in 1988 by AT&T's UNIX System Laboratories as `ksh`. The initial releases had some serious bugs in them, which were eventually removed.

The Korn shell also incorporates the features of the C shell (such as process control). The Korn shell was initially not available on all UNIX machines but is fast becoming the *de facto* standard for all later UNIX releases. One of the selling factors for the Korn shell is that it can run Bourne shell scripts without any modification at all.

During its first few releases, the Korn shell had to be purchased as an add-on to UNIX. Given its popularity, several shareware versions of the Korn shell were released after its birth. One is called `pdksh` and is a public domain Korn shell—thus, it is free.

The public domain version was written by Eric Gisin who made more enhancements to the original Korn shell. These include the `emacs` customizable keys and the tilde (~) command to default to items other than user names. All in all, this is a good alternative to the original Korn shell (if the original is not available to you on your system). However, it is not as complete as the original Korn shell.

Another later variation of the Korn shell is the windowing Korn shell from USL. This version incorporates the X Windows toolkit features and enables a programmer to write shell scripts that take advantage of the X Windows Xt toolkit. This is a major step toward developing shell scripts that take advantage of the X Windows environment and gives an alternative to the traditional character-based domain for shell scripts. For more information, contact Novell's UNIX System Labs at (800) 847-0240.

The Bourne-Again Shell

This is a freeware shell (called `bash`) from the Free Software Foundation (FSF) where it was developed by Brian Fox and Chet Ramey. The price (free) is a motivational factor for getting this powerful shell. Also, its "copyleft" decree is worth reading and comparing with a standard software copyright document. The downside to using this free shell is that there is no real support for it (such as you would get from a vendor). You probably wouldn't want to use this shell if you wanted a free alternative to the Korn shell. Remember that some UNIX releases either do not offer the Korn shell. If they do, they might charge you extra. For example, the Linux operating system variant comes with the `bash` shell as its default shell, and the only Korn shell look-alike is the public domain Korn shell, which is not the same as the original Korn shell.

Using the Shell

As stated earlier, UNIX starts a shell for you when you log in. When the shell starts up, it displays a command prompt as a way of requesting input from the user. The command prompt is generally a dollar sign (`$`), although the prompt can be different, depending on your mode and type of shell.

A shell can operate in two modes: *interactive* or *noninteractive* mode.

A shell is interactive when you, the user, interact with the kernel through this shell. A shell is noninteractive when it executes script files without user intervention. A *script file* is a set of commands stored in a file on disk. You will learn about script files in Days 8 and 9.

All of the shell scripts you have seen up to now are noninteractive scripts because they do not require any user input while running. In other words, they run from start to finish without requiring any input from the user. For a shell to be interactive, it must interact with the user. That is, it must be able to collect data from the user while running. Day 10 shows you how to determine whether your script is running in interactive mode.

```
# this is an example of a shell script
# that runs interactively
#
echo "Source File"
read src
echo "Destination File"
read dst
cp $src $dst
```

The first three lines in this script file are comments only. Comments are notes for the script writer and are ignored by the shell. The shell ignores all characters from the first unquoted `#` character to the end of the line.

The next line echoes a request for a filename. The line after that reads the user input into a variable `src`. See Day 10 for more information. You can see that the `read` command is used to read strings of input (user or via a pipe). This string is then assigned to the variable in the `read` statement. The input to the `read` statement is terminated with the Enter key. In this example, the variable `src` is assigned the string typed in by the user.

The shell then echoes a request for a destination file and reads it in via the next `read` statement for the `dst` variable. It then executes the `cp` copy command using the values in the variable `src` and `dst`.

Note: Note the `$` sign in front of `src` and `dst` to get the value stored in the variables `src` and `dst`. If the `$` were left out, the `cp` command would copy the file called `src` to the file called `dst`.

Each time the user types in a command, the shell searches a known set of directories for a file with the name of the command. If it finds such a command, it requests the kernel to execute the command. The kernel then loads the command into memory and runs it as a process. The shell then goes to sleep until it receives a response back from the process via the kernel. It then sends the response back to the requesting task or via a pipe to the next process in line.

Command-Line Syntax

UNIX shells are command-line driven. You type in a command and press the Enter key, and the shell processes the command for you and sends the results to where you requested them to go. All shell commands have to follow a syntax. The syntax for a command is:

```
command [argument1 [argument2 [argument3 ...]]] <Enter>
```

If present, the brackets around an argument (as in `[argument]`) indicate that an argument is optional. Special arguments are also called options when they affect the output of a command. All arguments to a command are referred to as the command's argument list. All commands are terminated when the user presses the Enter key. That means that a user can use the Backspace key to correct any typing mistakes.

Caution: If you see `^H` every time you press the Backspace key, try the command:

```
$ stty erase ^H
```

where `^H` is the character produced when the Backspace key is pressed.

DO	DON'T

DO remember to use the Backspace key to erase characters to the left of the cursor.

DON'T forget to press Enter to execute your command.

DON'T use the arrows keys on your keyboard; they do not always work.

You can get the control character (`^H`) by pressing the control key (usually marked Ctrl) and lowercase h simultaneously (Ctrl+h).

Single spaces or tabs are used to separate arguments to a command. Spaces are not allowed within arguments. If you have to give spaces within an argument name, use double quotes (`"`) or single quotes (`'`) around an argument.

Note: The accent grave (`` ` ``) character is a special character that forces the execution of a program of the name quoted between the characters and replaces the quoted string (between the grave characters) with the results of that command before proceeding.

Let's take a sneak preview at what quoting is all about in a shell. You will learn about quote characters and their special functions in Day 4.

Input/Output

```
$ echo I am learning                about                          you
I am learning about you
```

Analysis

The command in this case is the `echo` command. Also, there are five arguments to this command: `I`, `am`, `learning`, `about`, and `you`. The `echo` command simply echoes the arguments back out. Note how the extra spaces in the argument list are truncated to one space each.

If you were to put quotes around the entire sentence, you would be requesting the shell to preserve the whitespaces between any shell variables. Consider the output from the following command:

Input/Output

```
$ echo "I am learning you
I am learning about you
$
```

Analysis

The quotes allowed the white spaces between `learning` and `about` to exist as they were typed in. However, the white spaces between the words `about` and `you` were truncated since they were not within quotes.

What is Your Shell?

When you log into a UNIX system, UNIX automatically starts up an interactive shell for you. This is your default login shell. Type the following command.

Input
Output

```
$ echo $SHELL
/bin/sh
$ _
```

Analysis

The output of /bin/sh shows that the current shell is indeed the Bourne shell.

Caution: An easy way to determine what shell you are running is to echo the value of the SHELL variable. This may not be the safest way, however, because any process you run has the potential for changing the SHELL variable to a different value (although it's unlikely). The hard way is to use the ps command to see what shell process you are actually running:

```
$ ps
pid tty time command
19028 tty21 0:00 ps
(you will may see other processes listed here as well)
18943 tty21 0:00 sh
$
```

This output gives process id (pid) for the sh program.

The $SHELL environment variable tells you about what kind of shell you are running. You will learn all about environment variables in Day 4, so hang in there. Just remember that an environment variable is something that holds data with information about your login session.

The echo $SHELL command tells you about your login shell's executable program currently being used.

Some of the other outputs from the echo $SHELL command include the following:

For the Bourne-again shell:

```
$ echo $SHELL
/bin/sh
$
```

For the C shell (note the lowercase `$shell`):

```
% echo $shell
/bin/csh
$
```

For the Korn shell:

```
$ echo $SHELL
/bin/ksh
$
```

Another quick way to tell if you are in the C shell is to see if the prompt is a percent (`%`) sign. Both the Bourne and Korn shells provide the dollar sign (`$`) as a prompt. The shareware version of the C shell (notably the shareware version, `tcsh`) sometimes presents the greater than (`>`) as its prompt.

However, I caution, as I did before, to use the `SHELL` environment variable when you want to be sure (you will see ways of changing the prompt in Day 4).

Using Another Shell

If you are discontent with your shell or simply want to try another shell, enter the command to invoke that shell at the prompt. These commands will work only if the shell you are trying to invoke exists on your system. If the shell you are trying to create does not exist on the system, you will get a `command not found` message and not get a new shell. Because the Korn shell was a commercial shell on some older UNIX machines, these commands to invoke the Korn shell may not work. Similarly, if you do not have the BSD extensions, you may not have the C shell. If you are in doubt, use the `which` command to find out which version of the shell is available. For example:

Input Output

```
$ which csh
/bin/csh
$
```

Analysis

This command tells you that the C shell exists in the `/bin` directory. If the C shell did not exist in the path of executable files, the user would not see any output.

Note: The `which` command is a very useful tool to have in your toolbox. When writing shell scripts (later in this book), you will want to know which program is being executed. However, the `which` command may not be

> available on your system if you do not have the BSD extensions to UNIX. In this case, try the `type` command to find out which command is being executed. See Day 10 for more details on how to use the `which` command.

When you enter the command

```
$ /bin/csh
%
```

it will invoke the C shell on your terminal. The percent prompt is the shell's way of requesting input. When invoking the Korn shell from within the Bourne shell, you will see no real difference. You have now invoked a new interactive shell for yourself.

```
$ ksh
$
```

To get back to the original shell, type **`exit`** at the prompt and you will be returned to the calling shell. If the shell into which you typed **`exit`** had been your login shell, you would have been logged off the system. For more information, see the section later today titled "Logging Off."

These shells are like onion skins wrapped around the kernel. Each new shell is a layer on top of the previous shell; each `exit` command takes this layer off. The last layer taken off logs you off the system. See Figure 1.3 for this type of layering.

Input Output

```
$ csh
command not found: csh
```

Analysis

This tells you that the C shell, `csh`, does not exist on your current list of paths to look for commands. See Day 3 for details about setting this path.

> **Note:** UNIX offers a `find` command that locates files for you. For example, to find a file called `csh`, use the `find` command. An example follows this note.

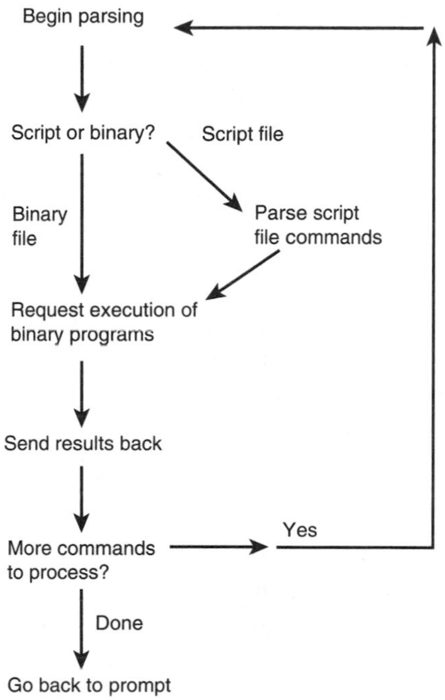

Figure 1.3. *The order of shells as they are wrapped around the shell.*

Input
Output

```
$ find   / -name csh       -print
/usr/ucb/bin/csh
$
```

Analysis

The arguments to the `find` command in this example are as follows:

- `/` is the directory in the tree from which to begin the search. The `/` signifies that the search will start at the root (the top) of the directory tree.
- `-name csh` requests that the `find` command search for a file called `csh`.
- `-print` is a request to the `find` command to print the full pathname of the file that matches with the name specified by the `-name` option. There are other actions that you could request the `find` command to do. Other actions include deleting the file and executing the file. Tomorrow's text discusses how to read the UNIX online man pages to get more information about most of UNIX utilities. You can use the man pages to get more information about the `find` command.

If you execute several shells, one after another, you would have to type the same number of `exit` commands (or Ctrl+d's) to back out of each shell. Think of each shell adding a new layer on top of the kernel. Look at the following command sequence.

Input/Output

```
$ sh
$ sh
$ sh
$ sh
$ exit
$ exit
$ exit
$ exit
$ exit

bye!
mpsi login: _
```

Analysis

The first four invocations of the Bourne shell (`sh`) required four exit commands. The fifth exit command logged you out completely because it terminated your original login shell. The `bye!` is a message from the system indicating that it has logged you off the system. You might see a different message, or nothing at all, depending on your system.

Caution: Note that Ctrl+d does not always work at logging you off a shell. Typing the `exit` command is the preferred, standard way of exiting a shell.

Working with Shell Commands

This section is a prelude to tomorrow and will familiarize you with using UNIX commands. You will use one of the most frequently used commands in UNIX, called `ls`, for a first trip through UNIX. Do not worry if you do not understand the introduced UNIX terms all at once. By the time you read Day 2, you will be very familiar with all the concepts of files and directories.

Issuing the `ls` by itself gives a directory listing of everything in your current working directory. Type **ls** at the prompt, followed by the Enter key.

Input/Output

```
$ ls
Xconfig
Xconfig.new
advs
chprog
```

```
chuser
docs
faq
quran
mkcdrom
sams
screen.dump
src
startx
tifs
xme
```

Analysis

The first command line was `ls` by itself. The results of that were a listing of all the files in the present directory. Now try the same `ls` command with an argument. Try the following example.

Input/Output

```
$ ls mkcdrom
mkcdrom
```

Analysis

This time, the command was of the form: `$ ls filename`. This format gives a directory listing of all the filenames specified in the command-argument list. In this case, the *`filename`* is an optional argument to the `ls` command.

Thus, because the file `mkcdrom` existed in my current directory, it was listed to the screen. You can request more than one file in the argument list as well.

Input/Output

```
$ ls /etc/passwd /etc/group
/etc/passwd /etc/group
```

Analysis

This command requests the listings for two files. The command name is `ls`. The first argument is `/etc/passwd`, and the second argument is `/etc/group`. This command will only list the two files in the `/etc` directory.

Now try the same command (as before) with the `-al` option.

Input/Output

```
$ ls -al /etc/passwd /etc/group/etc
-rw-r--r--   1 root    root         258 Jan 28 20:10 /etc/group
-rw-r--r--   1 root    root         601 Apr 23 22:42 /etc/passwd
```

Analysis

This is command requesting the listings for two files. The command name is `ls`, and the first argument is `-al`, which is the request to show all the file (a) and provide a long listing (`l`).

The second and third arguments are `/etc/passwd` and `/etc/group`, respectively. Since these are both files, this command will provide a long listing about these two files in the `/etc directory`.

Now try the same command, but this time use the `ls -al /etc` command.

Input/Output

```
$ ls
total
drwxr-xr-x    root    root        May
drwxr-xr-x    root    root        Apr
              root    root         Feb    DIR_COLORS
              root    bin          May    crond.pid
              root    root         Feb    csh.cshrc
              root    root         Feb    csh.login
drwxr-xr-x    root    root         Mar    default
              root    root         Jan    disktab
              root    root         Jan    fdprm
drwxr-xr-x    root    root         Apr    fs
              root    root         Apr    fstab
              root    root         Jan    gettydefs
              root    root         Jan    group
lrwxrwxrwx    root    root         Apr    inet
              root    root         Feb    inittab
              root    root         May    issue
              root    root         May    klog.pid
              root    root         Dec    ksh.kshrc
              root    root         May    ld.so.cache
              root    root         Mar    ld.so.conf
drwxr-xr-x    root    root         Apr    lilo
              root    root         Apr    lilo.conf
              root    root         Apr    lilo.conf.bak
              root    root         Dec    magic
              root    root         Sep    minicom.users
              root    root         Apr    minirc.dfl
              root    root         May    motd
              root    root         May    mtab
              root    root         Mar    mtools
              root    root         Apr    passwd
              root    root         Apr    passwd.OLD
              root    root         Apr    profile
drwxr-xr-x    root    root         Apr    rc.d
              root    root         Jan    securetty
              root    root         Mar    shells
drwxr-xr-x    root    root         Apr    skel
              root    root         Jan    syslog.conf
              root    root         May    syslog.pid
              root    root         Mar    termcap
              root    root         Nov    ttys
              root    root         May    utmp
```

Analysis

This is a very long listing of a `directory /etc`. The `-al` is the command's first argument and contains the options `-a` for all and `-l` for long. The `/etc` string is the second argument. In this case, `/etc` happens to be a directory; so all the files in the `/etc directory` are shown.

Day 2 examines the output from the `ls` command in greater detail.

More than One Command Per Line

1

By now you have dealt with many arguments to one command. Usually, commands are issued one a time at the prompt. However, if you want to issue more than one command on a line, you can separate the commands with semicolons (;).

Input
Output

```
$ ls who pwd
ls: who: No such file or directory
ls: pwd: No such file or directory
```

Analysis

This attempts to give you a listing of all `who` and `pwd` files.

Now, type in the command again with semicolons between the three words to get:

```
$ ls;who;pwd
```

The following code lines show this command with its output.

Input
Output

```
$ ls;who;pwd
ch01
ch02
ch03
ch04
ch05
ch06
ch07
ch08
ch09
ch11
dos2unix
dos2unix.c
nowkorn.asc
note
numlines
parlor
phone
pizza
sage
sams
sane
sate
saveme
sims
site
toc
whoout
kamran tty2 Jun 5 12:04
kamran tty1 Jun 5 12:00
/home/kamran/sams
```

Analysis

The `ls` command is executed first, the `who` command next, and then the `pwd` command.

The semicolons are what differentiates the previous two commands. The semicolons force the execution of the commands in order from left to right, one per command. Spaces are not necessary between the commands and the semicolons.

Because the semicolon is a special character to the shell, you have to put quotes around it to make it an argument instead of a command terminator. Consider the command:

```
$ ls grunch; bronchial
```

The command sequence will be to list the file `grunch` and then execute the command bronchial. However, the command

```
$ ls "grunch;" bronchial
```

will be interpreted by the shell as list the file `grunch`; (that is, with the semicolon as part of the name) and the file `bronchial`. Notice how the quotes are removed by the shell by the time the argument is passed to the `ls` command.

To see another feature in the shell, try the following command.

Input/Output

```
$ echo this is a "# " hash
this is
"#" hash
$ echo # Hi there I am a shell user
$ (nothing)
$
```

Analysis

The # character is the pound sign directly above the 3 on a keyboard. This is often referred to as the hash character, or the pound sign. As you can see from the output, the shell stopped parsing everything from the # character to the Enter keypress. The next line shows that nothing in the command after the # is interpreted.

This example shows that # is also a command interpreter terminator and takes precedence over the ; operator.

Input/Output

```
$ pwd #who
/usr/kamran/samples
(the who command is not executed)
```

Analysis

The shell will not execute the `who` command because the # has requested that all further input on the line be ignored until the next command is entered. This is of great significance to those writing shell scripts because the # is used to insert comments into a shell script. So, what if you want to display the # as part of the command structure? Put it in double or single quotes.

```
$ echo this is "#" hash
this is # hash
$ echo this is '#' hash
this is # hash
```

As before, the # can be displayed by putting quotes around it. Since the quotes are removed by the shell before the argument is sent to the command, the # is not parsed out and sent to the command.

This is a prelude to Day 4, which covers other complicated aspects of quoting.

Changing Your Password

Let's do some work with another command to change your password. This will help you familiarize yourself with using interactive commands. So far you know that once you issue the command (such as `ls`), the shell and the `ls` program do the work without requesting further input from you before returning the results.

Other tasks may require some user action during execution. Some examples include changing floppy disk drives for copying files, turning on a printer, and requesting actions required from a program (such as waiting for a keypress in a mail-reading program or changing your password).

Let's work with changing your password for this illustration. You might want to change your user-assigned password to one of your own preference. On some UNIX systems, it is mandatory to change your system-administrator-assigned password to one of your own when you first log in.

You can change your password by using the `passwd` command. See the following example.

```
$ passwd
Enter old password: (nothing is shown as you type)
Enter new password: (nothing is shown as you type)
Re-enter new password: (nothing is shown as you type)
$
```

The `passwd` program requires you to type your old password in before allowing a new one. This prevents someone changing a password on an unattended terminal. Also, you have to type the new password in twice to ensure that it is entered correctly.

Choosing a Password

Changing a password seems like an easy task when compared with choosing a password. Because your password is the only means of identifying you and your account to UNIX, guard it carefully and do not disclose to anyone else. Choose a password that is not easy to figure out. For example, it might be easy for someone to figure out your spouse's or children's names and birthdays. Combinations of first names, initials, and last names are very common and easy to guess. On the other hand, passwords like `2kde$5` are quite hard to guess but are a pain to remember. Almost universally, all UNIX systems require at least six characters in a password.

Use your judgment when choosing a password. Can it be kept secret? Is it long enough? Is this password written down somewhere, for example, like a driver's license number?

DO **DON'T**

DO mix upper- and lowercase characters (for example, KrYpToNite, SuPerBirD, and cLARkKeNT).

DO use alphanumeric (a through z and 0 through 9) characters.

DO check to see that your password is not in the online dictionary.

DO make sure that the password is not associated with your name.

DO make sure your password is at least six alphanumeric characters.

DON'T use a common name such as `jill`, `jack`, `roger`, or `mike`. It's easy to guess the name of a child, spouse, pet, or other loved one.

DON'T use your user, first, or last name. These are easy for others to guess.

DON'T use words found in UNIX's online dictionary.

DON'T keep your accounts with no passwords at all.

DON'T use passwords of project names.

Viewing Long Output on Your Screen

So far, the commands used produce output that is less than 25 characters. Often times, the output goes by too quickly. If you want to stop the output temporarily, type the Ctrl+s command to suspend the screen output. This is done by pressing the Ctrl and s key together.

The application generating the output continues to run; only the output to the screen is suspended. To restart the scrolling display, press Ctrl+q . The output scrolling is restarted until either the output is finished or another Ctrl+s is pressed.

> **Caution:** Pressing several Ctrl+q's at one time may disable the scroll-stopping capability of some terminals. So be cautious when using Ctrl+q. Also, Ctrl+q may not work on some terminals. Try using the `more` or `pg` command instead.

To stop the output from a command from scrolling any further, use the Ctrl+c command. This will generally stop the application from generating any more output to the screen.

Logging Off

After your session is over, it's best to log off UNIX. This frees up system resources, and you can walk away from your terminal without leaving a running session for someone else to use. Most UNIX installations log you off automatically if no key is pressed for a certain period. This is something that is a bit of a nuisance if you have a long process running, but for the most part this default is nice to have.

In some cases, your system administrator may have disabled this feature to allow an indefinite login period. In such a case, you cannot rely on UNIX cleaning up after you.

There are two ways to log off the UNIX system:

1. Type **`exit`** at the prompt.
2. Press Ctrl+d at the prompt.

The `exit` command instructs your shell to quit. This in turn causes your login session to be terminated, in which case you are presented with a login prompt.

The second command (Ctrl+d) at the prompt sends an end-of-file character to the shell. This tells the shell that there is no more input. Consequently, the shell just quits, leaving you with a login prompt. This is not the preferred way of logging off UNIX because it does not clean up after itself as well as the `exit` command. This method is included here if you find yourself looking at the login prompt after accidently typing in this combination.

As you learned earlier today, Ctrl+d does not always log you off on some UNIX systems. Typing the `exit` command is the preferred way of logging off UNIX.

Input Output

```
$ exit
bye!

Welcome to Emu

mpsi login:
```

Analysis

The `exit` command causes the shell to terminate. UNIX cleans up after you and then resets the terminal you were on to accept another user. You may see the word `bye` instead of the work `logout`, or some other string, to indicate that you have logged off the system.

On some systems, when you log out, you are presented with a message to indicate that you are indeed off the system.

Summary

You have learned a lot about UNIX today. Today's text introduced you to a broad number of concepts of UNIX rather than going into excruciating detail of one topic or another. As you proceed further, this book will cover each of today's topics in greater detail.

The topics covered today were the following:

- How to log onto UNIX. This is your starting point for all your future adventures in UNIX.
- Differences between programs and commands.
- Some concepts of UNIX users, login names, and passwords.
- UNIX commands such as the `ls` and `passwd`.

- Introduction to the shell and its role under UNIX.
- Types of shells and how to determine which type of shell you are using. You also now know how to start a new shell from within a shell.
- The syntax of commands under UNIX. You should now be comfortable with typing commands at the prompt and recognizing arguments to commands.
- How to stop scrolling output from a program to the screen in two ways: temporarily with Ctrl+q and permanently by stopping the program with Ctrl+c.
- How to change your password (a monthly task). You should now have enough information to select a good password.
- How to use the `exit` command.

UNIX Tools Learned Today

Today's text introduced you to these UNIX tools:

- `ls` Provides a directory listing
- `passwd` Changes your password
- `wc` Counts the number of words, lines, and characters in text
- `who` Finds out who else is logged on to the system

What's Next?

Tomorrow, you'll learn about files, directories, and commands. You will use the knowledge you have gained today to build on the next concepts. Tomorrow's text covers the `ls` command in more detail and discusses file and directory permissions, and other UNIX tools.

Q&A

Q What is a shell?

A The shell is your interface to the UNIX kernel.

Q How many types of shells are there for UNIX? Name three commonly found shells.

A There are many different types of shells in UNIX, each with its own special characteristics. The three most common shells are the Bourne, C, and Korn shells.

Q Why are there so many shells for UNIX?

A UNIX shells are programs that are independent of the UNIX kernel. You have the complete freedom to write your own personal shell if you want to. Given this freedom of choice, programmers with different tastes and preferences have written their own shells.

Q Why do we need login names and passwords?

A To uniquely identify yourself to UNIX. A password is your key into UNIX.

Q Can more than one login name have more than one password?

A No.

Q What is the command that lists all the files in a directory?

A The `ls` command is used to list all the files in a directory.

Q What is the preferred way of logging off the system?

A Type **`exit`** at the prompt.

Workshop

The Workshop provides quiz questions to help you solidify your understanding of the material covered. Some Workshop sections of this book also contain exercises to provide you with experience in using what you've learned. Try to understand the quiz and exercise answers before continuing on to the next chapter. Answers are provided in Appendix D, "Answers."

Quiz

1. What sequence of events happen when you log into UNIX?
2. What are the reasons for not showing the password?
3. Why are passwords stored in an encrypted form?

4. What's the difference between a command and a program?
5. What's the difference in doing the `ls -al` command on a directory instead of a file?
6. I cannot list two files and a chapter using the

   ```
   ls command:
   $ ls file; chapter
   ```

   Why? How can I change this command to remedy this situation?

Exercises

1. Type the `who` command and see who else is logged into your UNIX system.
2. Find out about the local time on your system. Use the `date` command.
3. Select a new password for your account. Be creative.
4. Try to use two different passwords with the first characters the same. For example, use `defer123bad` and `defer123good`. What happens when you try to log in with these passwords?
5. Try to select a password that is less than six characters long.
6. Try the following commands in your directory:

   ```
   $ ls file; chapter
   $ ls "file cat > help
   This is a help file
   ctrl-d
   $ cat > filename
   This is a file called filename
   ctrl-d
   ```

7. Then try the following commands:

   ```
   $ ls help; chapter
   $ ls "help;" chapter
   $ ls -al
   $ ls -a
   $ ls #
   $ who ¦ wc
   $ date
   $ ls; date; who;
   ```

WEEK
1

2

UNIX Tools

Today's text covers the basics of files and directories. These topics include the following:

- The UNIX file system
- What a file is
- What a directory is
- How to manipulate files
- How to manipulate directories

Today's text also covers some of the UNIX tools you will need to know before starting to learn the shell. These are tools with which you can build extra shell functionality. You will learn about the directory and file structures under UNIX.

The UNIX File System

The UNIX file system is a hierarchical file system. Files contain data or perform some special function. The file system enables you to organize your files into containers called directories. The name *hierarchical* is used since directory structures under UNIX look like hierarchical organizational charts of companies. Just as departments can contain smaller departments, so can directories contain other directories (called subdirectories), which in turn can contain more subdirectories.

The file system can best be conceptualized when compared with the root system for a tree. As you would expect, the thickest part of a tree branches from the root to thinner branches and finally to either leaves or barren branches.

The UNIX file system is also referred to as a directory tree. It's actually like a tree; you climb real trees, but traverse the UNIX directory tree. This makes sense if you think of the tree this way:

- The tree starts at the root. (Don't be concerned about the root system below the ground.) The top-level directory in UNIX is referred to as the root.
- The branches of the tree spread out as you climb the tree. In UNIX, you traverse the branches of the directory tree by going into subdirectories.
- If you correlate thickness to power, the trunk is thickest at the root and thins out as you go across branches. The closer you are to the root, the more important your function. The same is true for files and directories: The higher the location of a file in the directory, the more important it is.

- A leaf is the final point in a branch and serves the purpose of the data as a file.
- A branch devoid of leaves equals an empty directory.

In a real tree, things are a lot more complicated. It should be easy, however, to show you how to organize all your files and directories in this structure.

UNIX Files

Files are a collection of data items stored on disk. There are three types of files under UNIX:

- Ordinary
- Directory
- Special

An *ordinary file* contains data, text, program instructions, and so on. A *directory file* is a special file that includes other files. A *special file* is related to input and output (I/O) to UNIX and carries the special meaning to UNIX. It is special because it interacts with I/O devices. The last four days cover special files under UNIX.

In the most basic terms, a file is simply a holder for data. To refer back to this data, you have to identify the file. All files are given names to make them easier for a user and UNIX to identify. Given a file's name, you can modify the data and its file.

Just like everything in life, UNIX has a few rules about naming files:

- Filenames are generally composed of lower- or uppercase letters or numbers. UNIX differentiates between lower- and uppercase letters, so to UNIX, `prog1` and `Prog1` are two different files.
- Some limited punctuation marks are allowed, such as . or _, but, as a general rule, these should be reserved for special files.
- Some UNIX file systems enable filenames to be as long as you want, and some limit it to 14 characters (or less).

Note: If you plan to move files to a DOS machine, it's easier to use DOS filenames (up to eight characters). Longer filenames are usually truncated when moving them on to a DOS file system. For example,

> `BlackAndWhite.Doc` would be truncated to `BLACKAND.DOC`. When in doubt, use UNIX filenames that are 14 characters or less.
>
> A DOS filename is of the form *`XXXXXXXX.YYY`*, where *`XXXXXXXX`* is the base name of the filename, and the *`YYY`* after the period (.) is the extension of the filename. The base name must be eight characters or less, and the extension must be three characters or less. The period is not required if there isn't an extension.
>
> Unlike UNIX, DOS files are case-insensitive. Therefore, under DOS, `carpool` is the same `CARPOOL` or `CarPool`. In UNIX, they would be three distinct filenames.

So what are legal filenames under UNIX? Following are some examples using the `ls` command (from Day 1). Here's the output from the command:

Input Output

```
$ ls  /

bin
boot
cdrom
dev
dosc
etc
home
lib
lost+found
mnt
proc
root
sbin
tmp
usr
var
vmlinuz
vmlinuz.old
$ _
```

Analysis Your output may be completely different from the one shown here. This is the directory of all the typical files at the top-level directory. The sections titled, "Some Special Directories," and "File Permissions," cover the details of the root and these files.

> **Caution:** The output you see might not be in one column. In fact, you may see several filenames on one line. This might be due to the `ls` command defaulting to the `ls -C` option, which prints the listing out in as many columns as it takes to fit it in a columnar fashion.

Of particular interest should be the directory name called `lost+found`. Note how the plus sign (+) is used in a filename.

You also can use a hyphen (-) in a filename. For example, the following list of names are legal: `lost-found`, `cpio-2.3`, `ncurses-1.0.1`, `SysVinit-2.4`, and `i-spell-3.41.a`.

The key point to remember is that the file and directory names should not have spaces in them. Notice that I said should not—not cannot. It's not a good idea to put spaces in filenames because they create all sorts of problems for shell scripts using filenames. See Day 14 for shell tricks and creating filenames with spaces in the middle.

DO **DON'T**

DO use descriptive filenames when possible. Having filenames such as `t.dat`, `a.br` or `t.t.t` might be meaningful today but may not be so clear to you after a week or so. Examples of descriptive filenames are `BillsDueMarch`, `AnnualRpt94`, and `PhoneNumbers`.

DON'T use an asterisk (*), question mark (?), greater-than symbol (>), less than symbol (<), ampersand (&), or vertical bar (¦) in a filename. These symbols represent different things to the command interpreter. You will learn about the significance of each of these symbols later in this book.

DON'T use the hyphen (-) as the first character of a filename. Although such a filename is possible, it's a bad idea. For example, if you had a file called `-al`, how would you expect the command following the filename to work? In fact, if you create a file called `-a`, you may not be able to remove it from your directory. So be careful.

Directories

Directories are groups of files that collectively are given a name. Directories let you store your files by order of your choice. They also allow you to store other directories, or subdirectories, in them.

The fact that you can store files in directories becomes important when you have many files. It's easy to lose track of what files you have if everything is stored in one large directory. If you are a DOS user, files are generally cluttered on the top-level directory on the first drive.

Imagine directories as drawers in a filing cabinet, and files as file folders that contain the data that you need. (See Figure 2.1.) Of course, a file system has far more depth than a normal file cabinet's three levels (that is, cabinet to drawer to file to data) to get to the data. You can have several levels of subdirectories within subdirectories. It's common to have subdirectories that are five or six levels deep from the root.

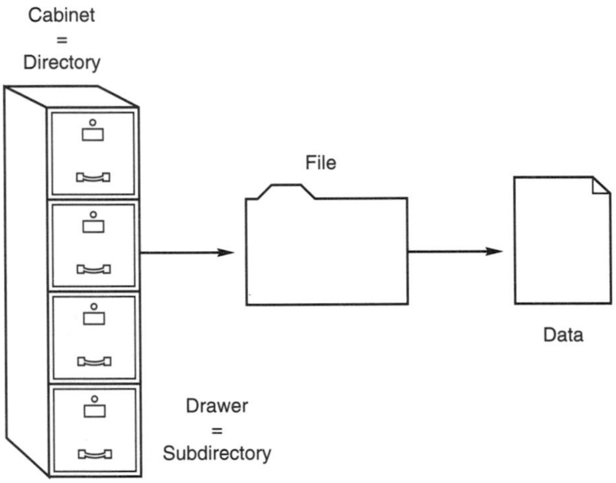

Figure 2.1. *Concept of a filing cabinet with annotations.*

The Directory Tree from the Root

Now, you can look at the directory tree from the root.

Try to think of the top-level directory as the root of a tree and its lower-level subdirectories as the branches of the tree. The forward slash (/) at the top of the tree is the root of the tree. All other directories are the subdirectories to that root directory.

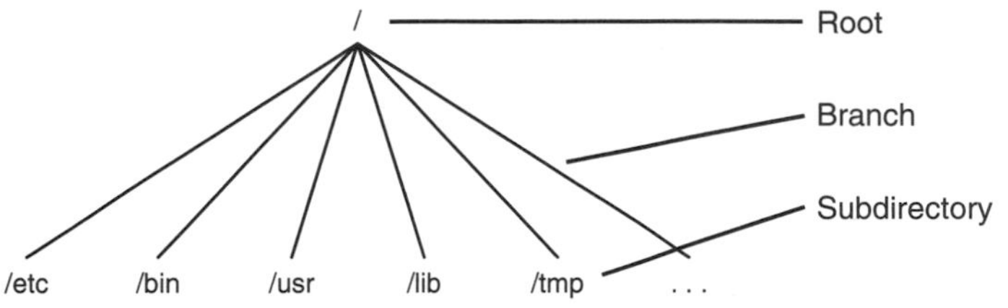

Figure 2.2. *Sample directories at the root.*

I have listed a few of the files in the directory tree shown in the Figure 2.2. This list is not complete; it only lists the common directories at the root level:

- `bin`: In UNIX programs, these files are called executables because a user can execute (run) them. When a program is the result of a compilation, it's in binary form and is called an *executable binary*. The `/bin` directory is the common place for executable *bin*aries.
- `dev`: This is the directory for all the special files in the UNIX file system, such as the keyboard or terminal device drivers.
- `etc`: As the name suggests, this is the catch-all directory for all the administrative files in UNIX.
- `lib`: This is the central library storage for files that are commonly used by other programs. A *library* is a collection of files (usually binary) that can be shared among many processes. The advantage of having a library is that it's a single source for data and/or modifications, and each program does have to have not a unique copy of these executable functions for itself (thus, using extra space).
- `lost+found`: This is the most likely place to find files after system crashes.
- `tmp`: Programs usually need extra space to store data on disk. The `/tmp` directory is such a storage place. In some cases, this `/tmp` directory resides on a faster disk than the rest of the system because this area may be used the most. It's also the location in which files tend to accumulate, especially by sloppy programs that do not clean out their files after they are finished.

What is a Path?

So how do you look at a directory tree branch? When you go to a branch from the root, you take a path. The following example shows a simple branch of a directory tree.

Input/Output

```
$ pwd
/home/author/sams
$ ls -x
ch01 ch02 ch03 ch04 ch05 ch06 ch07 ch08 ch09 ch10
ch11 ch12 ch13 ch14
$ _
```

Analysis

As covered in Day 1, the first command (`pwd`) tells you that you're in the `/home/author/sams` directory. The next command shows the files in the `/home/author/sams` directory. Here's one branch of this tree:

`/`	The root directory
`/home`	A subdirectory of the root directory
`/home/author`	A subdirectory of the `/home` directory
`/home/author/sams`	A subdirectory of the `/home/author` directory

Note: The `/home/author` directory is called the parent of `sams` directory.

Note: Note the use of the `-x` option to list the files in a row-by-row fashion. The default on most UNIX systems is to list the files in a column-by-column fashion using the `-C` option (as covered earlier today).

How did the shell know where to go list files? It used the current working directory because you did not specify a path as an argument to the command. So what is a path anyway?

A *path* is the route you would take to go from the root of the UNIX directory tree to the file or directory you want to specify.

The format pathname for a file is as follows:

`directory-tree-route/`*`targetfile`*

or

`/directory-tree-route/`*`targetfile`*

A pathname consists of a slash followed by a sequence of slashes and directory names. The *targetfile* is the file you want to specify. The first slash before the directory tree route (ignore the hyphens for now) makes a big difference in how this path is interpreted.

There are two kinds of pathnames: a full pathname and a relative pathname.

- A *full pathname* begins with a `/`, followed by the sequence of directories from the root to the target file or directory. The route thus begins from the root directory and progresses downward until the target file is reached.
- A *relative pathname* does not begin with a `/` and assumes a starting location of the current working directory. Therefore, it starts from the current directory and moves downward.

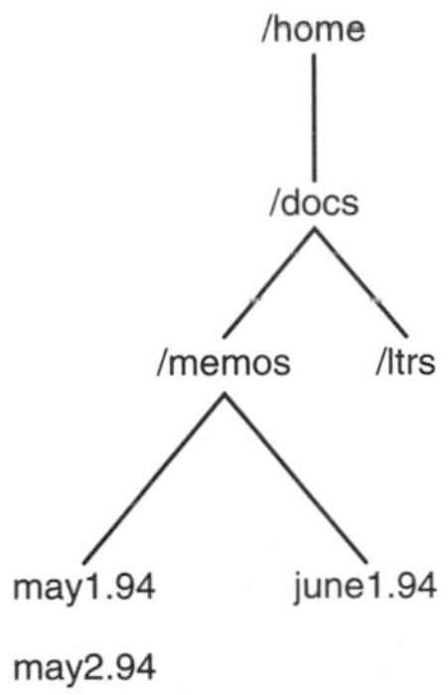

Figure 2.3. *Absolute versus relative pathnames.*

Look at Figure 2.3 for an example. If you are in the `docs` directory and want to get to `may1.94` from the root, you would have to specify `/home/docs/memo/may1.94` as the absolute pathname. To specify a relative path to this file, you would specify `memos/may1.94`.

You do not have to specify the `directory-tree-route` every time to get to a filename. If nothing is specified, your current working directory is selected as the `directory-tree-route`. The path (when you log in) would be the current working directory because you have not yet gone anywhere. This is shown via the print working directory (`pwd`) command. Type **`pwd`** at the prompt.

Input
Output

```
$ pwd
/home/kamran
$ _
```

Analysis

This command tells you about the current working directory. Now try an example with a subdirectory, called `alpha`, under your `home` directory. If you do not have an `alpha` subdirectory, do not worry. You will learn how to create one shortly. If you want to jump ahead and create one such directory, type the following command.

Input/Output

```
$ mkdir alpha
$ cp/etc/passwd alpha
$ ls -F
...alpha/
...
$
```

Analysis

You have just created a directory called `alpha` under your current working directory. Note the use of the `-F` flag. This lists the directory with a slash (`/`) after the name to indicate that it is a directory.

Note: The `ls -F` command on an empty directory will show nothing. If you had not copied `/etc/passwd` into `alpha`, `$ls -F alpha` would show nothing.

Caution: If you did not have permission to create a file in your directory, you would see an error message very similar to this one:

```
mkdir: cannot make directory "alpha". Permission denied
```

In this case, talk with your system administrator about setting your account right so you can create subdirectories.

You can refer to directories just as you do filenames:

- By using the relative pathname
- By using an absolute pathname

Some Special Directories

There are special directories in the directory tree in addition to ones discussed earlier:

- *The* `HOME` *directory:* UNIX places you into this directory by default when you first log in. This directory is your `HOME` directory. Note the uppercase. This is a special reserved word for the shell to remember where you logged in.
- *One period (.):* This is another name for your current working directory.
- *Two periods (..):* This is the directory above the current working directory. If you are at the root, this simply points to itself.

> **Note:** By now, you may have noticed how short all the UNIX commands are—for example, `cat` for concatenate, `ls` for listing, (`.`) for current directory, and (`..`) for its parent directory. This is because when UNIX was first developed on very slow terminal devices, it took quite long to type in commands. The shorter the name, the fewer characters to type.

2

File Permissions

Because UNIX was designed to be a multiuser system, there are provisions for making the file system personal for each user. You are given a specific area in which you can keep personal files. You can, at your discretion, lock these areas from other users reading or writing into them, or you can open your files to allow others' access. The parameters that allow such access are called *permissions.*

There are three types of permissions that you can grant to a file:

Read	Permission to read a file
Write	Permission to write into a file
Execute	Permission to execute a file that contains executable code

The scope of these permissions is based on the type of user:

User	Permission is granted to the owner.
Group	Permission is granted to the group of users to which this owner belongs.
Other	Permission is granted to all other users.

If you want any user on the system to read your file, you grant the file read permission for Other.

Here is the output of the `ls -al` command. This gives a mass of information about a file.

Input
Output

```
$ ls -al chap1
total 5
drwxr-xr-x   2 kbh      users        1024 Aug  7 08:32 ./
drwxr-xr-x   4 root     root         1024 Aug  7 07:54 ../
-rw-r--r--   1 root     root          217 Aug  7 08:19 bashful
-rw-r--r--   1 kbh      users          38 Aug  7 08:04 chap1
-rw-r--r--   1 kbh      users          44 Aug  7 08:05 chap2
$ _
```

Analysis

There are nine columns in this output.

Caution: Some variations of the `ls` command give fewer columns of information. For example, sometimes the time of creation, group, or both is not shown.

The first column is the mode of the file. This is the permissions structure.

The second column gives the number of links to this file. Links are ways to make other files in other directories point to this one. This enables more than one directory to have the same file without the added space of copies for each directory.

The fifth column shows the size (in bytes) of the file.

The output of column six sometimes shows the time and the date of the last modification of the file shown in column seven.

Following is a look at the permissions of chap1 in a bit more detail. There are 10 characters in the permissions field:

```
-rw-r--r--   1 kbh      users          38 Aug  7 08:04 chap1
```

The first hyphen (-) specifies the type of file. It can take the following values:

Value	Description
`-`	Ordinary file
`d`	A directory
`b`	A block device, such as a floppy disk drive
`c`	A character device, such as a terminal
`l`	Links to another file

The next group of three characters each specify the type of permission for this file. Three of these permission types are specified for each group type:

`r` for read
`w` for write
`x` for execute

The groups to which these types of permission apply are as follows:

- User
- Group
- Other

Users are individual users or login accounts. *Groups* are used to collect users who need to share data—for example, all the programmers on the same project. *Other* implies everyone in the system.

Now I'll discuss permissions. Basically, you need to have one of the three levels of permissions to be able to work with a file or directory, in order.

If a permission for this operation is not granted, the corresponding character is replaced with a `-`.

The next two sets of three characters have the same format but apply to the group and other, respectively. See Figure 2.4.

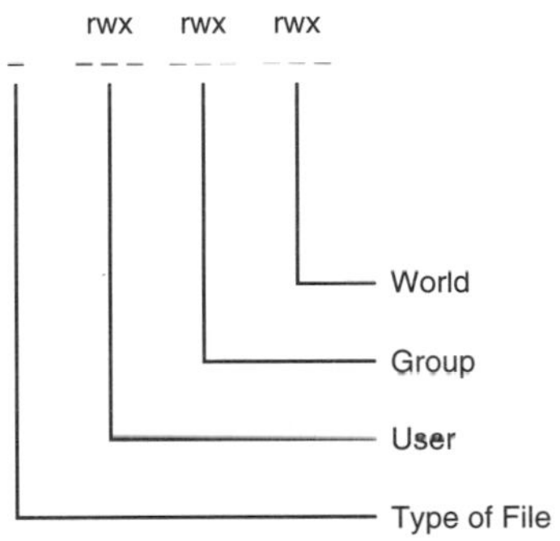

Figure 2.4. *File permissions.*

The format is as follows:

```
[type][owner][group][other]
```

Following are some sample permissions structures to illustrate these points:

```
-rwx------
```

implies that the file has write permissions only for the owner. The six dashes tell you that no group or world user has permission to read, write, or execute this file.

```
-rwxr-xr-x
```

implies that anyone can read or execute this file but only the owner can overwrite it. Note the missing `w`s in the second and third placeholders for the write permissions.

```
drwxrwx---
```

implies that the directory has all permissions for the owner and all users in the group, but others cannot read, write, or even look in this directory. Note the `d` for directory.

> **Note:** For a normal file, the `x` implies execution permission for the contents of the file. If you see an `x` in the user permissions, you can execute the contents of that file; otherwise, you cannot. For directories, however, the significance of the `x` changes to access permissions. If you remove the world `x` permissions from a directory entry, no one outside your group can even change directory (`cd`) into the directory. This is helpful if you do not want to show the contents of a directory to the rest of the world.

```
cr--r--r-
```

shows an entry for a character device that can only be read from, such as a keyboard.

```
br--r--r--
```

shows an entry for a CD-ROM drive, a block character device that can only be read from.

Changing File Permissions

The `chmod` command enables you to modify the permissions on a file. The syntax of the command is as follows:

```
chmod [ugoa][+-][rwx] filename
```

The following options are available to the `chmod` command:

`+w`	Gives write permission
`-w`	Takes away write permission
`+r`	Gives read permission
`-r`	Takes away read permission
`+x`	Gives execute permission
`-x`	Takes away execute permission
`u`	Applies to user
`g`	Applies to group
`o`	Applies to other (world)
`a`	Applies to all (default)

Input/Output

```
$ ls -al ss
-r--r--r--    1 kamran   users         2380 Jun 10 21:17 ss
$ chmod u+w ss
$ ls -al ss
-rw-r--r--    1 kamran   users         2380 Jun 10 21:17 ss
$ _
```

Analysis

The first line shows the current permissions on the file `ss`. The next command gives write permissions to the user for `ss`.

The permissions for the world and group for writing, as well other permissions (read/write for all), remain unchanged.

Input/Output

```
$ chmod a+w ch02
& ls -al ch02
-rw-rw-rw-    1 kamran   users        34520 Jun 10 22:02 ch02
$ _
```

Analysis

This gives the file write permission for you, the group, and the world. Anyone can remove the file with an `rm` command if the directory that this file resides in gives the user write permissions.

Input/Output

```
$ ls -al ss
-rw-rw-rw-    1 kamran   users         2380 Jun 10 21:17 ss
$ chmod a-w ss
$ ls -al ss
-r--r--r--    1 kamran   users         2380 Jun 10 21:17 ss
$ _
```

Analysis

This takes the file's write permission for you, the group, and the world. Now, even you cannot remove the file with the `rm` command. You also can specify the permissions with octal numbers. See the following Input/Output section for an example.

Input/Output

```
$
$ chmod 777 ss
$ ls -al ss
-rwxrwxrwx    1 kamran   users         2380 Jun 10 21:17 ss
$ _
```

Analysis

This gives the file read, write, and execute permissions for the world, group, and user. Now anyone can execute the file `ss`. Note that the shell uses this execute permission to run binary or shell script programs. If you do have execute permissions for a file, the shell will not execute the file, even if the file contains valid code or shell statements.

Note that `777` is an octal number. UNIX's age shows in some of the options to its command. The bits in octal numbers correspond to the permissions on a file in the following manner:

`-r--------`	0400 read permission for user
`--w-------`	0200 write permission for user
`---x------`	0100 execute permission for user
`----r-----`	0040 read permission for group
`-----w----`	0020 write permission for group
`------x---`	0010 execute permission for group
`-------r--`	0004 read permission for world
`--------w-`	0002 write permission for world
`---------x`	0001 execute permission for world

Note: In UNIX, you have to specify octal numbers with a `0` (zero) as the first digit.

You can specify the permissions explicitly as an octal number (listed previously). By combining these numbers, you can create the exact permissions structure for your file. For example, 0664 implies the following permissions:

`-r--------`	Read permission for user
`--w-------`	Write permission for user
`----------`	No execute permission for user
`----r-----`	Read permission for group
`-----w----`	Write permission for group
`----------`	No execute permission for group
`-------r--`	Read permission for world
`----------`	No write permission for world
`----------`	No execute permission for world
`0 6 6 4 <--`	The bits for permissions.

The Superuser Root

There is a special user name under UNIX called *root.* This user can read, write, or execute any file without regard to permissions. This user type is called the *superuser.* It's also referred to as the *root account, su,* or *being root.* Being a superuser lets you do things that mere mortal users cannot do, such as going into directories you do not have permission for and reading files at abandon.

If this sounds great, hold that thought. Being a superuser also can be dangerous because UNIX will not question any actions taken by the super-user. It is a privileged account, which only a few administrative accounts are allowed. It is not wise to leave this account without a password. If you see such an account on your site, please contact your system administrator.

Note: The left-most `0` in a permissions field is also used to set the sticky bit, group 10 bit, and user ID bits. The sticky bit tells the system to keep a copy of the program in memory after it's done (for a quicker load in the future). The group ID and user ID bits specify the permissions of the owner, and can be used to access files; otherwise, use the users permission. A discussion of these bits is beyond the scope of this book.

Even though I have an su account, I do perhaps 90 percent of my daily tasks as a regular user. The risks of causing irrevocable errors is too great for me to allow myself to run as root all the time.

You can become root by logging in by doing the following:

- Logging in as root
- Typing the su command and then the password

Working with Files

Now I'll discuss some of the most common file and disk operations you will use in UNIX. These will be the basic tools use to create, modify, or delete files and directories on a UNIX system.

Looking at the Contents of a File

To display the contents of a file use the `cat` command, use the following:

Input
Output

```
$ cat f1
The contents of file f1
$ _
```

Analysis

`cat` is short for concatenate, an archaic term for append. What UNIX does is append the contents of the file to the terminal. Note that the terminal is simply a file as far as UNIX is concerned. Therefore, when viewing a file, you are concatenating the contents of that file to the terminal file.

Copying One File to Another

To copy the contents of file `f1`, for example, over to another file called `f2`, use the `cp` command:

```
$ cp f1 f2
```

If `f2` does not exist, create it. If `f2` already exists, overwrite its contents with the contents of `f1`, if you have permissions. If you do not have permissions, you will get the following message:

```
cp: cannot create regular file `f2`: Permission denied
```

If you do not want to keep a copy of `f1` after copying it to `f2`, you can use the `mv` (for move) command. This renames the file `f1` to `f2`. Again, if `f2` already exists, it's removed from the disk if you have the permissions set correctly.

Deleting Files

You can remove files from UNIX with the `rm` command. Once removed, these files are generally not recoverable without help from special software. Even so, some files are generally not recoverable because the space they were using is freed for use by others in the system. Contact your UNIX system vendor for a list of such supported hardware.

You can specify more than one filename as an argument to the `rm` command.

```
$ rm f1 f2 f3
```

removes the files `f1`, `f2`, and `f3` from the directory tree.

Working with Directories

You have already seen directories in action. Now you will learn how to work with these directories.

Changing Your Directory

The following code shows how to change directories.

Input
Output

```
$ cd /etc
$ pwd
/etc
$ _
```

Analysis

You just changed your working directory to /etc. The current working directory then becomes the memos directory. The /etc directory must exist on the UNIX file system. Locate your current place in the directory tree with the pwd command.

Creating and Deleting Directories

To create a directory diet under your current working directory, do the following.

Input Output

```
$ mkdir diet
$ pwd
/home/kamran
$ ls diet
diet/
$ pwd
/home/kamran
$ mkdir /home/kamran/eat
$ ls eat
eat
$ _
```

Analysis

In the first instance, you created a directory diet with a relative pathname from your current directory. A listing with an -F option confirmed your command.

In the next line, you gave an absolute path to the new directory, /home/author/eat. Remember that you must have the forward slash (/) in front of the directory name for the absolute command.

Removing a Directory

To remove a directory, use the rmdir command, as shown in the following example.

Input Output

```
$ rmdir diet
$ ls diet
ls: diet: No such file or directory
$ pwd
/home/kamran
$ mkdir /home/kamran/diet
$ ls diet
diet
$ _
```

Analysis

You first removed the directory d1. This works only if the directory has no files or subdirectories in it. If you do not care what's in the subdirectory, use the rm -rf command:

```
$ rm -fr diet
```

The -r option causes the rm command to recursively remove all the files. Recursively, rm means that all files, subdirectories—if any—and all files in those subdirectories will be removed. The -f option forces the deletion of files even if the file is a read-only file. As long as you have permissions to write to the read-only file, you can delete it.

If you are unsure about your files, use the -i option to the rm command. This will interactively ask you before deleting each file.

Input/Output

```
$ rm -i myfile
myfile: ?
$ _
```

Analysis

The rm command prints the name of the file it's about to delete, a colon, and a question mark. If you want to delete the file, type the lowercase y key; otherwise, press any key (which indicates not to delete the file).

DO | **DON'T**

DO use the rmdir command often; it will at least force you to look in a directory that you are attempting to remove. If the directory isn't empty, you might accidently remove some important files with the rm -fr command.

DO use the -i option when you're not sure whether you are deleting important files.

DON'T use the rm -fr command unless you are sure that the directory you are deleting does not have important files in it.

Copying Files into Directories

The following shows an example of how to copy a file into a directory.

Input/Output

```
$ ls memos
f3
$ cp f2 memos
$ ls memos
f2 f3
$ ls f2
f2
$ ls f0
f0
$ mv f0 memos
$ ls f0
ls: f0: No such file or directory
$ ls memos
f0 f2 f3
$ _
```

Analysis

This copies the contents of `f2` (in your current directory) into the file with the name `f2` in `memos` directory. If `f2` does not exist, create it. If `f2` exists, overwrite it if you have permissions. You will be given an error message if you try to copy a file onto itself.

If the `memos` directory does not exist, `f2` will be copied on top of a file called `memos` in your current working directory. The `f2` file will still exist in the original directory. Similarly, the `mv` command moves the `f0` file into `memos`. However, `f0` will no longer exist in the original directory.

More About Working with Files

Working with files is just as easy as working with directories. You can create, modify, copy, move, delete, and list files. With executable files (with execute permission), you can run files as programs.

Creating Files

Now create a file from the `$` prompt. This is sometimes useful when you want to write something straight to disk.

Input Output

```
$ cat > newfile
Hello world
This is another user
ctrl-d
$ ls newfile
newfile
$ _
```

Analysis

I will discuss the significance of the > symbol later. For now, all you need to know is that > simply redirects whatever you type into a file called `newfile`. The Ctrl+d is the typing of the control key with the lowercase *d* key.

This is interpreted as an end of input file to the shell and causes the shell to close the file.

```
$ ls newfile
newfile
$ _
```

To see if the contents are indeed what you typed in, type in the following command.

Input Output

```
$ cat newfile
Hello world
This is another user
$ cp newfile copyfile
$ cat copyfile
Hello world
This is another user
```

Analysis

Now copy `newfile` to another file called `copyfile`. Note that UNIX doesn't tell you if it succeeded or not. If there were no errors, UNIX says nothing. Now look at contents of `copyfile` to confirm that it is identical to `newfile`.

Comparing ASCII Files

In the previous example, the files were small enough to do a visual comparison by looking at them on screen. This does not work very well with large files and subtle differences.

There are several ways to compare files. Here are two common ways to compare files:

- Count the number of words using the `wc` command.
- Compare the files line by line using the `diff` command. Day 10 covers this command in more detail.

Counting the Words in a File

First, count the number of words, lines, and characters in newfile. Then do the same for copyfile. Do they match?

Input
Output

```
$ wc newfile
2    6 33   newfile
$ wc copyfile
2    6 33   copyfile
$ wc copyfile newfile
2    6 33   newfile
2    6 33   copyfile
4 12 66   total
$ _
```

Analysis

`newfile` has 2 lines, 7 words, and 32 characters in all. Now count the number of words, lines, and characters in `copyfile`. Then count the number of words, lines, and characters in both files. Note that this command gives you the total number of lines, words, and characters in all the files you specified.

This is a quick way of determining the difference between two files. However, for a more detailed output, you should use the `diff` command.

The *diff* Command

Now let's create a `newfile` and `copyfile` with different text strings to see the differences with the `diff` command.

Input
Output

```
& cat > newfile
this is one
this is two
this is three
this is four
ctrl-d
$ cat > copyfile
this is one
this is two
this is three
this is four
this is five
Ctrl-d
$ diff newfile copyfile
2,3c2,3
< this is two
< this ie three
---
> this is 2
> this is three
4a5
> this is 5
$ _
```

Analysis

Note the difference between the two files. One has the word `two`, and the other has the numeral `2` in it. Obviously, this is a convoluted example with only a few lines. The `diff` utility is very useful in comparing long files with subtle differences.

The output from this command has several distinct parts:

- The first `2` in `2,3c2,3` indicates that lines 2 through 3 of the first file differ from the lines 2 through 3 of the second file.
- The different lines are shown with a less-than sign (`<`) sign for the lines in the first file passed to the `diff` command, and the greater-than (`>`) sign for the second file.
- The `4c5` with only the greater-than sign indicates that the first line does not have any more lines that can be compared with the fifth line in `copyfile`. This is the way to tell if one file is longer than the other if you do not want to use the `wc` command to count.

The *man* Command

One of the biggest hurdles in UNIX is that its command set is very cryptic. This is probably attributed to the laziness of programmers. The smaller the number of keys to type, the better the command. Added to that is the designer's notion that *if a command*

has no errors or has nothing to report, it should not say anything—or at least as little as possible. You might find it a bit annoying when a command does not behave the way you expect it to.

This is where UNIX's online documentation comes in—via the `man` command. In some situations, it's best to look up the online manual pages under UNIX.

The `man` command is the online manual command. This could be the most important command for you, whether you are learning the UNIX system or are an experienced user. The syntax for the command is as follows:

```
man command
```

The UNIX online documentation is divided into eight general sections. The sections are ordered as shown here:

Section	Topics covered
1	User commands
1M	System maintenance commands for administrators
2	System calls
3	Library routines
3N	Network routines
4	Administrative file information
5	Miscellaneous
6	Games
7	Special files
8	Administrative

Note: Your system's `man` command may produce a different list for the topics previously listed. Your system may not support the `man -k` command.

If you are unsure of the type of command, you can use the `man -k` option to list all types of commands. For example, to get information about the types of `who` commands, type the following command.

Input/Output

```
$ man -k who

mkuuwho (8)         - Make a database suitable for the uuwho command
rwho (1)            - Who's logged in on local machines
rwhod (8)           - System status server
uuwho (1)           - Show map entry for a site
w (1)               - Show who is logged on and what they are doing.
whoami (1)          - Print effective userid
$ _
```

Analysis The first item shows the command name, the second item shows the section number, and the rest of the line gives a short description of the command.

To get more details about a command, use the `man` command. For example, look at man page for the `who` command:

```
WHO(1L)                                                  WHO(1L)

NAME
       who - show who is logged on

SYNOPSIS
       who  [-imqsuwHT]  [--count]  [--idle] [--heading] [--help]
       [--message] [--mesg] [--version] [--writable]  [file]  [am
       i]

DESCRIPTION
          This  manual  page  documents  the GNU version of who.  If given no
          non-option arguments, who  prints  the  following information for each
          user currently logged on:

              login name
              terminal line
              login time
              remote hostname or X display

       If given one non-option argument, wwhhoo uses that instead of /etc/utmp as
       the name of the file containing the record of users  logged on.  /etc/wtmp
       is commonly given as an argument to who to look at who has previously logged
       on.

       If given two non-option arguments,  who prints  only  the
       entry  for  the user running it (determined from its stan-
       dard input), preceded by the hostname.  Traditionally, the
       two arguments given are `am i', as in `who am i'.

OPTIONS
       -m     Same as `who am i'.

       -q, --count
              Print  only the login names and the number of users
              logged on.  Overrides all other options.

       -s     Ignored; for compatibility with other  versions  of
              who.

       -i, -u, --idle
              After the login time, print the number of hours and
              minutes that the user has been idle.  `.' means the
              user  was  active  in last minute.  `old' means the
              user was idle for more than 24 hours.

       -H, --heading
              Print a line of column headings.
```

```
-w, -T, --mesg, --message, --writable
       Like -s, plus after the login name print a  charac-
       ter indicating the user's message status:

       +      allowing wwrriittee messages

       -      disallowing wwrriittee messages

       ?      cannot find terminal device

--help Print  a  usage message on standard output and exit
       successfully.

--version
       Print version information on standard  output  then
       exit successfully.
```

The first line indicates the section number and name of the command. The middle of the line tells you what version of the software you are running. The next few sections are consistent in their description of the command.

- `NAME` tells you in one line what the command is about.
- `SYNOPSIS` tells you how to run the command.
- `DESCRIPTION` gives a detailed description of the command.
- `COMMAND LINE` describes the options in detail.
- `OPTIONS` describe the options to this command.

You also can see some other fields in a `man` listing.

- `FILES` lists the related files to this command.
- `SEE ALSO` directs you to other related commands.
- `AUTHORS` credits the authors or other related parties.
- `BUGS` lists the known bugs (if any have been reported) in the command.

More About the *ls* Command

You have already used this command by now. This will soon become your most powerful tool in navigating the directory. Now look at the `-C` option.

To look at the files in the `/etc` directory, use the following command.

Input
Output

```
$ ls -C /etc
DIR_COLORS      fstab      ld.so.cache    motd       shells
crond.pid       gettydefs  ld.so.conf     mtab       skel
csh.cshrc       group      lilo           mtools     syslog.conf
csh.login       inet       lilo.conf      passwd     syslog.pid
default         inittab    lilo.conf.bak  passwd.OD  termcap
disktab         issue      magic          profile    ttys
fdprm           klog.pid   minicom.user   rc.d       utmp
fs              ksh.kshrc  minirc.dfl     securetty  wtmp
$ _
```

Analysis

The `-C` option gives you a multicolumn output suitable for editing. Look at the man pages for a load of options to this command. As this book progresses, many options to this command in are discussed.

Hiding a File or Directory from an *ls* Listing

UNIX provides a simple method for keeping files from being visible in an `ls` output listing. If the first letter of a filename begins with a period (`.`), the file is not listed in the output from the `ls` command. To list this command, use the ls `-a` option. For example, the file `.manual` will not be listed via the `ls` command, but with `ls -a`, `.manual` will be listed.

The `-a` option used in conjunction with the `-l` option on a directory will reveal all the files in that directory. Try the command `ls -a $HOME` to see how the `-a` option works.

Input
Output

```
$ ls -a $HOME
.               .kermrc       .term         chuser     screen.dump
..              .less         .xinitrc      docs       src
.Xauthority     .lessrc       .xserverrc    faq        startx
.Xdefaults      .mcwd         Xconfig       mkcdrom    t.t.t
.Xresources     .mwmrc        Xconfig.new   ml         tifs
.bash_history   .pdksh_hist   advs          quran      unvmnu
.emacs          .profile      chprog        sams       xme

$ ls $HOME
Xconfig      chprog  faq      quran        src     tifs
Xconfig.new  chuser  mkcdrom  sams         startx  unvmnu
advs         docs    ml       screen.dump  t.t.t   xme
$ _
```

Analysis

The `-a` command prints out all the files in your home directory to get a listing of all the files in that directory. Note how the output from the command without the `-a` option does not show the files with names beginning with a period.

The *more*, *less*, *head*, and *tail* Commands

These commands are helpful when you want to view parts of text files. The `more` and `less` commands enable you to page through a file. The `less` command enables you to move backward and forward while viewing a file, whereas the `more` command enables you to move forward only. The `head` and `tail` commands let you slice lines from the front (head) or back (tail) of a text file.

What's Better, *more* or *less*?

The `more` command is useful when viewing long files. See the following code for an example.

Input/Output

```
$ more numlines
This is line 0
This is line 1
This is line 2
This is line 3
This is line 4
This is line 5
This is line 6
This is line 7
This is line 8
This is line 9
This is line 10
This is line 11
This is line 12
This is line 13
This is line 14
This is line 15
This is line 16
This is line 17
This is line 18
This is line 19
This is line 20
This is line 21
This is line 22
--More--(12%)
```

Analysis

The `more` command prints one screenful at a time. The last line on the screen indicates the percentage of the file you are currently viewing. The previous example shows that you are viewing 12 percent of a file with 100 lines. The file `numlines` is a canned sample file with 100 lines in it, with each line indicating its line number from the start of the file.

Pressing the spacebar advances text by one screenful. The original `more` command only enables scrolling forward by using the Enter key to advance one line at a time, or the spacebar to advance the text one screenful at a time. Some UNIX systems also offer the `less` command.

The `less` command is based on the adage "less is always better than more." This command is similar to `more` but, among other features, it allows the user to scroll backward. The man pages are generally viewed through either the `more` or `less` utilities. The scrolling commands default to the `vi` editor, but this is modifiable. The man page for the `less` command gives an impressive array of customizable features for the `less` command.

Unfortunately, not all UNIX installations offer the `less` command. If it's not available, you should almost certainly have the `more` command. The best way to find out is to try and use it.

head and *tail*

The `head` command is particularly useful for printing very long files. It prints the first 10 lines of a file by default. This works best with text files. To print more than 10 lines, use the `-n` option.

Input
Output

```
$ head -n 13 numlines
This is line 1
This is line 2
This is line 3
This is line 4
This is line 5
This is line 6
This is line 7
This is line 8
This is line 9
This is line 10
This is line 11
This is line 12
This is line 13
$ _
```

Analysis

This prints the first 13 lines of the file `numlines`. The `head` command is especially useful for looking at the beginning of long files rather than using the `cat` or `more` commands, especially in script files.

Another way of specifying the number of lines is to use the `head` command with the alternate option, `--lines`, for specifying the lines. This is a new option available with the later versions of the `head` command.

Input/Output

```
$ head --lines 13 numlines
This is line 1
This is line 2
This is line 3
This is line 4
This is line 5
This is line 6
This is line 7
This is line 8
This is line 9
This is line 10
This is line 11
This is line 12
This is line 13
$ _
```

Analysis

Note how the `--lines` option gave the same output as the `-n` option.

> **Note:** The `--` option may not be available on your UNIX machine. Try the option anyway to see if it does exist.

You can print the head of more than one files by specifying all the filenames at the prompt. In this case, the files are printed out in succession with each file's head separated by => and <=.

Input/Output

```
$ head pizza parlor

==> pizza <==
Mr. Gatti       265-3419
Dominoes        256-1000
Pizza Hut       345-2174
Dirty's         980-2314
Gut Wrench      980-3184
Pizza Inn       265-2213
Slimey's        266-9876
Jorges' Pub     265-1987

==> parlor <==
Mr. Gatti
Dominoes
Pizza Hut
Dirty's
Gut Wrench
Pizza Inn
Slimey's
Jorges' Pub
```

Analysis

You can see the contents of the two files, one followed by another.

The ==> and <== signify the name of the file whose contents are being shown. The best way to use this feature is to catalog large numbers of files in a directory. If you type the files' descriptions in the first 10 lines of all the files in that directory and take the heads off the file, you will get the listing of all the files. For example, if you have several text files, you would use the `head *.memo` to get the heads of all the files with an extension of `.memo` as a catalog.

The `tail` command is the inverse of (and is more useful than) the `head` command. The `tail` command prints the last 10 lines of a file by default. This is especially useful when looking at debug listings—for example, when you want to see the output from a program right before it crashed.

As with the `head` command, you can specify the number of lines to display from the output by specifying the lines options.

Input
Output

```
$ tail --lines 12 numlines
This is line 88
This is line 89
This is line 90
This is line 91
This is line 92
This is line 93
This is line 94
This is line 95
This is line 96
This is line 97
This is line 98
This is line 99
$ _
```

Analysis

In this case, the last 12 lines of the file were shown. Note that I used the `--lines` option. I could also have used the command:

```
$ tail -n 12 numlines
```

to get the same results.

Caution: When using UNIX, you will see that there can be more than one option for a command to get the same thing done. Sometimes commands are compatible and take both forms of arguments; sometimes they do not. When in doubt, try both versions of a command and then use the one that works and with which you are comfortable.

The *file* Command

Occasionally, you have to know about the contents of a file. If you `cat` a non-text file to your terminal, you might be faced with a long series of loud beeps and squeals as the control characters play havoc with your terminal's line settings. This is somewhat embarrassing if you are seated next to others. It's also quite irritating because sometimes your terminal gets hung up (because of all the random control characters it is receiving).

It's best to check out the contents of the file before doing a `cat` on an unknown file by using the `file` command.

To find out about an item in the directory listing, look at the results of the commands, shown in the following example.

Input/Output

```
$ file pizza
pizza: ascii text
$ file .
.:directory
$ file /etc
/etc:directory
$ file /bin/ls
/bin/ls: Linux/i386 demand paged executable
$ _
```

Analysis

The first line tells you that the file `pizza` contains ASCII text. The next line queries about the item period (.), which implies the current working directory. Similarly, it recognizes the `/etc` item as a directory. The next two lines test the contents of the `/bin/ls` file, which is shown as a binary file. This command tells you that it's not a good idea to `cat` the contents of the `/bin/ls` file to your terminal.

Summary

Today's text covered the following items:

- This was a primer on the UNIX file system. It introduced you to the concept of files and directories under UNIX.
- You have worked with the basic tools in the UNIX system. These tools are required for working with the shell and will help you get a feel for how UNIX tools work.

- The man pages are very useful sources of information when starting out with UNIX. You should now know how to read man pages and be familiar with the ordering of the man sections.
- You learned how to create and remove files and directories.
- You learned how to navigate directory trees and to know where you are in a tree.
- You learned how to read and set the permissions.
- It's possible to create files that are hidden from normal listings. It's also possible to create files that are nearly impossible to get rid of. (`-a` is a good example of such a file.)
- The `more`, `less`, `head`, and `tail` commands are useful when looking at small, manageable sections of large text files.
- The `file` command is useful when checking whether or not a file contains ASCII text.

UNIX Commands Learned Today

`cp`	Copies files
`mkdir[name]`	Makes a directory below your current directory
`mv`	Renames files and/or moves them to different directories
`diff`	Looks at differences between two text files
`rm`	Removes a file (or with `-r`, removes a directory)
`rmdir`	Removes a directory
`more`	Enables you to view a text file one screen at a time
`less`	A better version of the more command
`head`	Lets you look at (and cut) the lines from the front of a file
`tail`	Lets you look at (and cut) lines from the back of a file
`file`	Lets you guess the type of file, directory, and so forth, when given a filename

What's Next?

Tomorrow's text covers shell variables and introduces you to a user environment. You will get started with the basics of the shell programming language.

Q&A

Q How do you get to list files row-by-row instead of column-by-column?

A Use the `ls -x` command to list multiple files row-by-row. Use the `ls -C` command to list multiple files column-by-column.

Q Can directories have other directories under them? What are these called?

A Yes they can, and these are called subdirectories.

Q What's the disadvantage of the `less` command?

A It may not be available on your UNIX installation.

Q How do I know it's safe to concatenate a file?

A Use the `file` command to test the type of file before displaying it.

Q How do I ask `rm` to confirm each delete?

A Use the `-i` option on the command line.

Workshop

The Workshop provides quiz questions to help you solidify your understanding of the material covered. Some Workshop sections of this book also contain exercises to provide you with experience in using what you've learned. Try to understand the quiz and exercise answers before continuing on to the next chapter. Answers are provided in Appendix D, "Answers."

Quiz

1. Give some characteristics of filenames. Is any punctuation allowed?
2. What is the limit on the length of filenames under UNIX?
3. What is the UNIX directory tree?

4. What is a path?
5. What is the difference between an absolute path and a relative path?
6. What are the types of permissions on a file and for access?
7. What is the difference between comparing two text files with `wc` and `diff`?
8. How can you look at small sections of text files? How do you know if a file contains text?

Exercises

1. Try to use some of the options in the `ls` command. What does the `-C` option do? What's the difference between the `-a` and `-l` options? Try these commands on your `HOME` directory.
2. Compare the output from the two commands:

```
$ ls -x
$ ls -C
```

3. You will learn about I/O redirection later in Day 4. However, given that

```
head oldfile > newfile
```

creates newfile with 10 lines from `oldfile`, how would you create a file that has lines 10 through 20 only from `oldfile`, which is greater than 20 lines?

Tip: Take the tail of one and the head of another.

4. What permissions would you give to a file that anyone can execute the file but not read or write it?
5. What do the following permissions mean for a file?

```
644 _ _ _ _ _ _ _ _ _ _
711 _ _ _ _ _ _ _ _ _ _
777 _ _ _ _ _ _ _ _ _ _
505 _ _ _ _ _ _ _ _ _ _
444 _ _ _ _ _ _ _ _ _ _
400 _ _ _ _ _ _ _ _ _ _
```

WEEK 1

3

Shell Variables

This section covers shell variables and introduces you to your user environment. This will get you started with the basics of the shell programming language.

- Shell variables
- Choosing variable names
- Working with shell variables
- Substitution operators
- Local versus environment variables
- Special shell variables
- Evaluating shell variables
- Simple math operations
- Built-in shell variables

Shell Variables

As with any other language, the shell provides the user with the ability to define variables and assign values to them. A shell variable has a format similar to that of a filename. The names for variables begin with an alphanumeric character or an underscore (_), followed by one or more alphanumeric or underscore characters. Some valid shell variables include the following:

```
HOME
DOS_SHELL
DIR1
S1
S_PI_BY_2
1234T
MR_TOE
```

You can assign values to variables using the following syntax:

```
variable=value
```

Note that there are no spaces on either side of the equal sign.

```
$ count=2
```

sets the value of the shell variable `count` to 2. To check the value of the variable, use the `echo` command:

Input
Output

```
$ count=2
$ echo count
count
$ echo $count
2
$ _
```

Analysis

The first line set the value of count to 2. The next command requested the shell to echo the string count. The third command requested the shell to echo the value of the shell variable count.

Notice that we preceded the variable with a $ to ask the shell to specify that we wanted the value of the variable. The $ tells the shell that the strings after the $ character are the name of a variable and the shell uses the *value* assigned to this variable.

Choosing Variable Names

When choosing variable names, you must follow some rules. You cannot use any punctuation characters at all. So, a variable name of t.n.t is not a valid name. If you have to separate words, use the underscore character, as in t_n_t.

Also, shell variable names are case-sensitive. This is consistent with filenames as discussed earlier, in Day 2. So, the words extra, eXtra, and EXTRA are three completely different variables as far as the shell is concerned.

The shell does not recognize a digit as the first character of a variable. So, 1234 is not a valid name.

DO | **DON'T**

DON'T use any other punctuation marks than the underscore.

DON'T put any spaces on either side of the equal sign when assigning a value to a variable.

DO realize that shell variables are also case-sensitive, just like filenames.

DO use meaningful variable names as you did with filenames. Names such as zzzz do not mean much to another user, or even yourself if you come back to look at it after some time.

DO use uppercase names for environment variables if you want them to stand out in listings and to not be confused with lowercase UNIX commands.

Uses for Shell Variables

Shell variables are very useful in a lot of ways. Two of the more common uses are as follows:

- As placeholders for pathnames
- As options to common commands

The first use shortens the typing required to traverse multiple directory paths. Look at the following listing:

```
$ adir=/home/another/prog2/data
$ echo $adir
/home/another/prog2/data
$ pwd
/home/this
$ cd $adir
$ pwd
/home/another/prog2/data
$ _
```

To assign the directory name to a variable, you can use the following command:

```
$ adir=/home/another/prog2/data
```

The `pwd` command confirms where you are in the directory tree.

Then you can switch over to directory by specifying the value held by the variable `adir`. The shell substituted the value of `adir` for the part of `$adir` before passing the argument to the `cd` command.

The shell does variable substitutions *before* it executes a command. For example, consider the output of the following commands (that is, when `count` was set to `2` and `adir` was set to `home/another/prog2/data`).

Input
Output

```
$ echo count adir
count adir
$ echo $count adir
2 adir
$ echo $count $adir
2 /home/another/prog2/data
$ _
```

Analysis

Notice how the shell does variable substitution before the `echo` command is executed. All variables preceded by a `$` character are replaced with the shell before being passed to `echo` command. In the last example, both `count` and `adir` are evaluated and the values resulting from these applications are passed to the `echo` command.

Shell Variable Considerations

The Bourne shell has no concept of numeric values. All values are strings as far as it is concerned. The values of `1`, `One`, and `1.23` are all stored in variables as strings. Later today, you will learn a technique for doing some very simple mathematics.

Unlike variables in higher programming languages such as C or Pascal, you do not have to declare a shell variable before you use it. If you use a shell variable without first setting it, the shell will merrily declare it for you and proceed with an empty string value. So, when in doubt about the value of a shell variable, use the `echo` command to display the contents of the variable.

It's up to you to confirm that the variable you are using has a value in it. Keep in mind that the shell does this substitution before it passes the arguments to the command. So what happens when you try to echo a variable that does not have a value? Try the following command:

```
$ echo $unknown

$ _
```

You cannot tell if the blank line was an extra carriage return or some other typo. To see if the value is indeed blank, put colons around it to get the following:

```
$ echo :$unknown:
::
$ _
```

As you can see, the shell did nothing with this variable. This variable now contains a `NULL` value. Shell variables with a `NULL` value are completely removed from the command line without a trace. So a command like the following:

```
$ ls $unknown -al $unknown $unknown *.c
```

will be reduced to

```
$ ls -al *.c
```

after all the `NULL` values for the unknown variable are removed. If the value of unknown had been set to something, the command may not have worked.

Customizing your shell environment can be a snap once you are familiar with shell variables. For example, you do have to type **`ls -C`** every time you want a nice columnar listing. Instead of typing this sequence all the time and subjecting yourself to typos, use a substitute for that command with an environment variable:

```
$ command="-C"
```

Then type

```
$ ls $command
```

to get the same results. Note that this is a taste of what shell scripts are about. Shell scripts provide many more features, such as arguments and consistency, and they are much more reliable. Plus, you do not have to type the `$` before the command name to invoke them.

> **Note:** The `-C` option example might not show you a real benefit of the substitution. Consider another example in which you have to print several text files with the extensions `.txt`, `.doc`, `.wp`, and `.man`. If you set the variable `MYFILES` to `*.txt`, `*.doc`, `*.wp`, and `*.man`, all you have to do is run your formatter with this command:
>
> ```
> $ formatter $MYFILES
> ```
>
> instead of
>
> ```
> $formatter *.txt *.doc *.wp *.man
> ```
>
> which takes longer to type and leaves more room for typos.

Input/Output

```
$ count="-C"
$ ls $count /
bin       dev     home         mnt     sbin    var
boot      dosc    lib          proc    tmp     vmlinuz
cdrom     etc     lost+found   root    usr     vmlinuz.old
$ _
```

Analysis

Note how the `$count` variable is expanded to the option `-C` before being executed.

Now let's try a more complicated example.

Input/Output

```
$ VOOT=/
$ NOTHING=bad
$ ls -al $NOTHING $VOOT
ls: bad: No such file or directory
total 644
drwxr-xr-x  18 root     root         1024 Apr 30 16:18 .
drwxr-xr-x  18 root     root         1024 Apr 30 16:18 ..
drwxr-xr-x   2 root     bin          1024 Apr 23 16:59 bin
drwxr-xr-x   2 root     root         1024 Apr 30 21:16 boot
dr-xr-xr-x   2 root     root         1024 Apr 30 21:16 cdrom
drwxr-xr-x   2 root     root         5120 Jun 12 05:34 dev
drwxr-xr-x   2 root     root        16384 Dec 31  1969 dosc
drwxr-xr-x   7 root     root         1024 Jun 12 05:34 etc
drwxr-xr-x   5 root     root         1024 Jun  4 10:55 home
```

```
drwxr-xr-x    2 root     root          1024 Apr 23 22:54 lib
drwxr-xr-x    2 root     root         12288 Apr 23 16:51 lost+found
drwxr-xr-x    2 root     root          1024 Mar 16 13:23 mnt
dr-xr-xr-x    5 root     root             0 Jun 12 00:34 proc
drwxr-x--x    4 root     root          1024 Apr 23 22:42 root
drwxr-xr-x    2 root     bin           1024 Apr 23 16:59 sbin
drwxrwxrwt    3 root     root          1024 Jun 12 07:11 tmp
drwxr-xr-x   18 root     root          1024 Apr 23 17:17 usr
drwxr-xr-x   10 root     root          1024 Apr 23 17:21 var
-rw-------    1 root     root        264708 Apr 30 21:19 vmlinuz
-r--------    1 root     root        346628 Apr 30 21:13 vmlinuz.old
$ _
```

In this example the `VOOT` variable is first set to point to the root `/`. Then you issue the `ls` command to find the file with the value of `$NOTHING`, called bad. After that, it proceeds to provide long listing of the files listed in the directory specified by `$VOOT`, the `/` directory.

The moral of the story is that setting shell variables as synonyms for arguments is an effective and very powerful way of selectively passing parameters to a command.

If you are using a particular set of parameters to a command, you could set a variable to that set of flags and save yourself some typing effort. For example, when compiling a C program in UNIX, you might have to set four options for every compile: `-g`, `-m486`, `-ansi`, and `-v`.

So the command to type for every source file would be as follows:

```
$ gcc -g -m486 -ansi -v myfyl.c -o myfyl
```

Typing this in every time would be difficult and prone to error. Obviously, the ideal solution would be to make a shell script out of it. However, if you were to change one of the flags, you would have to change every shell script to reflect the new flag. Instead, it would be faster to set up the environment variable once and have all the commands and shell scripts refer to it.

So, set a variable called `CFLAGS` to the list of options.

```
$ CFLAGS="-g -m486 -v"
$ gcc $CFLAGS t.c -o t.out
Reading specs from /usr/lib/gcc-lib/i486-linux/2.5.8/specs
gcc version 2.5.8
   /usr/lib/gcc-lib/i486-linux/2.5.8/cpp -lang-c -v -undef
   ➥D__GNUC__=2D__GNUC_MINOR__=5 -Dunix -Di386 -Dlinux -D__unix__ -
   ➥D__i386_-D__linux__ -D__unix -D__i386 -D__linux -Asystem(unix) -
Asystem(posix) -Acpu(i386) -Amachine(i386) -g -D__i486__ ../t.c /tmp/cca00155.i
GNU CPP version 2.5.8 (80386, BSD syntax)
#include "..." search starts here:
#include <...> search starts here:
 /usr/local/include
/usr/i486-linux/include
/usr/lib/gcc-lib/i486-linux/2.5.8/include
```

Input Output

```
/usr/include
End of search list.
 /usr/lib/gcc-lib/i486-linux/2.5.8/cc1 /tmp/cca00155.i -quiet -dumpbase ➥t.c -
m486 -g -version -o /tmp/cca00155.s
GNU C version 2.5.8 (80386, BSD syntax) compiled by GNU C version 2.5.8.
 as -o /tmp/cca001551.o /tmp/cca00155.s
 ld -dll-verbose -m486 /usr/lib/crt0.o -static -L/usr/lib/gcc-lib/i486-➥linux/
2.5.8 /tmp/cca001551.o -lgcc -lg -lgcc
Fixup count 0
Removed 0 symbols from symtab
Fixup table address: 7488
$ _
```

Analysis

The verbose command gave the verbose listing, whereas the shell executed the compiler command, `gcc`.

Unfortunately, this variable is set only for the duration of your current session. In Day 5, when you work with customizing your environment, you learn of ways to save this information for all subsequent sessions in a `.profile` file. The `.profile` file is the standard file to which the shell saves such parameters.

Note: The variable `CFLAGS` is the standard shell variable used by the standard C compiler on UNIX when compiling C program files.

Resetting a Variable

When a variable has no value, it defaults to `NULL`. You can think of `NULL` as an empty string. To set the value of a shell variable to `NULL`, you can choose from at least three different ways, shown in the following Input/Output section.

Input Output

```
$ myvalue=
$ echo $myvalue

$ myvalue=#
$ echo $myvalue

$ myvalue=""
$ echo $myvalue
$ _
```

Analysis

All three ways are equivalent. The first assignment is terminated with a return immediately following the equal sign. The second assignment is terminated with a comment character. The third assignment is set to two double quotes with no spaces between them.

Using Shell Variables

For example, your HOME shell variable is set to the directory into which you are placed when you log in. So, wherever your current working directory may be, you can go to your login directory by typing the following:

```
$ cd $HOME
```

In the case of cd, if no pathname is specified, the value of $HOME is implied as the input directory name.

Perhaps you wanted to copy the file at your current location to your home directory:

```
$ cp file $HOME
```

This would copy the file in your current directory to your HOME directory, regardless of where you are in the directory tree.

Assigning values to shell variables can be confusing at times, because it's easy to forget about the $ sign when referencing a variable. For example, try the following command.

Input Output

```
$ value1=88
$ value2=value1
$ echo $value2
value1
$ _
```

Analysis This was probably not what you expected. The value of value1 was assigned to the variable value2, instead of the value contained in the variable called value2. You should have used the following:

```
$ value2=$value1
$ echo $value2
88
$ _
```

This worked now because the $ was placed before the variable name. In the first case, you forgot to put the $ in front of the variable value1.

The following is a more useful example.

Input Output

```
$ s=/home/kbh/documents/memos/jan92
$ d=/home/kbh/reports/annual92
$ ls $s
...,"output of /home/kbh/documents/memos/jan92",...
$ echo $s
/home/kbh/documents/memos/jan92
$ echo $d
/home/kbh/reports/annual92
$ ls $d
...,"output of /home/kbh/reports/annual92",...
```

Input/Output

```
$ cp $s/*.doc $d
$ cp $s/*.doc $HOME/backup
$ _
```

Analysis

As you can see, by setting the variables `s` and `d` once, you ease the burden of typing long pathnames. It's a lot easier to type **`$s`** than to type **`/home/kbh/documents/memos/jan92`**, and you are less likely to make mistakes.

Also, the shell expands these variables. The `$ cp $s/*.doc $d` command, expands correctly to `$ cp /home/kbh/documents/memos/jan92/*.doc $d` when it's actually executed.

In the last line, I sent a copy of all the same files to the backup directory under my home directory.

Constructing New Variables

Frequently, you'll want to append some letters to filenames. For example, to copy `oldFlame.old` to the filename called `oldFlame`, shown in the variable `BUGSYS`, you might be tempted to use the following command:

```
$ mv $BUGSYS $BUGSYSold
```

Of course, you must ensure that `BUGSYS` is set to `oldFlame`. The command is translated using the following translation:

```
$ mv oldFlame (the value of BUGSYSold )
```

This command translates to the value of `BUGSYS` into the first argument. The shell then attempts to translate the second variable to the value of `BUGSYSold`. If that variable does not exist, you get an error. If it exists, you may move this file to a completely different location than you expected.

To achieve this, use the following:

```
$ mv $BUGSYS ${BUGSYS}old
```

The curly braces (`{}`) remove the ambiguity. This command works because the shell first replaces the value within the curly braces before it appends the `old` string to it.

This feature of the shell enables you to create new variables from another. For example, you could get a set of files with different extensions from the same base name. Let's say you want to write three chapter files with extensions 1, 2, and 3. See the following example.

Input Output

```
$ bname="Chapter"
$ chap1=${bname}.1
$ chap2=${bname}.2
$ chap3=${bname}.3
$ echo $chap1
Chapter.1
$ echo $chap2
Chapter.2
$ echo $chap3
Chapter.3
$ _
```

Analysis

Notice how the three filenames are created from the base name. These names can now be used to cat, rename, copy, move, or otherwise manipulate files.

Evaluating Variables

To evaluate the results of a shell command you must use the eval command. This command scans the command line twice. You use the eval command when you start writing shell scripts that create new variables or have to parse a line twice. See the following example.

Input Output

```
$ pipe="¦"
$ ls $pipe wc -l
ls: ¦: File or directory not found
ls: wc: File or directory not found
$ eval ls $pipe wc -l
 296

$ _
```

Analysis

The first part of the command did not work because the pipe variable was evaluated by the shell on its one and only pass on the command line.

The shell substituted the ¦ for the string $pipe and sent all the parsed arguments to the ls command.

In the second command, however, the command line was parsed twice by the shell because of the eval command. Note that the number you see may be different, depending on the contents of your directory.

In the first pass, the eval command received the arguments with the $pipe substituted by the ¦ symbol. It then rescanned the line, this time recognizing the ¦ symbol as a piping directive and passing the results of the message to the wc command.

Now try to extend the value of the eval command to actually reference another variable.

Input
Output

```
1. $ x=1
2. $ px=x
3. $ echo \$$px
   $x
4. $ eval echo \$$px
   1
5. $ echo this is a semicolon \;
   this is a semicolon ;
   $
```

Analysis

This is a special example that warrants line numbers for the code. Lines 1 and 2 simply set the variable `x` to `1` and `px` to the string `x`, respectively.

Line 3 shows how to explicitly echo the `$` as part of the argument. The backslash character in front of the `$`, in `\$`, forces the shell to not evaluate the `$` and let it go through unchanged.

Line 4 shows how the `$` is first sent through the `eval` command to give the command `echo $x`. The second time around after the `eval` command, the `$x` is evaluated to its value of `1`.

Line 5 shows that the special command separator character, the semicolon, also can be printed out for you as part of a command instead of being interpreted as a command separator.

Note: The implication of this is tremendous. You can now change the reference to x without changing x, just as with a pointer to a location. For the C programmers among you, this has the same behavior as a pointer in C. For assembly language programmers, this should remind you of a double indirection statement.

The information you have learned about the backslash character is especially useful when writing shell scripts that create commands for other shell scripts. Yes, some sophisticated shell scripts can actually create and execute command lines, or even more shell scripts. This powerful feature is covered in detail on Day 14.

Doing Simple Math with Shell Variables

Shell variables take only strings as their arguments. As you learned earlier today, the value of `1` is the string `1`, not the number 1. You can work with strings by concatenating, resetting them, and so forth, but sometimes it's helpful to count items in variables.

The shell does not explicitly provide this feature, but you can use the quoting feature to circumvent this shortcoming. For the moment, just learn how to do this; in Day 4, you'll learn why this works on quoting mechanisms. Let's see how this works in the following example.

Input/Output

```
$ count=1
$ echo $count
1
$ count=count+1
$ echo $count
count+1
$ count=$count+1
count+1+1
$ _
```

Analysis

Perhaps this is something you did not expect. The `count+1+1` is not a very useful way to describe the number 3! Describing 3 as `1+1+1` is a bit crude for us. So, use the `expr` command.

The `expr` command is the shell's way of evaluating an expression.

Input/Output

```
$ count=1
$ echo $count
1
$ count=`expr $count + 1`
$ echo $count
2
$ _
```

Analysis

At last—the light at the end of the tunnel. The `expr` command performed the magic addition of variables with help from the grave quote character. The accent grave character (`) is the backward single quote generally found on the key under the tilde (~) on PC-compatible keyboards. On Sun workstation keyboards, it's near the Enter key. Basically, anything between the two grave quotes is passed on to a new shell. The double quotes and everything in between are then replaced with the results of that command.

So, the command

```
expr $count + 1
```

returns the result of 1 + 1 since `$count` is interpreted as the *number* 1 by `expr`. Note that the spaces below the `+` and `1` are required by `expr`.

The `expr` command has other operations as well. It can multiply, divide, subtract, and give the modulus (`%`) result. The following Input/Output section shows an example.

Input/Output

```
$ count=1000
$ div=50
$ ans=`expr $count / $div`
$ echo $ans
20
$ echo `expr $count / $div`
20
$ count=hello
$ echo `expr $count \* $div`
expr: Non-numeric argument
$ count=2.2
$ echo `expr $count \* $div`
expr: Non-numeric argument
$ echo `expr $count * $div`
expr: syntax error
$ echo `expr $count \* $div`
50000
$ _
```

Analysis

The results of the division command worked as planned. The values of the variables in `count` and `div` were coerced into numbers by `expr`. The `count` and `div` are evaluated by the shell into the strings **`1000`** and **`50`**, respectively. They are forced to numbers 1000 and 50 by the `expr` command.

If neither `count` nor `div` could be coerced into numbers, you get an error. The word `hello`, for example, did not evaluate into a number and gave an error.

Also, `expr` only works with integers. It does not handle floating point numbers. On Day 10, you learn about the desk calculators for working with data in UNIX.

> **Note:** Look at how the multiplication character, the asterisk (*), is handled with the backslash. If the backslash is missing, the shell expands these out to list all the files in the directory.

If this sounds confusing, wait until tomorrow where it becomes clear as to why this happens, when I discuss filename expansion.

DO	DON'T
DO expect math operations to be cumbersome and slow.	
DO escape the multiplicaton asterisk (*) with the backslash.	

DO put a space between the variables and the mathematical operator. That is, do not use `$a+$b`; use `$a + $b` instead.

DON'T expect to do many mathematical operations with the shell. (Do integer math only.)

DON'T use real numbers in shell variables.

DON'T put a space on either side of the equal sign when assigning values to the shell variable.

Local Versus Environment Variables

By now you should have an idea about what an environment variable is. The environment variables refer to those shell variables that UNIX sets for you when you log in and the ones you set for shortening your commands. I'll discuss the specific environment variables in much more detail on Day 6, when I discuss how to customize your environment.

Local variables in the shell are variables that are local to your shell, which no other standard UNIX process really needs to know about. Local variables could be variables that exist for a short time during a shell script and are not valid, or that reset to `NULL` after they are used. In other words, they are local to your shell environment. For example, you could set a variable called `count` to whatever you desire, without it affecting the way your standard commands work.

Your shell environment contains a set of variables that identify specific files, paths, and other information for you. Technically, you can override all system defaults, but it's probably not a good idea to change some of these unless you know what you want. For example, changing the value of the HOME directive changes the reference to your login directory. However, some UNIX variables such as HOME are default parameters for a lot of UNIX programs.

Input
Output

```
$ echo $HOME
/home/myself
$ cd /usr/lib/X11
$ pwd
/usr/lib/X11
$ cd
$ pwd
/home/myself
$ _
```

Analysis Note how the `cd` command returned you back to your home directory when no argument was specified to the `cd` command.

The `$HOME` variable is used by many system scripts as the default directory of where you log in. It's generally not a good idea to change the value in this variable, since a lot of standard UNIX script files might not work. For example, a special file, `.profile` (discussed on Day 6), exists in your `HOME` directory.

> **Warning:** Some programs require certain environment shell variables to be set to a certain value. For example, a package for an application may require that the library files for its programs be specified in the `LIBPATH` or a combination of the `HOME` environment variable. If this variable is not set correctly, your application might not run correctly, if at all. Before you change an environment variable's value, check its impact first.

Some interesting environment variables include the following:

- `HOME`: This is your home directory. As you saw earlier, this is the directory that `cd` sends you to if you do not specify any parameters.
- `SHELL`: When UNIX programs invoke a shell command, they check this variable to see what program to invoke. For example, in the `vi` editor, if you type **`! ls`** at the colon prompt, `vi` will start up a new copy of the shell specified in the `SHELL` environment variable. After typing **`exit`** from this new shell, you return to the `vi` application that you were originally in. This variable may all be called `SH` on some systems.
- `TERM`: This defines the type of terminal you are using. It is required to service your keyboard input and screen output. By setting the `TERM` variable, you are ensuring that your current session will work. Common values for this variable are `vt100` and `vt102`. On remote lines, you'll probably see the value of `vt100`, since this is the most common type of terminal available to date. By setting the `TERM` value to an incompatible terminal type, you run the risk of locking out a terminal from the shell.
- `MAIL`: This specifies the directory containing my mailbox for UNIX's mailbox facility. You can change this variable to point to another existing file location without really harming anything. Check your man pages for more details.

- USER: This is the predefined variable used to specify your account name and is set by the `login` command.
- LOGNAME: This is another name for USER.

Take a look at some of the shell variables in my account.

Input Output

```
$ set
SH=/bin/sh
DISPLAY=softland:0
HOME=/home/kamran
LOGNAME=kamran
EDITOR=/bin/vi
MAIL=/var/spool/mail/kamran
MANPATH=/usr/man:/usr/man/preformat:/usr/X11/man:/usr/openwin/man
MINICOM=-c on
OPENWINHOME=/usr/openwin
PATH=/etc/local:/etc:/local/bin:/usr/bin:/bin:/usr/local/bin:/usr/bin/➥X11:/usr/
openwin/bin:/user/kamran/bin:.
PWD=/home/kamran/sams
SHELL=/bin/sh
TERM=console
$ _
```

Analysis Note that the `set` command displays many more variables than the list I gave earlier. This is because you have full liberty to change any of these variables or add your own. For example, the EDITOR variable could be set to `/usr/bin/emacs` to specify the editor to be invoked by other programs that use this variable. Your output will look different than the one shown here.

Built-In Shell Variables and Commands

The shell has several built-in commands and variables. Built-in commands and shell variables increase overall performance of the shell scripts and its capability to access its internal data structures. The commands are designed to have semantics indistinguishable from external disk-based commands. So, in some systems, these commands might actually exist on disk as files instead of as part of the shell itself.

For instance, the `echo` command is built into the shell I use, so you won't find an executable called echo on your disk. However, on my UNIX system at work (linux .99.p5), I have an echo executable on my disk. Some commands such as those loop constructs (for example the `for` command) is almost always guaranteed to be built in to the shell, and consequently you will not find an executable for it.

Summary

Today's text covered shell variables and how to use them:

- You can customize your environment by setting your shell's environment variables, in addition to making life easier for yourself with simple names for extensive commands.
- You learned how shell variables are set and evaluated.
- The curly braces provide a faster way of creating new variables.
- You can re-evaluate a command line using the `eval` command to parse newly created variables.
- You know the difference between local and environment variables.
- It's possible to do simple mathematical operations in the shell by using the `expr` command. These operations are limited to integers only.
- The backslash character provides the means to pass arguments with special meanings to the shell without evaluation to a command.
- Some shell variables and commands are built into the shell to save the time required to load them from disk. However, this is generally transparent to the user.

UNIX Commands Learned Today

- `eval` For evaluating shell variables and expressions one extra time
- `expr` For integer math operations in the shell
- `set` For setting environment variables

Q&A

Q Are these valid shell variable names?

```
1234
ASAP
NEW_1
_1_2
#232
0123
ee.ff
ee123
```

A	`1234`	No. (Don't use a digit as the first character.)
	`ASAP`	Yes.
	`NEW_1`	Yes.
	`_1_2`	Yes.
	`#232`	No. (The pound sign is not valid.)
	`0a12`	No. (Don't use a digit as the first character.)
	`ee.f`	No. (Don't use the period as part of the name.)
	`ee123`	Yes.

Q Why would you assign shell variables with double quotes?

A If the value you want to specify contains spaces, you'll have to put spaces around it.

Q Name some of the environment variables.

A `HOME`, `PATH`, `USER`, and `MAIL`. (You can name a whole lot more.)

Q How do I pass the `$` as an argument into a program?

A Using the backslash escape character, `\$`, overrides the shell's desire to evaluate the text following the `$` sign as a variable.

Workshop

The Workshop provides quiz questions to help you solidify your understanding of the material covered. Some Workshop sections of this book also contain exercises to provide you with experience in using what you've learned. Try to understand the quiz and exercise answers before continuing on to the next chapter. Answers are provided in Appendix D, "Answers."

Quiz

1. What are shell variables?
2. How do you choose variable names?
3. What are two common uses for shell variables?
4. What are the data types in shell variables?
5. How do you construct a new variable?
6. What are the differences between local and environment variables?

Exercises

1. Verify that the answers to the first question are correct. To test these out, try assigning values to these variables in your shell and check the results. For example:

   ```
   $   1234=test
   ```

   Does this give you an error? (It should.)
2. Try to come up with more ways to set `NULL` values to shell variables.
3. You will be learning about regular expressions next, but here is a head start for tomorrow. Try the following sequence of commands:

   ```
   $ ls
   $ x=*
   $ echo $x
   ```
4. How do you explain the output from the previous list of commands in Exercise 2?

5. Try the following command sequence. (Note how the cases are mixed in the environment variables.)

```
$ med="Medical"
$ echo $medHISTORY
$ echo ${med}HISTORY
$ echo "Dow "${med}"College"
```

6. Type the command to echo the string: `"My $.02"`. Print the quotes too. (Hint: use the `\` character.)

4

WEEK 1

Using Metacharacters

Today you will learn about one of the most important features of the shell—the use of metacharacters as a shorthand for arguments to user commands. This lesson covers the following subjects:

- Metacharacters
- Syntactic metacharacters
- Quotation characters
- Filename metacharacters
- Substitution metacharacters
- Input/output special characters

Along the way, you will be learning how these metacharacters apply in all of the previous cases. A metacharacter is a character that has a special meaning to the shell. Where you see the word *metacharacter*, think "special," and you should understand what I mean.

Metacharacters

So far, I have dealt with single arguments to UNIX commands. Metacharacters enable you to use a "shorthand" to describe more than one item in one argument. Using the shell's shorthand notation, you can specify files in the form "all the files in my current directory," or "all files with the letter *x* in their name," or "all files that begin with the letter *c*," and many more such combinations.

You can use this feature of the shell through the special metacharacters. You can think of these metacharacters as the joker cards in a rummy game; they can take different values depending on their usage.

Syntactic Metacharacters

The metacharacters in the shell are the following:

- The asterisk (`*`) character, which expands to zero or more instances of a character.
- The question mark (`?`) character, which expands to one character.

- Square brackets ([and]) characters, for which the match is on any character within the list of characters specified between the brackets. In fact, you can specify a list of characters by using the hyphen character (-). If, for example, you wanted to match all the lowercase characters *a* through *z*, you would use [a-z] as the special character set.

After a command has been interpreted into its separate words, the shell scans each word for these metacharacters. If the shell recognizes any of these metacharacters, the shell replaces the word with an alphabetically sorted list of filenames that match the pattern. If the shell does not find these metacharacters, the word for the argument is left unchanged.

Consider the following example.

Input
Output

```
$ ls -C c*
ch01    ch03    ch05    ch07    ch09    ch14
ch02    ch04    ch06    ch08    ch11    chap1
```

Analysis

The `ls` command was typed to have two words, `-C` and `c*`, as arguments to it.

The shell left the first word alone, even though the `-C` argument contains a metacharacter hyphen (-). This is because the hyphen must be between the `[ ]` brackets to be interpreted as a special character.

The shell recognized the asterisk in the second word, `c*`, as a metacharacter. The asterisk then was expanded to a list of zero or more characters in order to match all existing filenames that begin with the letter *c*.

The shell's flow of progress can be summarized in these steps:

1. Find the command to execute.
2. Expand all the typed words, one at a time, into arguments. If the typed word contains metacharacters and is not quoted, expand the word into a list of sorted words as specified by the metacharacters. Otherwise, leave the word alone.
3. Pass all the arguments to the command.
4. Return or display the results to the user.

I will cover the use of metacharacters and how to disable their expansion by means of quotes, escape characters, and shell flags later today.

Note: Even though today's lesson focuses on using the `ls` command to illustrate the use of metacharacters, this does not mean that metacharacters are limited to a few select UNIX commands. Metacharacters are used to specify the expansion to the shell, which in turn, while it evaluates a command line, expands the metacharacters into a list of arguments that are then sent to the requested command. So when you see a command such as

```
$ ls c*
```

which lists all the files beginning with the letter *c*, (the next section explains how this works), you should realize that you also can use the `wc` command *with same arguments* to count all the words, lines, and characters in all files beginning with the letter *c*:

```
$ wc c*
```

Filename Metacharacters

Filename metacharacters enable you to expand one metacharacter or a combination of metacharacters to full filenames or directories. The best way to illustrate the filename metacharacter features and describe them in detail is through examples. Consider the following directory listing.

Input/Output

```
$ ls -C
a.out     ch06    d-h.fi        n             sa        sims
ch01      ch07    dos2unix      newkorn.asc   sage      site
ch02      ch08    dos2unix.c    numlines      sams      ss
ch03      ch09    kk            parlor        sane      t-g.awk
ch04      ch11    me.ps.out     phone         sate      toc
ch05      ch14    mech01        pizza         saveme    whoout
```

Analysis

This output shows you a listing of the directory you will be working with in the following examples. Your own directory listing may not look anything like this. This one is simply the starting point for all the examples that follow.

The `ls` command should be the command most familiar to you by now. It is also a simple command to use when illustrating the use of metacharacters for filename expansion. You are not limited to the `ls` command, of course, and may use any other command you want.

The Asterisk (*)

The asterisk (*) character expands to an arbitrary string of zero or more characters. Following is an example.

Input Output

```
$ ls -C c*
ch01   ch03   ch05   ch07   ch09   ch14
ch02   ch04   ch06   ch08   ch11   chap1
$ ls -C d*
d-h.fi        dos2unix   dos2unix.c
$ ls -C n*
n         newkorn.asc  numlines
$ ls -C *m*
me.ps.out  mech01     numlines sams     saveme     sims
```

Analysis

Four commands and their outputs are shown. In all four commands, I have requested a columnar listing of my current directory, giving different metacharacters. The -C option provides the columnar listing, which fills the output one column at a time.

Look at the `ls -C c*` command in a bit more detail. The asterisk by default expands to a string of zero or more characters. The `c*` string therefore expands to mean "all files with the letter *c* as the first character in their name."

The second command (when you specify the string `d*`), lists all the files with the letter *d* as the first character in their names.

In the output from the third command, you see that `n*` has expanded to `n`. This is done because the asterisk can expand to nothing; hence, `n` by itself will be interpreted as expected by the shell.

The fourth command requests a list of files with names based on the `*m*` argument. This argument tells `ls` to find all files with the letter *m* in their names. This argument shows that the asterisk can be positioned before or after a specification, or both.

To see some of the filename expansions that are available to you, see Table 4.1.

Note: It's important to remember not to use a space between the asterisk and its other modifiers. If you use a space, the results may not be what you expect.

Table 4.1. Filename expansions.

Pattern	Meaning
`*.c`	Finds all files with names with the extension `.c`
`*c`	Finds all files with names ending in the letter `c`
`c*`	Finds all files with names beginning with the letter `c`
`*c*`	Finds all files with names having at least one letter `c` somewhere in the name
`*memo*`	Finds all files with the word `memo` somewhere in the middle of the filename
`*`	Finds all files
`a*b`	Finds all files with names beginning with the letter `a` and ending with the letter `b`

Consider the following command and output.

Input Output

```
$ ls c *
ls: c: No such file or directory
a.out*   ch07   ch14         n              sage     ss
ch01     ch08   d-h.fi       newkorn.asc    sams     t-g.awk
ch02     ch09   dos2unix*    numlines       sane     toc
ch03     ch10   dos2unix.c   parlor         sate     whoout
ch04     ch11   kk*          phone          saveme
ch05     ch12   me.ps.out    pizza          sims
ch06     ch13   mech01       sa             site
```

Analysis

Note the shell recognized two words (`c` and `*`) when it parsed the command. The shell tried to list the file `c`, and then, because of the asterisk, the shell listed all the files.

The asterisk character also expands to subdirectories. For example, the `ls -F /etc` command shows you the contents of the `etc` directory and points out all the subdirectories underneath it with a forward slash.

However, if you try the command ls `-F /etc/*`, you might get a very long listing of all the files and subdirectories under `etc`.

Input Output

```
$ ls -F /etc
DIR_COLORS        gettydefs      lilo/           passwd        syslog.pid
crond.pid         group          lilo.conf       passwd.OLD    termcap
csh.cshrc         inet@          lilo.conf.bak   printcap      ttys
csh.login         inittab        magic           profile       utmp
default/          issue          minicom.users   rc.d/         wtmp@
disktab           klog.pid       minirc.dfl      securetty
fdprm             ksh.kshrc      motd            shells
fs/               ld.so.cache    mtab            skel/
fstab             ld.so.conf     mtools           syslog.conf
$ ls /etc/*
/etc/DIR_COLORS   /etc/inittab        /etc/minicom.users  /etc/securetty
/etc/crond.pid    /etc/issue          /etc/minirc.dfl     /etc/shells
/etc/csh.cshrc    /etc/klog.pid       /etc/motd           /etc/syslog.conf
/etc/csh.login    /etc/ksh.kshrc      /etc/mtab           /etc/syslog.pid
/etc/disktab      /etc/ld.so.cache    /etc/mtools         /etc/termcap
/etc/fdprm        /etc/ld.so.conf     /etc/passwd         /etc/ttys
/etc/fstab        /etc/lilo.conf      /etc/passwd.OLD     /etc/utmp
/etc/gettydefs    /etc/lilo.conf.bak  /etc/printcap       /etc/wtmp
/etc/group        /etc/magic          /etc/profile

/etc/inet:
DIR_COLORS     gettydefs     lilo           passwd        syslog.pid
crond.pid      group         lilo.conf      passwd.OLD    termcap
csh.cshrc      inet          lilo.conf.bak  printcap      ttys
csh.login      inittab       magic          profile       utmp
default        issue         minicom.users  rc.d          wtmp
disktab        klog.pid      minirc.dfl     securetty
fdprm          ksh.kshrc     motd           shells
fs             ld.so.cache   mtab           skel
fstab          ld.so.conf    mtools          syslog.conf

/etc/default:

/etc/fs:
fsck.ext2    fsck.minix    fsck.xiafs    mkfs.minix
fsck.hpfs    fsck.umsdos   mkfs.ext2     mkfs.xiafs

/etc/lilo:
install

/etc/rc.d:
rc.0   rc.6     rc.K     rc.M        rc.S       rc.local   rc.serial

/etc/skel:
$
```

Analysis

The output from the `ls -F` command has a forward slash (`/`) after the name of any listed subdirectories.

In the `etc` directory, I have five subdirectories: `default`, `fs`, `lilo`, `rc.d`, and `skel`. Ignore the `wtmp` for now; it's a link to another file. Links are shown with an "at" symbol (`@`).

Note: A link is a directory entry that points to another file. There are, therefore, two ways to get to this file from a directory tree. In the case of `/etc/wtmp` I use the `-al/etc/wtmp` to find out where the file actually exists.

```
lrwxrwxrwx   1 root  root  13 Apr 23 16:56 /etc/wtmp -> /usr/adm/wtmp
```

The string

```
/etc/wtmp -> /usr/adm/wtmp
```

shows me that the actual file exists on the branch `/usr/adm/wtmp`. I can, however, access the file through both the `/etc/wtmp` and the `/usr/adm/wtmp` branch.

In the second command, `ls /etc/*`, I have asked the shell to expand everything under `/etc`. In this case, the entire contents of the `/etc` directory and all its subdirectories are listed.

The moral of the story is that you should be careful how you specify the asterisk when you request it in listings. Using the asterisk as I did in the second command would only result in a long listing for you to look at. If you use the `rm` command to specify this parameter, you may wind up losing more files than you expect. For this reason, the `rm` command does *not* recurse the asterisk down subdirectories unless you specify the `-r` switch at the command line.

This safeguard in `rm` will also not remove subdirectories unless the `-r` switch is specified. Unfortunately, this safety feature will not save you from mistyping or from an erroneously specified wildcard match. When in doubt, use the `ls` command to check the expansion before you use it with the `rm` command.

DO | **DON'T**

DO use `echo` to check the asterisk expansion on sample files and directories before using a command that will affect your files. For instance, echo `"m*"` will give you an idea of what files or directories will be affected.

DON'T use the asterisk by itself with `ls` on the command line unless you explicitly want it to expand to list all the filenames.

DON'T use the asterisk as an argument to the rm command unless you first check it out with the ls command. Using the wildcard in the rm command without first checking it may cause you to delete some files that you did not really want included in the match.

Matching Single Characters

The asterisk tells the shell to find zero or more occurrences of a match. What if you want to see all the files that match exactly one character? The question mark (?) metacharacter matches one character in a filename or directory.

Consider the following example.

Input
Output

```
$ ls -CF
a.out*     ch07   ch14          n             sage     ss
ch01       ch08   d-h.fi        newkorn.asc   sams     t-g.awk
ch02       ch09   dos2unix*     numlines      sane     toc
ch03       ch10   dos2unix.c    parlor        sate     whoout
ch04       ch11   kk*           phone         saveme
ch05       ch12   me.ps.out     pizza         sims
ch06       ch13   mech01        sa            site
$
$
$ ls c?01
ch01
$ ls s*
sa   sage sams sane sate saveme    sims site ss
$ ls s?
sa  ss
$ ls s??e
sage  sane  sate  site
$ ls s*e
sage sane sate saveme    site
```

Analysis

The ls c?01 command requests a listing of all the files that both begin with the character c and also end in the string 01. The command comes up with one filename, ch01.

The next command (ls -CF s*) expands to all the files in the directory that begin with the letter s and can have any number of letters after the s. Notice how this gives nine files in the output.

The next command (ls -CF s?), however, gives only two files in its output. This is a shorter list than the output of the previous command because in the directory only two files exist whose names begin with an s and are only two characters long. Since I have defined the length of the filename to search for two characters, one character is for the letter `s` and the other is by the wildcard question mark, which expands to only one character.

The command `ls s??e` shows how a two-character wildcard can be specified. In this case, the shell is expanding the two question marks to one character each, next to each other. The output is `sage sane sate site`, as you can see in the example.

Notice how the output of the last command (`ls s*e`) compares with the one using the question marks. In this last case, the output includes an extra file called `saveme`. This file was displayed because the asterisk expands to zero and more occurrences, whereas the pair of question marks limits the expansion to two characters only.

The paired question marks will equate to two characters next to each other. You can try the question mark in different combinations to define many different relative locations.

Input/Output

```
$ ls c?0?
ch01  ch02  ch03  ch04   ch05  ch06  ch07  ch08   ch09
$ ls ?h?4
ch04  ch14
$ ls ?h*
ch01  ch03  ch05  ch07   ch09  ch11  ch13  phone
ch02  ch04  ch06  ch08   ch10  ch12  ch14  whoout
```

Analysis

The first combination (`ls c?0?`) matches all the filenames that have a `c` as the first character and `0` as the third character.

The second command (`ls ?h?4`) expands to match all the filenames with an `h` in the second position and `4` in the fourth character position.

Compare the second command's output with the output of the next command (`ls ?h*`). You would read this `ls` command as meaning "list all the files that have names at least two characters long and with an `h` as the second character." Note the length of all the filenames in the output, including filenames such as `phone` and `whoout`.

It's usually easy to forget the subtle difference between the asterisk and the question mark when expanding filenames. Look at the next example.

Input/Output

```
$ ls n*
n         newkorn.asc  numlines
$ ls n?
ls: n?: No such file or directory
```

Analysis

The first command (`ls n*`) showed the filename `n` because the asterisk expanded to an empty string at the start. The second command (`ls n?`) did not show the filename `n` because the command searched for a two-character filename beginning with the letter `n`.

In other words, the question mark forces an extra character to be searched for, whereas the asterisk allows the single character to stand alone.

Using Brackets

You can specify which characters to choose from for an expansion by enclosing the list of possible characters in brackets, `[]`. The characters in the brackets can be

- Lowercase characters, *a* through *z*
- Uppercase characters, *A* through *Z*
- Digits, 0 through 9
- Special characters, such as the period (.) or the underscore (_)

Why would you want to use brackets? It's perfectly legal to specify the command

```
$ ls s* c* m*
```

to indicate that you want to look at all the files that begin with the letter `s`, `m`, or `c`. If you wanted to look at all files that begin with the letter `m` through `w`, you would be tempted to try

```
$ ls m* n* o* p* q* r* s* t* u* v* w*
```

Yes, this method is legal, but it is also quite awkward to use. A better way—one without a large number of keystrokes—would be to use the bracket wildcards.

Input
Output

```
$ ls m* n* o* p* q* r* s* t* u* v* w*
me.ps.out    numlines     sa       sate       ss
mech01       parlor       sage     saveme     t-g.awk
n            phone        sams     sims       toc
newkorn.asc  pizza        sane     site       whoout
$ ls [m-w]*
me.ps.out    numlines     sa       sate       ss
mech01       parlor       sage     saveme     t-g.awk
n            phone        sams     sims       toc
newkorn.asc  pizza        sane     site       whoout
```

Analysis

Note that the shell has picked up all the filenames that begin with the characters `m` through `w`. The second command is a lot easier to understand.

Just as with the question mark, the brackets are replaced with the matched characters of the filenames being listed. In fact, you can pair some of the brackets together to further specify filenames.

The brackets are used to indicate a list of specific characters that should be used to replace the brackets. With the question mark, however, where the shell is given freedom to choose replacement characters from the entire alphanumeric set, `a-zA-Z0-9_`.

Brackets differ from the asterisk in the sense that they specify one occurrence only. Specifying `[0-9]` means that you are asking to substitute one digit, 0 through 9 only. If you want to specify all the numbers from 10 to 29, you would use two bracket pairs: `[12][0-9]`. The first pair would specify the tens by two digits, either 1 or 2. The second pair would specify the ones, using the digits from 0 to 9.

Input/Output

```
$ ls ch0[2-5]
ch02  ch03  ch04  ch05
$ ls ch[01][2-5]
ch02  ch03  ch04  ch05  ch12  ch13  ch14
```

Analysis The first command (`ls ch0[2-5]`) listed all the filenames with `ch0` as the first three characters, followed by a character anywhere in the range from `2` through `5`.

The second command (`ls ch[01][2-5]`) illustrated that two pairs of match characters can be specified. In this command, the first pair of brackets `[01]` specified the tens; the second pair `[2-5]` specified the digits `2`, `3`, `4`, and `5` for the ones.

As you recall, you should not use spaces with the asterisk; likewise, you should be careful with brackets. Consider this example.

Input/Output

```
$ ls [m-w] *

a.out*    ch07    ch14          n             sa        site
ch01      ch08    d-h.fi        n             sage      ss
ch02      ch09    dos2unix*     newkorn.asc   sams      t-g.awk
ch03      ch10    dos2unix.c    numlines      sane      toc
ch04      ch11    kk*           parlor        sate      whoout
ch05      ch12    me.ps.out     phone         saveme
ch06      ch13    mech01        pizza         sims
```

Analysis The command `ls [m-w] *` will attempt to list two sets of files: one set with filenames of only one character in length, with the `[m-w]` expansion; and a list of all the files, with the asterisk. For this reason, the filename `n` appears twice in the output.

No number of examples can fully explain the many combinations of filenames and search parameters you can specify with these metacharacters (`?`, `*`, `[]`, and others). The best way to learn about these expansions is to see the examples in this book as you progress and try them out.

One of the best tools for learning about these expansions is the `echo` command, which enables you to see whether your selections are indeed correct.

Input
Output

```
$ echo ?
n
$ echo ??
kk sa ss
$ wc ch0*
   1425    9185    52924 ch01
   1318    7044    41167 ch02
    657    4407    26483 ch03
    606    3269    20326 ch04
     86     355     1973 ch05
    221    1025     5848 ch06
    152     580     3247 ch07
     96     367     2082 ch08
    115     389     2380 ch09
   4676   26621   156430 total
```

Analysis

This command (`wc ch0*`) shows you how to use other UNIX commands with the wildcard characters.

Turning the Filename Expansion Off

At times, it may be necessary to turn off the filename expansion. This is true of shell scripts in which you may want to create other shell scripts from within. It's helpful to know how to use the `-f` flag.

By turning off the `f` flag, you instruct the shell not to expand the filename expansion metacharacters. You turn off the `f` flag with the command

```
$ set -f
```

To turn on the `-f` flag, use the command

```
$ set +f
```

By default, the filename expansion is turned on when you first log in.

Input
Output

```
$ echo ??
kk sa ss
$ set -f
$ echo ??
??
$ set +f
$ echo ??
kk sa ss
```

Analysis

When expansion is turned off, the `echo` command will not expand the double question marks and will echo them out.

Turning off the expansion is an alternative to quoting everything in a long series of commands. Instead of having to quote all the special commands, you just turn expansion off, do your thing, and then turn expansion back on later.

This brings me to another feature of the shell used to group items together and prevent arguments from expanding in a shell. I'll cover these subjects in the next section.

Quoting

The way the shell interprets quote characters is one of the shell's unique features. As you progressed through the first three days of this book, you were introduced to the quote characters. Now you will learn about them in detail.

There are four basic quote characters:

- The single quote character, `'`
- The double quote character, `"`
- The back quote character, `` ` ``
- The backslash character, `\`

The first three must occur in pairs; the last one is unary in nature.

Before I discuss quotes any further, let me introduce a special command under UNIX called `grep`. This stands for *global regular expression print.* You will learn about it in more detail when you learn about regular expressions in Day 5. For today, I will use the `grep` command to find strings within text files and also to provide the basis for the examples in the next two days.

The syntax for the `grep` command is

```
grep [options] pattern [filename1] [filename2] ...
```

As you saw in Day 1, the brackets `[ ]` indicate that the arguments are optional. For a complete list of options to the `grep` command, use the `man grep` command and also see Day 5.

For today, you will use only the `-n` option. This option prefixes each line of input with its line number. The *`pattern`* is a string that you are searching for.

The filenames are those files in which you want to look for the string. The filenames given in the syntax can include the asterisk or any other filename expansion metacharacter. If you do not specify a filename, `grep` will default to reading from the standard input, the keyboard in this case.

Let's say that you want to find all the lines with the word `Pizza` in the file called `parlor`. First check the `parlor` file for the list of names and then search for `Pizza` in the list of names.

Input Output

```
$ cat parlor
Mr. Gatti
Dominoes
Pizza Hut - West
Pizza Hut - East
Dirty's
Gut Wrench
Pizza Inn
Slimey's
Jorges' Pub
Billy Bobs
Cici
$ grep -n Pizza parlor
3:Pizza Hut - West
4:Pizza Hut - East
7:Pizza Inn
```

Analysis

Look at output from the second command. The `grep` command took two arguments: `Pizza` and `parlor`.

This command tells `grep` to search for the pattern `Pizza` in the file `parlor`. The `-n` option requested the line numbers of the match, lines 3, 4, and 7. These are the numbers preceding the colon. If you do not specify the `-n` option, the line numbers will not be printed.

4

The Single Quote

What if you want to look up two words in this `grep` search? Suppose you simply want to hunt for the words `Pizza Hut` in this file. Trying the command `grep Pizza Hut` would not help.

Input Output

```
$ grep Pizza Hut parlor
grep: Hut: No such file or directory
parlor:Pizza Hut - West
parlor:Pizza Hut - East
parlor:Pizza Inn
```

Analysis

This command resulted in three arguments being sent to the `grep` command—`Pizza`, `Hut`, and `parlor`. This happened because the shell uses whitespace characters to separate the arguments to a command.

Note that the second word of the command (`Pizza`) was interpreted properly, but the third word was in the place where `grep` expects to see a filename. The file `Hut` does not exist, and so `grep` generated an error message.

`grep` does, however, find the file called `parlor`, opens it, searches for the string `Pizza`, and dutifully prints the output.

> **Note:** Notice that this time I did not specify the `-n` parameter, and thus `grep` printed only the filename followed by a colon.

Now, to see the usefulness of single quotes, you should group the arguments together between single quotes and try the command again.

Input/Output

```
$ grep 'Pizza Hut' parlor
Pizza Hut - West
Pizza Hut - East
```

Analysis

This time, because of the single quotes, the arguments are indeed grouped together when they are passed to `grep`. In other words, `grep` receives two arguments: `Pizza Hut` as one and `parlor` as the other.

The shell ignores all special characters between the single quotes. So the space between `Pizza` and `Hut`, which normally would have been treated as a whitespace character, is now ignored. No matter how many whitespaces are between the quotes, the words enclosed in the quotes are interpreted as a single argument and the spaces are preserved.

Input/Output

```
$ echo 'I  am learning                  about you'
I  am learning                  about you
```

Analysis

This is very similar to the example presented in Day 1 concerning the preservation of whitespaces while using double quotes.

Here are some more examples of the use of the single quote.

Input/Output

```
$ echo *
a.out ch01 ch02 ch03 ch04 ch05 ch06 ch07 ch08 ch09 ch10 ch11 ch12
$ echo '*'
*
$ echo '< > ¦ ;'
< > ¦ ;
$ echo 'I will insert a new line here:
> and keep typing here'
I will insert a new line here:
and keep typing here'
$
```

Analysis

Notice how the newline was ignored while between the quotes. The shell changed the prompt from a `$` to a `>` to indicate that it's expecting more input from the same line.

> **Note:** When you are continuing the input on a newline for the same command, the shell changes the prompt from the value set in the environment variable `PS1` (`$`) to that in the environment variable `PS2` (`>`). The value in `PS2` is known as the *secondary prompt.*

Single quotes are also required when you assign values to shell variables.

Input Output

```
$ message='Hello I am an assignment'
$ echo $message
Hello I am an assignment
$ message='This is an assignment with * '
$ echo $message
This is an assignment with a.out ch01 ch02 ch03 ch04 ch05 ch0...
```

Analysis

Notice the last line:

```
This is an assignment with a.out ch01 ch02 ch03 ch04 ch05 ch0....
```

The asterisk was expanded before it was sent to the `echo` command. This raises an important point to remember: the shell does filename substitution *after* variable name substitution.

After the `message` variable was substituted, the shell expanded the asterisk when it did filename expansion. Then it requested that the `echo` command be executed. The fact that variable name substitution precedes filename substitution is a nuisance, but it is something you must deal with when working with single quotes.

The Double Quote

The double quote (`"`) performs almost the same functions as the single quote, with a few glaring exceptions. Although the single quotes cause the shell to ignore just about every special character between the single quotes, when the double quotes are used, the shell does not ignore the following characters:

- Dollar signs
- Backslashes
- Back quotes

The result of not ignoring dollar signs is that variable substitution is done within the double quotes.

Input/Output

```
$ x=*
$ echo $x
a.out ch01 ch02 ch03 ch04 ch05 ch06 ch07 ch08 ch09 ch10 ch11 ch12
$ echo '$x'
$x
$ echo "$x"
*
```

Analysis

This output best shows the differences between not using quotes, using single quotes, and using double quotes.

When quotes are not used, `echo $x` is expanded to echo all the filenames in the directory. The `$x` is first substituted with the asterisk `*`, which in turn is expanded by filename substitution.

With single quotes, the shell completely ignores the special meaning of the dollar sign and instead displays `$x`. Neither filename substitution nor variable substitution is performed.

In the case of double quotes, the shell substitutes `$x` with the asterisk `*`. The filename substitution portion, however, is suppressed within double quotes, so the value of `*` is sent to the echo command to be printed.

To illustrate the point further, here's another example.

Input/Output

```
$ message="I am line 1
> I am line 2
> I am line 3"
$ echo $message
I am line 1 I am line 2 I am line 3
$ echo "$message"
I am line 1
I am line 2
I am line 3
$ echo '$message'
$message
```

Analysis

The first line assigned a string with two newline characters to the variable `message`.

In the line that I requested the value of `message` be printed, the shell did the variable assignment and removed all extraneous whitespaces. This includes the newline characters, which the shell interprets as an argument separator. Thus the `echo` command sees only one long argument without the newline characters. So I got one long line instead of three.

However, the next command (`echo "$command"`), which used the double quotes, requested that whitespaces not be removed even if the `$` was recognized. This preserved the newlines, and thus the `echo` command received the newlines, giving me three lines of output.

DO | **DON'T**

DO realize that the `$` sign is ignored when it's between single quotes and is not ignored when between double quotes.

DON'T use double quotes if you don't want the asterisk expanded.

The Backslash

4

The backslash character (`\`) is a *unary* quote character and is equivalent to placing single quotes around one character, with one exception. (The word *unary* means that it does not have to be paired as are single quotes or double quotes.) Let's see how the backslash works before dealing with the exception.

Input Output

```
$ echo >
sh; syntax error near token '>'
$ echo '>'
>
$ echo \>
>
$ echo \\
\
```

Analysis

The basic syntax for quoting by means of backslashes is to use the `\` character before the character being quoted. A backslash simply removes the special meaning of the character it precedes.

The backslash itself can be escaped with the backslash character itself. See the `echo \\` command.

The backslash character generally behaves like the single quote. The only exception to this rule occurs when the character being escaped is a newline. Consider the following example.

Input Output

```
$ lines='one
> two'
$ echo "$lines"
one
two
$ lines=one\
> two
$ echo "$lines"
onetwo
```

Analysis

Notice that the shell completely removes the occurrence of the newline when the backslash is used. In the case of single quotes, the newline was preserved.

The backslash is very useful when you are typing long lines of a command at the prompt and the command must continue on the next line. Using single quotes would introduce an extra newline into the command being typed.

> **Note:** When the backslash character is used to remove the special meaning of a character `c`, you can say that the shell is "escaping the character `c`."

Within double quotes, the backslash is interpreted as removing the special meaning of dollar signs, newlines, and the quoting characters—single quotes, double quotes, or other backslashes. If none of these special characters precedes the backslash, the shell does not interpret the backslash as a special character and leaves it alone. For this reason, you have to be selective in how you use the backslash character.

Input
Output

```
$ echo "\$dollars"
$dollars
$ echo " this is a \ character"
this is a \ character
$ x=3
$ echo "the value of x is \'$x\""
the value of x is '3"
```

Analysis

In the first command (`echo "\dollars"`), the dollar sign is quoted, or *escaped.* In the next command (`echo " this is a \ character"`), the backslash character is quoted out to be displayed. Because the shell did not see a special character (`$`,`"`,`'` or `\`) in front of the backslash, it left the backslash alone and printed the backslash as it was in the original string.

The third command (`echo "the value of x is \'$x\""`) illustrates how to quote the double and single quotes themselves by using the quote character. In this case, the shell did see the special characters and did display the special character while removing the backslash character.

You also can display quotes within quotes by using one type of quote around another.

```
$ echo "this is a single quote'"
this is a single quote'
$ echo 'This is a double quote "'
This is a double quote "
```

The Back Quote

The back quote offers a function completely different from that of the quoting mechanisms you have seen thus far. In this special case, the shell interprets everything between the back quotes as a shell command. The shell then executes the command as a subshell and replaces the text and the paired back quotes with the results of that command. These subshells are *child invocations* of the shell program. (See Day 1.) In the case of back quotes, the subshell runs only for the duration in which it executes the command given between the back quotes.

> **Note:** It's easy to confuse the back quote with the single quote. On most keyboards, the single quote, or apostrophe, (') is below the double quote (") key. The back quote, or accent grave, (`) is on the key with the tilde (~).

Consider the following examples.

Input/Output

```
$ which rm
/bin/rm
$ ls -l `which rm`
-rwxr-xr-x    1 root     bin          5612 Nov 16  1993 /bin/rm
$ ls -l /bin/rm
-rwxr-xr-x    1 root     bin          5612 Nov 16  1993 /bin/rm
$
```

Analysis

The `which` command found the command `rm` along the path using the `which` command. It then replaced the back quotes with the results and created the command `ls -l /bin/rm` and executed it.

The command executed between the back quotes is done with the same environment as the original shell, but only those shell variables that are explicitly *exported* are available to this program. In Day 6, when you learn about conforming your environment, you will learn about the use of subshells and exporting of values. Look at another example of using the back quotes. Suppose you wanted to count all the words and characters in the files that have the extension `.t`. You could do it this way.

Input/Output

```
$ ls *.t
i.t
x.t
$ ls *.t | wc
      2       2       8
$ wc `ls *.t`
     21      171     1184 i.t
     20      184     1099 x.t
     41      355     2283 total
```

Analysis

Consider the output of the second command (`ls *.t ¦ wc`). The pipe command sent the output of the `ls` command to `wc`, which counted two lines.

The third command (`` wc `ls *.t` ``) first used the back quote to list all the files `*.t` in the directory and then passed the list on to the `wc` command.

Obviously, this is a contrived example because the command `$ wc *.t` would have achieved the same result. A more complex example is when you do a backup using the `find` command.

Input Output

```
$ tar -cvf ../myfile ` find . -name "*.[ch]" -print
```

Analysis

The `tar` command is UNIX's version of the tape archiving utility to do backups and restorations of files to disk. You have already dealt with the `find` command.

This command would call the `tar` command with the following options:

- `c` to create
- `v` to be verbose
- `f ../myfile` to create the archive called `myfile` in the directory above the current one

The names of the files that are input to the `tar` command are provided from the output of the find command between the single quotes.

The `find` command takes the following arguments:

- `.` (the period) to use the current directory.
- `-name "*.[ch]"` to search for all the files with a `.c` or `.h` extension. Notice the quotes around filename description.
- `-print` to request that all the matched filenames are printed.

The `find` command then recursively traverses the entire tree path and finds all the files with the extension `.c` or `.h` and prints the output. The shell collects all these names and passes them on to the `tar` command. The `tar` command creates the archive with all the filenames.

Metacharacters in Filenames

Metacharacters are not good candidates for filenames because it is very awkward to manipulate them. Though creating filenames and directory names with these characters is not impossible, it's still not a good idea to do so unless you deliberately want to confuse the user or keep the user from working with the file.

Generally, you can use the permissions fields to keep someone from deleting a file. You also can hide a file or directory from the normal `ls` listing by specifying a period (`.`) as the first character of its name. (See Day 3.)

Input Output

```
$ ls
text
$ mv text '&lddr'
$ ls
&ddr
$ rm &lddr
[1492]
Try rm --help for more information
sh: lddr: command not found
+exit     rm
$ ls &lddr
&lddr          idbstk.txt    mtfscale.txt  vertxstr.c
cli            mk_kern       mytfook.txt   ximage.txt
finwiz5.zip    mtfdlg.txt    pl.exe
sh: lddr: command not found
$
```

Analysis As you can see, the `mv` command has created the file `&lddr` for you. However, it's confusing the `rm` and `ls` commands because they interpret the filename's `&` as a request to run everything before the command as a background process.

In almost all cases, you can eliminate the annoyances of such names by quoting the name in single quotes to shield it from the shell. Some commands, however, especially `cp` and `rm`, do not treat an initial hyphen (`-` as the first character) in a filename very kindly. So be careful.

In fact, by using the single quotes, you can use tabs or whitespaces as part of the filename. You learned some of this in Day 3.

Although including special characters in filenames and directory names may be great when you are trying to impress your peers and loved ones, it's generally not standard practice. In some cases, you may wind up with weird directory names because of erroneous typing. In such cases, you may have to resort to living with the files in that directory or to removing the entire directory after you move your important files to another directory.

The moral of the story is that UNIX is very flexible—to the point of letting you do things to harm yourself.

DO	DON'T

DO keep backups of the files you are modifying, preferably in a separate directory tree.

DO use the single or double quotes with echo when you're in doubt about how the metacharacters will expand.

DO make sure that the quotes are balanced. That is, the number of the same type of quote marks should be divisible by two.

DON'T use any of the filename extension shortcuts at the root directory, even if you have permission to do so.

Metacharacter Reserved for Input/Output

Other special characters for the shell are those reserved for use when handling input and output in the shell. These are the `>`, `<`, `&`, and `¦` characters. You will learn about these in greater detail in Day 7 when you learn file input and output redirection.

Summary

Today, you examined many important aspects of using metacharacters in the shell.

- Metacharacters are characters that carry a special meaning to the shell.
- The shell uses filename substitution to expand the value of a shell variable into filenames or directory names.
- Without quotes, the shell interprets the value of a shell variable before it does filename expansion.
- When you use double quotes, the `$`, `\`, and `` ` `` characters are interpreted as metacharacters.

- When you use single quotes, the `$`, `\` and `` ` `` characters are not interpreted as metacharacters.
- The backslash is a unary operator (not paired) and works on one character only.
- The shell does not preserve any newlines marked by the backslash character. It does preserve them when they are marked by the paired quotes.
- Quoting mechanisms enable you to display metacharacters in many forms.
- You were introduced to the `grep` command and learned how to use it to extract strings from a file.
- You can use special characters in filenames and directory names by using the quoting mechanisms in UNIX.

What's Next?

Tomorrow's lesson covers the `grep` command in more detail as you learn about regular expressions. This will be the basis for the tools for extracting strings from within files and for performing string functions.

4

Q&A

Q What is a metacharacter?

A A metacharacter is a special character that expands to filenames.

Q How can I count all the words in files with two or more characters in the filename?

A You can use the command `wc ??*`.

Q How do I stop the shell from expanding the filename expansion?

A You can do so by quoting the filename or by setting the `-f` flag.

Q How can I print quotes within quotes?

A You can print single quotes from within double quotes and vice versa. You can also escape the quote using the `\` operator.

Workshop

The Workshop provides quiz questions to help you solidify your understanding of the material covered. Some Workshop sections of this book also contain exercises to provide you with experience in using what you've learned. Try to understand the quiz and exercise answers before continuing on to the next chapter. Answers are provided in Appendix D, "Answers."

Quiz

1. How would you list all files that have two or more characters in their names?
2. How would you list all files that have either an underscore or a period anywhere in their name?
3. How would you list all files that have a digit anywhere in their filename?
4. How would you create a file with an asterisk in its name? How about with a $ symbol?
5. How would you get a complete listing of all the files and subdirectories under your current working directory? How would you stop the listing to display one page at a time?

Exercises

1. Try the following commands:

   ```
   $ echo *
   ```

   ```
   $ echo ?
   ```

   ```
   $ echo ??
   ```

   Can you explain what each command shows you?

2. Try the following command:

   ```
   $ echo "*"
   ```

   What is the output from this command and why?

3. Discover two ways of typing the following line from an echo statement:

   ```
   This is a "double quote" and this is a 'single quote'
   ```

4. Create a file called `bad file`. (Be sure to include the space in the middle of the name.)

5. Try the commands and see what outputs you get:

```
ls *
ls .
ls -X
ls -x
ls -aXl
ls -F
```

5

Life with Regular Expressions

Today, you will learn about one of the most important features of UNIX—regular expressions. Along the way, you will learn about the following:

- ☐ Pattern-matching operators
- ☐ The dollar sign operator (`$`)
- ☐ The caret operator (`^`)
- ☐ The period operator (`.`)
- ☐ The asterisk operator (`*`)
- ☐ The parentheses operators (`()`)
- ☐ Closures
- ☐ The plus operator (`+`)
- ☐ The asterisk operator (`*`)
- ☐ The question mark operator (`?`)
- ☐ The `grep` command
- ☐ More on using `grep`
- ☐ The `grep` family
- ☐ The `glob` command

By the end of the day, you will have learned all about `grep` and how to use regular expressions to do a search operation. This information will be the basis for writing specialized search-and-replace filters for programs, for the streaming editor `sed` (see Day 11), and for `awk` (see Day 12).

Regular Expressions

In Day 4, you were introduced to `grep` as a means of locating text strings within files. Today, you will learn about specifying complex strings using a technique called *regular expressions.* The `grep` utility uses regular expressions to search for complex strings. The utility derives its name from the fact that it is a *g*lobal *r*egular *e*xpression *p*rinter.

Searching for complex strings can take many forms, for example:

- ☐ Find all five-letter words that begin with *c*.
- ☐ Find all words ending in *tion.*

- Find all two-digit numbers at the beginning of a line.
- Find all words that start with *w* and end with *h*.

The pattern you would use to specify these searches is called a regular expression.

You will work with `grep` in the same manner as you did in Day 4. The only difference is that you will specify a regular expression instead of a text string.

Pattern-Matching Operators

The following are the pattern-matching operators. They are used to specify the type of data you are looking for:

- The caret (^) and dollar sign operators ($)
- The period operator (.)
- The asterisk operator (*)
- The parentheses operators (( ))
- The plus operator (+)

The Caret and Dollar Sign Operators

The caret (^) is used to specify the start of a line, whereas the dollar sign ($) signifies the end of a line. Some of these examples include the following:

`"public"`	The word *public* anywhere on a line
`"^public"`	The word *public* at the start of a line
`"public$"`	The word *public* at the end of a line
`"^public$"`	A single line with the word *public* in it

Note: Earlier in this book, you learned about filename expansion and the definition of metacharacters. The special characters for regular expressions also can be referred to as metacharacters.

Unfortunately, some metacharacters in `grep` have different meanings than those used by the shell. Also, some are the same as those interpreted by the shell—for example, the `$` or the `*`. Therefore, when you are passing parameters and you think the shell may misinterpret them, you should put double quotes or single quotes around them.

Look at the following examples, in which I try out these operators on a sample file, `farkle`.

Input
Output

```
$ cat farkle
The proposed acquisition is subject to satisfaction of customary
conditions, including completion of due diligence by both parties,
execution of a definitive agreement, approval by the shareholders of
both companies and certain regulatory filings, and is expected to be
completed by the end of 1994.

IDB Communications Group, Inc. is a global telecommunications company
that operates a domestic and international communications network
providing its customers with international private line and long
distance telephone services, radio and television transmission
services, facsimile and data connections, mobile satellite
communications capabilities and the design and integration of
satellite networks worldwide.

Peoples Telephone Company, Inc., one of the nation's leading public
communications companies, owns and operates approximately 50,000
public, inmate and cellular pay telephones in 46 states. For the year
ended December 31, 1993, the Company reported revenues of $121.8
million, an increase of 63%, net income of $5.3 million, an increase
of 64%, and cash flow from operations of $27.5 million, an increase of
54%, all as compared to the year ended December 31, 1992.
$
$ grep "public" farkle
Peoples Telephone Company, Inc., one of the nation's leading public
public, inmate and cellular pay telephones in 46 states. For the year
$
$ grep "^public" farkle
public, inmate and cellular pay telephones in 46 states. For the year
$ grep "public$" farkle
Peoples Telephone Company, Inc., one of the nation's leading public
$ grep "^public$" farkle
$
```

Analysis

The command `grep "public" farkle` used the string `"public"` to get lines with the word *public* anywhere on a line.

Note: The dollar sign (`$`) is by itself on the last line of the example because I entered an extra Return to generate an extra line to separate the command line and its output. This was for clarity only; the extra Return does not have to be entered.

The next command (`grep "^public" i.t`) used the caret (`"^public"`) to get lines with the word *public* at the beginning of a line.

After that, the next command (`grep "public$" i.t`) used `"public$"` to get the line with the word *public* at the end.

Lastly, I searched for a full line with the single word *public* in it by using the expression `"^public$"`.

You can specify complete lines with these two pattern matchers by enclosing the string between a `^` and a `$`, as shown in the preceding example with `"^public$"`:

```
"^I will match a line like this one$"
```

This expression selects a line that looks exactly the following:

```
I will match a line like this one
```

The number of spaces between words must match exactly for this match to work.

More than One File as Input

You can specify more than one file for a filename when using `grep`. The shell will expand the definition for you into a list of filenames, as you learned in Day 3. When `grep` is given a list of files, the output from `grep` shows at the beginning of each line the name of the file in which that matching line was found.

Input
Output

```
$ ls *.t
i.t x.t
$ grep "public" x.t
Two publicly-available programs which allow interactive definition of
$ grep "public" i.t
Peoples Telephone Company, Inc., one of the nation's leading public
public, inmate and cellular pay telephones in 46 states. For the year
$ grep "public" *.t
farkle:Peoples Telephone Company, Inc., one of the nation's leading public
farkle:public, inmate and cellular pay telephones in 46 states. For the year
x.t:Two publicly-available programs which allow interactive definition of
$ grep "public" farkle x.t
farkle:Peoples Telephone Company, Inc., one of the nation's leading public
farkle:public, inmate and cellular pay telephones in 46 states. For the year
x.t:Two publicly-available programs which allow interactive definition of
```

Analysis

When I used the `grep` command on one file, the output showed the matched lines. When I specified more than file, however, either explicitly or by filename expansion from the shell, `grep` prefixed each line with the name of the file where the line originated.

The Period Operator (.)

The period operator performs a function that is similar to the question mark for the shell during filename expansion. It matches either one character or no characters at its position, except that the question matches exactly one character.

The string `"gl. "` (notice the space after the period) matches all words that begin with the letters *gl*, followed by one character and a space.

Input/Output

```
$ grep "p....c" farkle
IDB Communications Group, Inc. is a global telecommunications company
Peoples Telephone Company, Inc., one of the nation's leading public
public, inmate and cellular pay telephones in 46 states. For the year
$
```

Analysis

The `"p....c"` string specifies a word with a *p* at the beginning, followed by exactly four characters, and a *c* at the end. The word *public* matches this pattern completely, and thus the output shows two lines that have the word *public* in them.

At first, it's a bit hard to see why the first line is printed out, because that line doesn't have the word *public* in it. Can you see why the line is printed? The match occurred in `Group, Inc.`; notice the *p* and the *c*, and you can see that the four characters between them—`, In`—match the four periods.

The Asterisk in Regular Expressions

An asterisk in a regular expression performs the same function as an asterisk in filename expansion. It matches zero or more occurrences of any patterns preceding it.

The following examples serve as a good starting point to understanding the use of the asterisk in regular expressions.

Input/Output

```
$ grep "a*ll" farkle
services, facsimile and data connections, mobile satellite
satellite networks worldwide.
public, inmate and cellular pay telephones in 46 states. For the year
million, an increase of 63%, net income of $5.3 million, an increase
of 64%, and cash flow from operations of $27.5 million, an increase of
54%, all as compared to the year ended December 31, 1992.
$
```

Analysis

The `"a*ll"` expression matches any word starting with the letter *a* and ending with the letters *ll*. This includes the words *satellite* and the word *all*. These are fairly obvious matches in the output. Remember to enclose this expression in double quotes to prevent the shell from expanding the asterisk.

What may not be obvious is why the other lines are printed. Consider this output line:

```
public, inmate and cellular pay telephones in 46 states. For the year
```

The word *inmate* has the letter *a* in it, and the word *cellular* has the *ll* pair. The asterisk specified any number of characters (including zero or spaces) between *a* and *ll*. Thus, the segment `ate and cell` satisfied the search pattern requirements. If you simply wanted to search for a word ending in *ll*, you should specify a space between the second *l* and the double quote, thus: `"a*ll "`.

Input Output

```
$ grep "a*ll " farkle
54%, all as compared to the year ended December 31, 1992.
```

Analysis

In this case, the space between the `l` and `"` prevent multiple words from being matched.

The Parentheses Operators

There are two types of parentheses operators that you can use to define the sets of characters on which matches should be done:

- Use `[]` for defining a set of characters from which to choose. They are often referred to as "brackets."
- Use `{}` for defining a count of repeated sets of matches on one line. They are often referred to as "curly braces."

5

The Set Operator ([ ])

The bracket operators `[]` define a set of characters to choose from for one or more characters in that position. For example, the expression

```
[Tt]elevision
```

matches the words *Television* and *television.*

The expression `"^[abc012]"` matches the characters *a,* or *b,* or *c,* or *0,* or *1,* or *2* at the beginning of a line for all lines in a file. The bracket operators also enable you to specify lists of characters by using the hyphen operator (`-`). You can specify the preceding statement by using the following equivalent statement:

```
^[a-c0-2]
```

The most common patterns that you will use are these:

`[a-z]`	The lowercase set of characters *a* through *z*
`[0-9]`	The digits 0 through 9
`[A-Z]`	The uppercase set of characters *a* through *z*

So when I was looking for words that match the pattern `"p....c"`, I could have specified `"p[a-z][a-z][a-z][a-z]c"` as the search pattern.

Input Output

```
$ grep "p[a-z][a-z][a-z][a-z]c" farkle
Peoples Telephone Company, Inc., one of the nation's leading public
public, inmate and cellular pay telephones in 46 states. For the year
$
```

Analysis This output shows two lines instead of three shown in the previous example, for which the pattern `"p....c"` was used. The obscure line that matched earlier did not show up this time.

Here's another example. If you need a way to find all the lines with digits in them, you would use this match pattern.

Input Output

```
"[0-9]"

$ grep "[0-9]" farkle
completed by the end of 1994.
communications companies, owns and operates approximately 50,000
public, inmate and cellular pay telephones in 46 states. For the year
ended December 31, 1993, the Company reported revenues of $121.8
million, an increase of 63%, net income of $5.3 million, an increase
of 64%, and cash flow from operations of $27.5 million, an increase of
54%, all as compared to the year ended December 31, 1992.
$
$ grep "[0-9]*\.[0-9]" farkle
ended December 31, 1993, the Company reported revenues of $121.8
million, an increase of 63%, net income of $5.3 million, an increase
of 64%, and cash flow from operations of $27.5 million, an increase of
$
```

Analysis The first command line (`grep "[0-9]" i.t`) prints out all the lines with at least one digit in them. The `[0-9]` matches one digit between 0 and 9.

The second command line, which uses the pattern `"[0-9]*\.[0-9]"`, finds all the numbers with at least one digit after the period. The first `[0-9]*` is used to match zero or more digits. The `\.` period matches the period literally, followed by one digit.

> **Note:** The backslash (\) escapes the period so that it is taken literally instead of being interpreted as a metacharacter. (See Day 4.)

The caret (`^`) before the brackets (`[ ]`) in a pattern is used to indicate the beginning of a line. If the same caret is used *between* the `[ ]`, the caret takes on a completely different meaning: it actually negates the selection process. Thus, the pattern

```
"^[^a-z]"
```

matches all lines that begin with a character *other than* the lowercase letters *a* through *z*.

If you want to use the hyphen as part of the matching characters, you must specify it either at the beginning or at the end of the set within the brackets. For example, the pattern

```
"[-af]" or "[af-]"
```

matches the characters `-`, `a`, and `f`.

DO	DON'T

DON'T use the pattern `[A-z]` to do the match `[a-zA-Z]`. The pattern `[A-z]` matches all the ASCII characters between *Z* and *a*.

DO use the pattern `[a-zA-0-9]` to match names for common shell variables.

The {} Operators

A number enclosed in braces following an expression specifies the number of times the preceding expression must be repeated. This is also known as a *closure*. For example, I could search for all three-digit numbers in my text by using `"[0-9]{3} "`.

The general form of a closure is `{s,t}`, where s specifies the minimum number of times that the pattern should be repeated and *t* specifies the maximum number of times. The expression also can be specified as `{s,}`, which implies that *t* is a huge number. Likewise, the expression `{,t}` implies 1 for the variable `s`. The `{s}` by itself implies an exact occurrence of `s` times for the preceding expression.

Note: The curly braces operators `{}` will not be available to you in certain older versions `grep` because the original `grep` does not support all of the features of regular expressions.

The later versions of `grep`, `egrep`, and notably the `grep` from GNU provide a large number of options and *do* provide the support for the `{}` operators. See the section on "Grouping Patterns in `egrep`," later today.

> Whether or not the curly braces are available to you with your version of grep, you do need to know about the curly braces for other UNIX tools and get an understanding of how regular expressions are parsed in UNIX.
>
> Knowing how to use these expressions will be especially useful for you when you work with text editors such as sed to do search-and-replace from within shell scripts (see Day 11) or when you use the awk command (see Day 12).

When you use closures with the grep command, be careful to escape the braces with a backslash character to prevent the shell from interpreting them. Consider the following example.

Input Output

```
IDB Communications Group, Inc. is a global telecommunications company
that operates a domestic and international communications network
communications capabilities and the design and integration of
communications companies, owns and operates approximately 50,000
million, an increase of 63%, net income of $5.3 million, an increase
54%, all as compared to the year ended December 31, 1992.
$ grep "com" farkle
conditions, including completion of due diligence by both parties,
both companies and certain regulatory filings, and is expected to be
completed by the end of 1994.
$ grep "com{2}" farkle
$ (nothing)
$ grep "com\{2\}" farkle
IDB Communications Group, Inc. is a global telecommunications company
that operates a domestic and international communications network
communications capabilities and the design and integration of
communications companies, owns and operates approximately 50,000
$
```

Analysis The command to list two occurrences of the string "com" (the command grep "com{2}" i.t) failed without the braces because they were not escaped with the backslash character.

As I stated earlier, not all closures are available for all versions of grep. The next section on the grep family introduces you to an enhanced version of grep, called egrep, which does support the closure features.

Some shortcuts, however, are always available for grep to get the most common closure types. These shortcuts are the following:

- The + operator: This is a shorthand for describing a closure of {1,}, meaning that the preceding expression must be repeated 1 or more times. For example, the expression "[a-z]+" will specify as the match pattern all words that are one character or more in length.

- The `*` operator: This is a shorthand expression describing the closure `{0,}` for zero or more occurrences of the preceding pattern. The pattern `'\$[0-9]* '` specifies searching for patterns that begin with a dollar sign, followed by zero or more digits, followed by other characters.
- The `?` operator: This is the shorthand expression for the closure `{0,1}`, which specifies either one or zero. You could use `"\$[0-9]?"` to specify patterns containing single digits or no digits after a dollar sign.

  Note the escaped dollar sign. This is necessary if you intend to use this pattern at the command line with double quotes. Had this been between single quotes, you would not need to escape the `$` character.

Note: You will be learning about the use of these expressions in greater detail in Days 11 and 12 when you study the streaming text editor `sed` and the `awk` programming language.

More on Using *grep*

In the previous sections, you dealt with specifying regular expressions for `grep` to match. In this section, you will learn more about the output features of `grep`. On the man page for `grep`, you will see many options to the `grep` command:

- `-i` ignores case distinction.
- `-n` prints the line number of each match.
- `-v` prints all lines except those that match prints.
- `-c` prints only a count of the number of lines that match.

Let's look at some examples of these options on a short file.

Input
Output

```
$ cat x.t
The xwd client in the X11 distributions can be used to select a window
or the background. It produces an XWD-format file of the image of that
window. The file can be post-processed into something useful or printed with
the xpr client and your local printing mechanism. To print a screendump
including a menu or other object which has grabbed the pointer, you can use
this command:

  sh$ sleep 10; xwd -root > output.xwd &
```

```
and then spend 10 seconds or so setting up your screen; the entire current
display will be saved into the file output.xwd. Note that xwd also has an
undocumented (before R5) -id flag for specifying the window id on the
command-line. [There are also unofficial patches on ftp.x.org to xwd for
specifying the delay and the portion of the screen to capture.]

Two publicly-available programs which allow interactive definition of
arbitrary portions of the display and built-in delays are asnap and
xgrabsc.
There are several versions of xgrabsc; version 2.3, available on ftp.x.org
[9/93] is the most recent. xgrab, part of the package, is an interactive
front-end to xgrabsc.
$
$ grep "xwd" x.t
The xwd client in the X11 distributions can be used to select a window
  sh$ sleep 10; xwd -root > output.xwd &
display will be saved into the file output.xwd. Note that xwd also has an
command-line. [There are also unofficial patches on ftp.x.org to xwd for
$
$ grep -i "xwd" x.t
The xwd client in the X11 distributions can be used to select a window
or the background. It produces an XWD-format file of the image of that
  sh$ sleep 10; xwd -root > output.xwd &
display will be saved into the file output.xwd. Note that xwd also has an
command-line. [There are also unofficial patches on ftp.x.org to xwd for
```

Analysis The esc commands show you how grep catches the extra line (the line with *XWD*) when case is ignored.

To number the lines that are printed out, use the `-n` option.

Input/Output

```
$ grep -n "public" farkle
15:Peoples Telephone Company, Inc., one of the nation's leading public
17:public, inmate and cellular pay telephones in 46 states. For the year
$ grep -n "public" x.t
16:Two publicly-available programs which allow interactive definition of
$ grep -n "public" x.t farkle
i.t:15:Peoples Telephone Company, Inc., one of the nation's leading public
i.t:17:public, inmate and cellular pay telephones in 46 states. For the year
x.t:16:Two publicly-available programs which allow interactive definition of
```

Analysis Notice that the line numbers are preceded by filenames when more than one file is specified on the command line.

To list the lines that did not match a pattern, you can use the `-v` option. For example, to find all the lines in `i.t` where the pattern *and* is not used, use the command `grep -v "and" i.t`.

Input/Output

```
$ grep -v "and" farkle
The proposed acquisition is subject to satisfaction of customary
conditions, including completion of due diligence by both parties,
execution of a definitive agreement, approval by the shareholders of
completed by the end of 1994.
```

```
IDB Communications Group, Inc. is a global telecommunications company
satellite networks worldwide.

Peoples Telephone Company, Inc., one of the nation's leading public
ended December 31, 1993, the Company reported revenues of $121.8
million, an increase of 63%, net income of $5.3 million, an increase
54%, all as compared to the year ended December 31, 1992.
$
$ grep -vn "and" farkle
1:The proposed acquisition is subject to satisfaction of customary
2:conditions, including completion of due diligence by both parties,
3:execution of a definitive agreement, approval by the shareholders of
5:completed by the end of 1994.
6:
7:IDB Communications Group, Inc. is a global telecommunications company
13:satellite networks worldwide.
14:
15:Peoples Telephone Company, Inc., one of the nation's leading public
18:ended December 31, 1993, the Company reported revenues of $121.8
19:million, an increase of 63%, net income of $5.3 million, an increase
21:54%, all as compared to the year ended December 31, 1992.
```

Analysis Notice how you can combine the two options `-v` and `-n` into one for this output. The `-v` option reversed the search pattern. Instead of searching for and printing all the matched lines, `grep -v` printed the lines that do not match the pattern.

Notice how grep caught the empty lines 6 and 14 where the word *and* was not found.

Dealing with Blank Lines in a File

You can remove all the blank lines from a file by specifying a pattern that looks for a space or tab at the start of a line, followed zero or more such occurrences. So, `$ grep -v "^[ ]*" i.t` removes all the blank lines from the file. The brackets contain one space and one tab (you cannot see them).

To remove all the empty lines from a file, use `$ grep -v "^$" i.t`. By *empty lines*, I mean that the line has only a carriage return (or, in the case of DOS files, a carriage return and line feed). A *blank line* may have whitespaces (space and tabs) but no other characters.

Sometimes you are interested in only the files in which you found a pattern; you're not interested in seeing the lines themselves. A good example is when you search all your memos for the word *malpractice* to find out which memos contain this word. Rather than list every line in every such memo, you want simply to list all the filenames of memos containing this word. In this case, you can use the `-l` option to `grep`. The following example searches for the word *shell* in all the chapters of this book.

Input/Output

```
$ grep -l "shell" ch*
ch01
ch02
ch03
ch04
ch05
ch06
ch07
ch08
ch09
ch10
ch11
ch12
ch13
ch14
$ grep -l "shell" ch* ¦ wc -l
      14
$
```

Analysis

The first command (`grep -l "shell" ch*`) listed all the files with word *shell* in them. The second command used the `wc` command to count the number of lines from the `grep` command.

If you had not used the `-l` option to the `grep` command in the second command, `wc` would have printed out a count of the number of lines that use the word *shell* in all the files `ch*`.

You can generate a count of the number of lines that, in any groups of files, uses a particular word. To count the number of all the lines with the word *and* in *.t files, you can use the commands shown in the following example.

Input/Output

```
$ grep -c "and" i.t
9
$ grep "and" i.t ¦ wc -l
      9
$ grep -c "and" *.t
i.t:9
x.t:6
$ grep "and" *.t ¦ wc -l
     15
```

Analysis

Notice how I counted the number of lines in the `i.t` file in two ways.

As before, the use of more than one filename causes `grep` to prefix its output with the associated filename. Also, the last command in the sequence (`$ grep "and" *.t ¦ wc -l`) shows the total number of times the word and was used in all the files with the `.t` extension.

DO | **DON'T**

DO use the -c option to count lines per file.

DO read the man pages to see more options to the grep command and to check what options are available to the version of grep at your site.

DON'T use the wc command on the output from the -C option to grep.

Note: The fast portion of grep is now really a myth. Generally, you're better off using grep. The fgrep is listed here only for the sake of completeness.

The *grep* Family

The grep command is not alone. There are two similar commands: egrep and fgrep.

The fgrep does not offer the options of parsing closures, but it does offer these additional options:

- -h suppresses the printing of preceding filenames when multiple lines are selected.
- -x matches the pattern exactly.
- -f specifies a file that could contain a list of patterns for you to choose from. This way you can store several search patterns in one file and specify this file for your search.

The command is called fgrep because it uses fixed strings to do the matching, and it does not do regular expression parsing on the special characters for grep: {,}, [,], *, ?, and +. The name fgrep stands for either "fast grep" or "fixed grep" (because it works with fixed strings only), depending on the text you happen to be reading.

The `egrep` command is the enhanced version of `grep`. It offers all the features of `grep`, plus support for the `+`, `*`, `?` and closure `{ }` operators in addition to all the extra features offered by the `fgrep` command.

DO | **DON'T**

DO use the options you think will work with the `fgrep` command on large files first, because `fgrep` is generally faster than `egrep`.

DO use `egrep` for complex regular expressions.

DO think of breaking up a complex regular expression into two separate regular expressions. Pipe the output from one `grep` command into the input of the other, instead of trying to come up with a complex expression. For example, use `$grep "hello" *.txt | grep "World"`.

DON'T use `egrep` if you can use `fgrep` or `grep`, both of which execute faster than `egrep`.

Grouping Patterns in *egrep*

Let's say you want to look up the name of a pizza parlor but you don't remember whether it was *Pizza Inn* or *Pizza Hut*. Rather than do two searches, you could do one search by grouping the matching patterns together.

Input/Output

```
$ egrep "Pizza (Hut|Inn)" parlor
Pizza Hut - West
Pizza Hut - East
Pizza Inn
```

Analysis The parentheses in the `egrep` command grouped together several patterns. Had you typed in

```
$ egrep "Pizza Hut|Inn" parlor
```

you would have searched for *Pizza Hut* and *Inn*—quite a different pattern than what you expected.

The `|` operator is the logical `OR` operator in this case and enables you to select a pattern on either side. You can concatenate several patterns on either side of the pattern. The parentheses group the `OR` patterns together.

Note: The GNU Project's version of `grep` offers `grep`, `egrep`, and `fgrep` all in one package called `grep`. The type of `grep` is selected by means of options:

- `-G` (the default)
- `-F` `(fgrep)`
- `-E` `(egrep)`

So, `grep -E` would invoke the `egrep` program, and `-F` would invoke the `fgrep` program.

Dealing with Complex Expressions

Note: This section looks ahead at solving complex problems with regular expressions with tools I have yet to discuss. So be warned that some of the terms may not make sense to you until Day 7. I have already covered a bit about input/output redirection, so the following material should not be very difficult.

Sometimes you need to search for special string patterns that are problematic; they simply cannot fit on one line or describing them would create a very convoluted regular expression. In such cases, it's sometimes better to break the problem into two separate files and run `grep` twice with a simpler expression each time.

Suppose you want to get all lines with the word *on* but not with the word *ion.* Instead of describing a complex expression to do this, you could use pipes to extract the lines with the word *on* but not the word *ion.*

Input/Output

```
$ grep ion farkle ¦ wc
     13      118     859
$ grep on farkle  ¦ wc
     14      130     930
$ grep on farkle ¦ grep -v ion
public, inmate and cellular pay telephones in 46 states. For the year
```

Analysis

From the output from the first command (`grep ion i.t ¦ wc`), you saw that the word *ion* occurs 13 times. From the second command's output, you saw that the word *on* occurs 14 times. Therefore, one line has the word *on* but not the word *ion.*

To get this line, you would strip out the lines with the word *on* and then use the UNIX pipe symbol to pass these lines to another `grep` command that will print only the lines that do not have the word *ion* in them.

This is a simple example for you to look over, but think of using UNIX commands, pipes, and I/O redirection commands as tools that you can use to build up complex commands.

The *glob* Command

The UNIX shell is very capable of working with regular expressions. However, some shell look-alikes, especially those designed for DOS machines, cannot use the simple expansion capabilities of `command.com`.

> **Note:** On DOS systems, especially when you are using the MKS toolkit, you will run across a command called `glob`. Contact MKS directly at (800) 265-2797.

This `glob` command is used by the shell to match pathnames to the expression passed to the shell command. You are not supposed to call `glob` directly from the command line, but almost all the UNIX utilities under DOS will call it on an as-needed basis.

So, if you are working on DOS machine with a shell look-alike and find that your regular expressions are not being parsed correctly by this shell, check to see if you need the `glob` command.

Summary

Today's text introduced you to the concept of regular expressions and how to use them. Regular expressions are used to describe complex strings.

- The UNIX `grep` utility is used to search for strings given regular expressions.
- The `*` matches zero or more occurrences of a preceding pattern.
- The `?` matches zero or one occurrence of a preceding pattern.
- The `+` matches one or more occurrences of a preceding pattern.
- Special characters can be escaped with the `\` character.

- The brackets `[ ]` offer a way of specifying a set of characters from which to choose.
- The `-` operator between characters within `[ ]` specifies the range of ASCII letters between the characters.
- The `^` (caret) matches the beginning of a line when it's used outside the `[` and `]`. When used within the `[` and `]`, the caret negates the list that follows it.
- The `$` signifies the end of line.
- Empty lines are specified by using the expression `"^$"`.
- Blank lines are specified by using the expression `"^ *$"`.
- The `grep` command uses regular expressions to search for types of strings. It has two other versions: `fgrep` and `egrep`.
- The `fgrep` utility offers more features than the standard `grep` command, including the capability to specify more than one pattern in a file.
- A closure specifies the number of times a pattern may be repeated. User-defined closures are not supported by the standard `grep` command or by `fgrep`.
- The `egrep` utility offers the support for closures in addition to those features offered by `fgrep`.
- The `egrep` utility also provides support for grouping several patterns together with the `|` operator in expression. This enables you to specify an `OR` operation of patterns to match.
- On DOS machines, the `grep` command may call a special command called `glob.exe` to do the regular expression parsing. If things do not work right on a DOS version of the shell, check the manual for that shell to see if you need `glob.exe` installed from by your vendor.

Today's text is by no means a complete discussion of all the possible combinations of regular expressions you can use to match and search patterns. As you progress through the next days' texts, you will cover more and more of these expressions as they are needed.

What's Next?

Tomorrow, you will learn about your environment and ways customize your shell.

UNIX Commands Learned Today

- `grep` Global regular expression printer
- `egrep` Enhanced
- `fgrep` Faster version of `grep` (although you might not be able to tell the difference)

Q&A

Q What does `grep` stand for?

A It stands for global regular expression printer.

Q What is a regular expression?

A A regular expression is a shorthand way of describing a complex string.

Q Can regular expressions include metacharacters, and how do I include them in a match pattern?

A Yes, they can include metacharacters, as long as they are between single quotes or are escaped with a backslash. (See Day 4.)

Q Can I simply list all the files with a regular expression in them?

A Yes, you can do so by using the `-l` option.

Workshop

The Workshop provides quiz questions to help you solidify your understanding of the material covered. Some Workshop sections of this book also contain exercises to provide you with experience in using what you've learned. Try to understand the quiz and exercise answers before continuing on to the next chapter. Answers are provided in Appendix D, "Answers."

Quiz

1. What do the following patterns match?

```
x*
x*z
x\{1,5\}
[0-9]
[0-9]+
[0-9]*
[Uu]nix
[Dd][eE][mM][Oo]
c?t
```

2. Describe in words the meaning of the following patterns:

3. How would you count the number of lines with the word *magnet* in all the files that have the extension `*.txt`?

4. How would you get a count of the number of times *magnet* was used in each file?

5. How would you count the number of empty lines in a file?

Exercises

1. Come up with regular expressions for the following patterns:

   All words ending in *tion*

   All words that begin with an *f* and end with a *e*

   Five-letter words beginning with *q*

   Four-letter words ending in *m*

2. Come up with a way to match blank lines.

3. Variables in the C language begin with a letter of the alphabet or an underscore, followed by zero or more than one occurrence of an alphanumeric or underscore character. Describe a regular expression for a C variable.

4. Given that you specify a curly brace per line of blocked text, with `{` at the beginning and a `}` at the end of each block, and you can nest blocks within one another, thus using the following:

```
{
    ...
    {
        ....
    }
    {
        ....
    }
}
```

how would you check to see whether the number of open braces was equal to the number of closed braces?

5. How would you see whether the user "root" is logged in your system? (Hint: Pipe the who command to `grep`.)

WEEK 1

6

Your Environment

Today you will learn about your user environment—what it is, how to work with it, and how to customize it. The topics covered here include the following:

- What your environment is
- What happens when you log in
- The `.profile` file
- Some important environment variables
- Customizing the user environment
- Some desktop utilities for you to work with

The Environment

The collection of shell variables, your home directory, and other related information about your login session is referred to as the *environment.* The shell variables that are part of this environment are called the shell's *environment variables.* Some of the most important environment variables include the following:

- `HOME` — This is the path to your home directory.
- `SHELL` — This is the default program that is called when other programs execute UNIX commands.
- `PATH` — This is a colon-delimited list of directory names that are searched when the shell processes a command. If the command is not found along this path and is not built into the shell, the shell responds with a `command not found` message. However, the shell requests the kernel to execute the first occurrence of the command in any one of the `PATH` directories.
- `TERM` — Your terminal type is set to this variable. By default, your terminal value is set to *unknown,* but when you log in the first time, it's set to a value defined for the phone line or terminal type on which you are logged in.
- `USER` and `LOGNAME` — These are your user identifiers to UNIX. Under BSD (Berkeley's version of UNIX), your identifier would be `LOGNAME`, and under AT&T's versions of UNIX prior to SVR4, your identifier would be `USER`. Instead of agreeing on just one word, most UNIX systems now define both these variables.
- `PWD` — The shell sets this variable to your present working directory.

- IFS — This is the interfield separator for splitting arguments into words. Normally, this variable is set to a space, tab, or newline.
- MAIL — This is the location for the default mail box. A host of mail utilities use this variable.

Of course, there are other shell variables that define your environment as well. I will cover them in a later section.

The way you can look at the environment variables is shown in the following example.

Input Output

```
$ set
DISPLAY=mpsi:0
EUID=501
HOME=/home/kamran
HOSTTYPE=i386
IFS=

LESS=-MM
LOGNAME=kamran
MAIL=/var/spool/mail/kamran
MANPATH=/usr/man:/usr/man/preformat:/usr/X11/man:/usr/openwin/man
MINICOM=-c on
OPENWINHOME=/usr/openwin
OPTERR=1
OPTIND=1
PATH=/etc/local:/etc:/local/bin:/usr/bin:/bin:/usr/local/bin:/usr/bin/X11:
➥/usr/openwin/bin:/user/kamran/bin:.
PPID=78
PWD=/home/kamran/sams
SHELL=/bin/sh
SHLVL=2
TERM=console
UID=501
USER=kamran
_=/usr/bin/vi
ignoreeof=10
```

Note: The output from your PATH variable may wrap around your screen several times on several lines.

Analysis You do not have to know about every environment variable in your login session. Just worry about the common environmental variables for now. The set command displays a long list of variables for my environment. Some of these variables are as alien to me as they are to you, whereas some are more familiar.

What Happens When You Log In

In Day 1, you learned about the login sequence. After UNIX verifies your identity, it starts your shell, which in turn presents you with a shell prompt and waits for your commands. Before the shell presents you with your first prompt, however, it runs two special programs:

- `/etc/profile`
- `$HOME/.profile`

The `/etc/profile` is a file set up by your system administrator. This file sets up all the environment variables that apply to all users in the system. This includes setting up prompts, the home directory, `TERM`, `PATH`, and so on. Your system administrator has the responsibility of setting up this file.

The second file, `./.profile`, exists in your `HOME` directory. Your system administrator will have set up this file for you. You can edit this file to set your own variables or to override (reset) some of the variables set by the `/etc/profile` command.

> **Note:** Remember from Day 4 that the period (.) in front of the filename causes the file to not be listed in a regular `ls` listing. You have to use `ls -a .profile` to list this file.

Let's look at my `.profile` file.

Input
Output

```
$ cat .profile
PATH=/etc/local:/etc:/local/bin:/usr/bin:/bin:/usr/local/bin:
/usr/bin/X11:/usr/openwin/bin:/user/kamran/bin:.
export PATH
DISPLAY=mpsi:0
export DISPLAY
```

Analysis

Look at the first line; it resets the `PATH` variable to my own version. I also set another environment variable, `DISPLAY`, for my X window system login. Notice how I have set only two variables in my `.profile` variable, but the `set` command (which you saw earlier) displayed a long list of variables. Those additional variables were set in the `/etc/profile` program.

Note: The *export* commands make the shell variables available to your login shell even after the `.profile` program is executed. I will deal with exporting shell variables to subshells in Day 7.

If you make some changes to the `.profile` file, these do not take effect unless you execute the file or log out and log in again. It's often simpler to execute the profile with the *period* command, . :

```
$ . .profile
```

The *period* command executes the `.profile` file as a shell script. In fact, your login sequence can be summed up as two commands:

```
$ . /etc/profile
$ . $HOME/.profile
```

Notice how the two are executed by your login shell. This way, the variables retain their values for the duration that you are logged in.

Some Special Environment Variables

In this section, you will look at some of the important environment variables.

HOME, Sweet *HOME*

Your home directory is the place to which you log in. A special variable called `HOME` is set to this directory when you log in. This is the default variable that the `cd` command uses when you do not specify an argument to `cd`.

Input Output

```
$ echo $HOME
/home/myself
$ cd /usr/lib/X11
$ pwd
/usr/lib/X11
$ cd
$ pwd
/home/myself
```

Analysis

Notice how the `cd` command returned me to my home directory when I did not specify an argument to the `cd` command.

The `$HOME` variable is used by many system scripts as the default directory to which you log in. It's generally not a good idea to change the value in this variable because if you do so, many of the standard UNIX script files may not work. For example, a special file `.profile` (to be discussed later in this chapter) exists in your `HOME` directory.

The *SHELL* Variable

When UNIX programs process their shell command (usually a `!`, followed by a shell command name), they check to see what the `SHELL` variable is set to. You can set the `SHELL` variable to whatever shell you want to be executed.

If the `!` is followed by a carriage return, you will get a new shell prompt to a subshell of your program. A sample program to test this on is `vi`, where you can issue the commands from the : prompt. The `:!ls` command in `vi` will list all the files in the current directory.

You can echo the `SHELL` variable with the `echo` command, as shown here:

```
$ echo $SHELL
/bin/sh
```

Your *PATH*

The `PATH` environment variable is set to the list of directories that the shell will search when it's trying to find a command to execute. To show your current `PATH` variable, issue the following command:

```
$ echo $PATH
/etc/local:/etc::/local/bin:/usr/bin:/bin:/usr/local/bin:/usr/bin/X11:.
```

It's likely that your output will be very different from the output shown here. Even so, you will see that the directories are separated by a colon (`:`). The special notation (`::`) is an equivalent notation for `:.:`, your current directory.

To add more directories to your `PATH`, you will usually append your directory to `PATH` using

```
$ PATH=$PATH:/new/dir
```

The `/new/dir` directory will be searched for all subsequent commands after all the directories in the previous `PATH` variable have been searched. If you want to search your `/new/dir` *before* all the regular versions are searched, you can use this command:

```
$ PATH=/new/dir:$PATH
```

What happens if you have more than one command with the same name? The shell executes the first command that is in the PATH and that matches your specification. To find out exactly which command you are executing, use the `which` command.

Note: A better command is the UNIX type command. `type` is portable, whereas the `which` command might not be as accessible. Try type to see which command is available and to your preference:

```
$ type pwd
pwd is a shell built in
$ type who
who is /usr/bin/who
```

Input
Output

```
$ which ls
/bin/ls
```

Analysis

The `which` command tells you that the `ls` command is in the `/bin` directory. You can replace the `ls` command with your own version either by modifying the `/bin/ls` command or by modifying the PATH variable. Modification of the `/bin` directory is usually reserved to the superuser, so it's difficult to put files there unless you have root access. I used this as an example only because it's not a good idea to modify the `/bin/ls` command, since all the users on your system use this command. What if you have a bug in your "new and improved" `ls` command? Rather than have irate users complaining to you, you might be better off modifying just your PATH variable.

Note: Modifying the PATH variable for a root command in order to put in a new program is the method sometimes used by hackers to break into computer systems.

Hackers will usually put an innocuous-looking program in place of a standard UNIX utility, and then put it in a global area. A good example is that the hackers rewrite the `ls` command and place it in a world-writeable directory. If you have the *period* `(.)` before the `/bin` in your path, and you were in this directory, you will run their version of the program as yourself. This could have very disastrous results if you were running as root, because their program would then run almost completely unchecked.

Consequently, it's a good to place the *period* . in your path after the standard directory paths.

Other examples of hacking include rewriting a shell script called `mail` so that it sends an extra copy to an industrial spy in addition to sending your mail for you through the regular `mail` command.

It's a good idea to see which command you are executing before you use a suspect command. Also, periodically check the dates on your most frequently used commands to see whether they have changed. For instance, if the `nroff` command has last week's date and all other related files for `nroff` have last year's date, you should ask your system administrator whether he or she recently updated the command.

DO	DON'T

DO use the `type` or `which` command to determine if you are using the correct file or if you suspect some foul play on your system.

DO use the `type` command to see if a command is built in or not; `which` will not tell you this.

DON'T assume that the `which` program exists on your system.

PS1 and *PS2*

Your shell's prompt characters are shown as the values set in `PS1` and `PS2`. Use the commands in the following example to see what your prompt setting is.

Input
Output

```
$ echo :$PS1:
:$ :
$ echo :$PS2:
:> :
```

Analysis

Your output should look very similar to the output shown in the example. You also can change the value of the `PS1` variable. So what are these two variables?

`PS1` This is the string for the first prompt. This prompt is displayed as your regular prompt.

PS2 This is the text for the secondary prompt. This prompt is displayed when the shell expects more input on a current command line.

Let's look at a few examples.

Input Output

```
$ echo "This is
> a new line
> or two"
This is
a new line
or two
$
$
```

Analysis

To see a new command that requires multiple lines, let's be adventurous and jump ahead to look at the `for` statement. The syntax for the `for` statement is

```
for variable in variable_list
do
   command1
   command2
   command3
   .....
done
```

The `for` command executes `command1`, `command2`, `command3`, and so on, once each for all the items in the list of variables specified in `variable_list`. Actually, the shell creates a subshell. See the following example.

Input Output

```
$ for i in Hi I am learning UNIX
> do
> echo $i
> done
Hi
I
am
learning
UNIX
$
```

Analysis

The > character is simply the shell's way of asking for more input. The `for` loop requires the `do` and `done` statements in order to be a complete command.

You can customize your prompts by modifying the values of `PS1` and `PS2`. You can change your prompt to `What next Boss?`

Input Output

```
$ PS1="What next Boss? "
What next Boss? (Press Enter a few times to see the prompt)
What next Boss?
What next Boss?
```

Analysis

The prompt has changed to the string! Remember, the prompt will remain at this value until I log off. If you want to make this change permanent, you should add the following lines in your `.profile` file:

```
PS1="What next Boss? "
export PS1
```

The `export` command guarantees that the `PS1` environment variable is set for all subsequent subshells. For this to make sense, you have to learn what a subshell is. You'll learn that later today, but for now, concentrate on customizing your environment.

Customizing Your Desktop

In UNIX, there are some utilities that can be used with the shell program to create nice desktop functions. These functions and commands are of great use to the shell programmer. One of these is the calendar-generating utility, `cal`. Take a look the output of a `cal` command. Type **`cal 7 1994`** at the prompt.

Input
Output

```
$ cal 7 1994
     July 1994
 S  M Tu  W Th  F  S
                1  2
 3  4  5  6  7  8  9
10 11 12 13 14 15 16
17 18 19 20 21 22 23
24 25 26 27 28 29 30
31
$
```

Analysis

This utility gives you the calendar for the seventh month of the year 1994. Abbreviations for the month name are not allowed. Using `cal` without any options prints the current month and year. Use `1994`, not `94`; otherwise, you will get the output for A.D. 94!

Input
Output

```
$ cal 94
                                   94

       January               February               March
 S  M Tu  W Th  F  S   S  M Tu  W Th  F  S   S  M Tu  W Th  F  S
          1  2  3  4                     1                     1
 5  6  7  8  9 10 11   2  3  4  5  6  7  8   2  3  4  5  6  7  8
12 13 14 15 16 17 18   9 10 11 12 13 14 15   9 10 11 12 13 14 15
19 20 21 22 23 24 25  16 17 18 19 20 21 22  16 17 18 19 20 21 22
26 27 28 29 30 31     23 24 25 26 27 28     23 24 25 26 27 28 29
                                            30 31
```

Input Output

```
        April                    May                     June
 S  M Tu  W Th  F  S     S  M Tu  W Th  F  S     S  M Tu  W Th  F  S
       1  2  3  4  5                 1  2  3     1  2  3  4  5  6  7
 6  7  8  9 10 11 12     4  5  6  7  8  9 10     8  9 10 11 12 13 14
13 14 15 16 17 18 19    11 12 13 14 15 16 17    15 16 17 18 19 20 21
20 21 22 23 24 25 26    18 19 20 21 22 23 24    22 23 24 25 26 27 28
27 28 29 30             25 26 27 28 29 30 31    29 30

        July                    August                September
 S  M Tu  W Th  F  S     S  M Tu  W Th  F  S     S  M Tu  W Th  F  S
       1  2  3  4  5                    1  2        1  2  3  4  5  6
 6  7  8  9 10 11 12     3  4  5  6  7  8  9     7  8  9 10 11 12 13
13 14 15 16 17 18 19    10 11 12 13 14 15 16    14 15 16 17 18 19 20
20 21 22 23 24 25 26    17 18 19 20 21 22 23    21 22 23 24 25 26 27
27 28 29 30 31          24 25 26 27 28 29 30    28 29 30
                        31
       October                 November                December
 S  M Tu  W Th  F  S     S  M Tu  W Th  F  S     S  M Tu  W Th  F  S
          1  2  3  4                       1        1  2  3  4  5  6
 5  6  7  8  9 10 11     2  3  4  5  6  7  8     7  8  9 10 11 12 13
12 13 14 15 16 17 18     9 10 11 12 13 14 15    14 15 16 17 18 19 20
19 20 21 22 23 24 25    16 17 18 19 20 21 22    21 22 23 24 25 26 27
26 27 28 29 30 31       23 24 25 26 27 28 29    28 29 30 31
                        30
```

Analysis

This is the calendar for A.D. 94. Try `cal 1994` instead. Another interesting month and year to look at is September, 1752, in which dates 3 through 13 are "missing" as casualties from the big calendar switch from the Julian to the Gregorian calendar. Try `cal 1752` for that year's calendar.

Now, if you want to see a "snapshot" of your current directory in a file, you would type in the following command.

Input Output

```
$ cal ; ls -al
     July 1994
 S  M Tu  W Th  F  S
                1  2
 3  4  5  6  7  8  9
10 11 12 13 14 15 16
17 18 19 20 21 22 23
24 25 26 27 28 29 30
31
total 731
drwxr-xr-x   2 kamran   users        1024 Jul  2 22:43 .
drwxr-xr-x  15 kamran   users        1024 Jul  3 05:42 ..
-rwxr-xr-x   1 kamran   users       45605 Jun 12 07:36 a.out
-rw-r--r--   1 kamran   users       52924 Jun  5 14:35 ch01
-rw-rw-rw-   1 kamran   users       41167 Jun 12 11:56 ch02
-rw-r--r--   1 kamran   users       26483 Jun 12 23:02 ch03
-rw-r--r--   1 kamran   users       41785 Jul  2 22:54 ch04
-rw-r--r--   1 kamran   users       33379 Jul  2 22:54 ch05
-rw-r--r--   1 kamran   users       20317 Jul  3 07:15 ch06
-rw-r--r--   1 kamran   users        3400 Jul  3 06:01 ch07
-rw-r--r--   1 kamran   users        2082 May 10 21:53 ch08
-rw-r--r--   1 kamran   users        2380 May 10 21:54 ch09
```

Input Output

```
-rw-r--r--   1 kamran   users        2380 Jun 19 11:12 ch10
-rw-r--r--   1 kamran   users        7643 May 21 20:41 ch11
-rw-r--r--   1 kamran   users        2380 Jun 19 11:12 ch12
-rw-r--r--   1 kamran   users        2380 Jun 19 11:12 ch13
-rw-r--r--   1 kamran   users        2480 Jun 10 21:22 ch14
```

Analysis The `cal` command prints out the current month and year. The `ls -al` command prints out a listing my current directory just after the calendar.

If you want to know what the time is at your terminal, use the `date` command.

Input Output

```
$ date
Sun Jul  3 07:21:50 CDT 1994
```

Analysis The `date` command has several options; to view them all, use the `$ date --help` command.

Note: On some UNIX system's, `date -help` will either give you a list of options or an error message such as `date: illegal option -h`. In this case, try the `$ man date` command to see your options.

Input Output

```
$ date -help
Usage: date [OPTION]... [+FORMAT] [MMDDhhmm[[CC]YY][.ss]]

  -d, --date=STRING         display time described by STRING, not `now'
  -s, --set=STRING          set time described by STRING
  -u, --uct, --universal    print or set Universal Coordinated Time
      --help                display this help and exit
      --version             output version information and exit

FORMAT controls the output.  Interpreted sequences are:

  %%   a literal %
  %a   locale's abbreviated weekday name (Sun..Sat)
  %A   locale's full weekday name, variable length (Sunday..Saturday)
  %b   locale's abbreviated month name (Jan..Dec)
  %B   locale's full month name, variable length (January..December)
  %c   locale's date and time (Sat Nov 04 12:02:33 EST 1989)
  %d   day of month (01..31)
  %D   date (mm/dd/yy)
  %h   same as %b
  %H   hour (00..23)
  %I   hour (01..12)
  %j   day of year (001..366)
  %k   hour ( 0..23)
  %l   hour ( 1..12)
  %m   month (01..12)
  %M   minute (00..59)
  %n   a newline
```

Input Output

```
%p    locale's AM or PM
%r    time, 12-hour (hh:mm:ss [AP]M)
%s    seconds since 00:00:00, Jan 1, 1970 (a nonstandard extension)
%S    second (00..61)
%t    a horizontal tab
%T    time, 24-hour (hh:mm:ss)
%U    week number of year with Sunday as first day of week (00..53)
%w    day of week (0..6);  0 represents Sunday
%W    week number of year with Monday as first day of week (00..53)
%x    locale's date representation (mm/dd/yy)
%X    locale's time representation (%H:%M:%S)
%y    last two digits of year (00..99)
%Y    year (1970...)
%Z    time zone (e.g., EDT), or nothing if no time zone is determinable

$
$ date +%A
Sunday
$ data +%B
July
$ This is a `date +"%A in %B of %Y"`
This is a Sunday in July of 1994
```

Note: These options may not be available on your system. If they aren't, skip to the next section.

Analysis

The number of options available from the `date` command enables you to set up various strings and formats to display. The most common place to insert this command would be in the `.profile` file. Thus the line

```
echo Hello! Today is `date +%A` and a great day to login.
```

would print you a nice welcome when you log in.

The `date` command is only one of a long list of commands available to you to customize your desktop. Among them are two types of desk calculators, bc and dc.

UNIX Calculators for the Desktop

No desktop is complete without a calculator, and the UNIX desktop is no exception. In fact, UNIX has two types of calculators: `dc` and `bc`. The `dc` version of the calculator is the postfix calculator most popular with HP aficionados; the `bc` calculator is an infix version. The `bc` version is somehow more prevalent in UNIX distributions; `dc` is not always distributed in some UNIX systems.

The differences between infix and postfix can be summarized this way.

Suppose you wanted to calculate the total cost of shipping 40 of your new widgets somewhere. Ten of these widgets cost $24.00 each; the rest cost $35.00 each. Also, there is a tax of 8 percent, and the total shipping cost would be $5.00.

Using infix notation, the calculation would be the following:

```
((24 * 10) + (30 * 35)) * 1.08 + 5
```

The 1.08 simply adds the percentage of tax to the total price.

Using postfix, the calculation would be this:

```
24 40 * 30 35 * + 1.08 * 5 +
```

Notice the absence of parentheses in this version. This method of calculation is most popular with Hewlett-Packard calculators and users who prefer fewer keystrokes. (When operations are counted, each parenthesis is included in the count.)

Using the *bc* Calculator

To use the bc calculator, type **`bc`** at the prompt:

```
$ bc
```

The program does not provide any prompt whatsoever. You have to assume that `bc` is waiting for input. Typing **`help`** at this "prompt" will yield an output of 0.

```
((24 * 10) + (30 * 35)) * 1.08 + 5
1398.2
```

You can set variables in this program. For example:

```
w1 = 24
p1 = 10
```

will set the variables `w1` and `p1` to 24 and 10, respectively. Now you can use the two variables in a calculation:

```
w1 * p1
240
```

Other math functions are also available in this calculator. The catch is that you have to load `bc` with the `-l` option to load the math libraries:

```
c(n)    Cosine
s(n)    Sine
t(n)    Tan
a(n)    arc tan
l(n)    natural log
```

```
e(n)    exponential function
sqrt(n) Square Root
^       exponent
```

Keep in mind that the cosine, tan, and sine functions take radians as arguments. Getting out of this program is easy. Type **quit** on one line, and you are returned to the prompt. You could also enter Ctrl+d, but if you accidentally enter it twice, you will be logged off. Remember that the shell interprets the Ctrl+d as a terminator of input to the shell. If either exit method fails, just enter Ctrl+c and bc will be forced to terminate.

Using the *dc* Calculator

To get the dc program, type the following command:

```
$ dc
```

As before, you see nothing that indicates whether or not you are in the program. Enter the following postfix commands.

Input
Output

```
24 40 * 30 35 * + 1.08 * 5 +
1398.2
```

Analysis

This command calculated the result of the postfix expression and printed it out when it saw the p token. The answer is 1398.2.

Quitting the dc calculator is very similar to quitting the bc calculator. Type **quit** on one line, and you will be returned to the prompt.

The dc calculator should be easy to use if you have worked with the HP calculators. After you type a line and press the Enter key, dc parses the line. Every time it sees a number, dc places the number on a stack. You can think of this as stacking plates on top of each other.

As soon as dc sees an operation—for example, the * in the line—dc removes two items from the stack and performs the action on them. Then dc the answer back on the stack. Consider this example:

```
25 4 * p
100
```

The dc command will first place 25 and 4 on the stack. When dc sees the asterisk, it will pop these two numbers off the stack and multiply them to get 100. Then dc will place the 100 back on the stack and get the next token, p. This token tells dc to print the topmost item on the stack.

Can you parse the entire line now?

```
24 40 * 30 35 * + 1.08 * 5 +
```

Multiply 24 by 40 and place the result on the stock, multiply 30 by 35 (placing the result on the stock), add the two answers together (again placing the result on the stock), and then multiply 1.08 by 5. Finally, add the numbers on the stack.

Now you know about some of the utilities available to you on your desktop. These are only a few of the utilities available. As you explore UNIX, you will come across more utilities and more functionalities of UNIX and of the shell that you can take advantage of.

One of the most powerful features of the UNIX shell is its capability to fire up copies of itself. These copies are called subshells.

Subshells

A *subshell* is an entirely new shell program that is run to execute a command. This new shell has its own set of environment variables. This shell is called a subshell, or a *child*, of the calling shell. The calling shell is called the *parent shell*, shown in Figure 6.1.

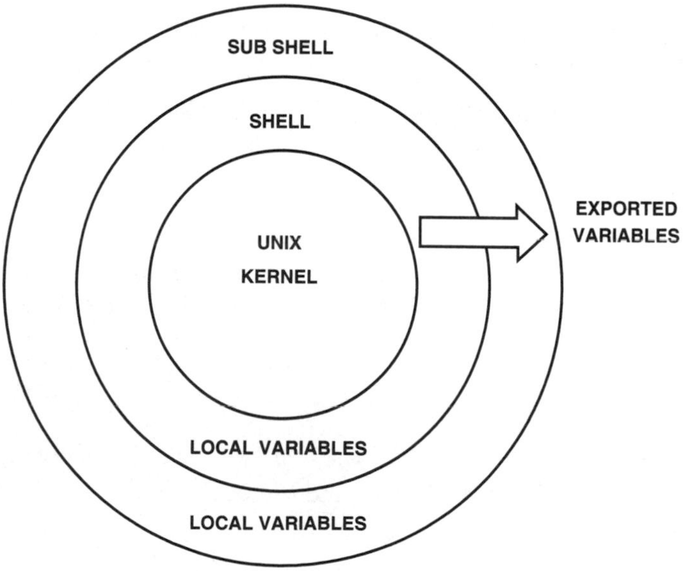

Figure 6.1. *The parent-child relationship.*

A subshell has absolutely no knowledge of any local variables of a parent shell; nor can it change the value of any variables in shells above itself.

Let's look first at what a shell script is. On Day 8, you will learn much more about shell scripts; for now, just note that a shell script is basically a series of commands in a text file. The text file containing the shell script has its execute bit set. When the shell executes the shell script, the shell will fire off a subshell. This subshell will read in the commands from the script file, one line at a time, and will execute the lines as they are read.

Look at the shell script `st1` here:

```
echo x at start= $x
x=100
echo x at end= $x
```

The following example shows the command being executed.

Input Output

```
$ cat st1
echo x at start= $x
x=100
echo x at end= $x
$ x=11
$ echo $x
11
$ st1
x at start=
x at end= 100
$ x=11
$ echo $x
11
```

Analysis The first command (`cat st1`) listed the program. Then I set a local variable `x` to 11. This is a local variable to the parent shell. I echoed it to confirm that is indeed set.

Then I ran the shell script, `st1`, by typing it at the command line.

The first thing that the st1 script does is echo the value of shell variable `x`. This is `NULL`, because the parent shell's local variables are *not* passed to the subshell executing the shell script. The *x* in the subshell is a shell variable totally different from the one in the parent.

Then I set the value of *x* to 100 and print it out to confirm that it is set correctly within `st1`. It is echoed as 100 from within the shell script.

However, when the shell has finished executing, the value of *x* is back to 11! Why? This is because the local variables in the shell no longer exist after the shell is executed. Also, because the variables were local to the shell, they did not influence the value of *x* in the parent shell.

Input Output

Now I'll execute the commands shown in the following example.

```
$ export x
$ st1
x at start= 11
x at end= 100
$ echo $x
11
$ cat st1
echo x at start= $x
x=100
echo x at end= $x
export x
```

Analysis

This time the value of *x* was exported down to the subshell correctly. However, on return from this shell, the value of *x* in the parent shell was not changed.

Notice how the value of *x* was exported in `st1`. This export directive to the shell exports the value of the shell variable to all subsequent subshells, but never to the parent shell. After a value is exported, it's exported for all occurrences of subshells during the course of the execution of the shell it was exported from initially.

Exported shell variables retain their status for all subsequent subshells. To get rid of this, you will have to log out and log in again to reset your environment variable *x* to nothing. You also can try an easier method by using the `unset` command:

```
$ unset x
```

- A variable can be exported at any time—either before or after it is assigned a value.
- After it is exported, a variable will remain exported for all subsequent subshells of the shell that initially exported it.
- Exported variables are copied into a subshell's environment when a subshell is created. Any changes to these variables have no affect on the calling shell's exported variables.
- Exported shell variables retain their status for all subsequent subshells.

Using (..) and {..;}

You can run subshells without writing a shell script; you can do so by using either `()` or `{ ;}` around the commands. These special characters work the same way as do the single quote, in that the command that is executed is the command between the pair of these special characters. Unlike single quotes, however, the output from this command is not inserted into a command line being executed.

The () directive groups all the commands together and executes them in a subshell. You separate commands by using semicolons. For example, to list the /var directory, use the following command:

```
$  (cd /var; ls)
```

The { ;} directive groups the commands to together and executes them using the current shell. You can also separate commands with the semicolon, as you see here:

```
$  {cd /var; ls;}
```

Note: Note the last semicolon, after the ls command. For the correct syntax, it's important that you put a semicolon there.

Look at the following examples.

Input Output

```
$ x=howdy
$ (x=hello)
$ echo $x
howdy
$ {x=hello}
$ echo $x
hello
```

Analysis

The first command—(x=hello)—executed the hello assignment in a subshell. The value of x did not change in the parent shell. In the second command, ({x=hello}), the assignment was done in the same shell; the value of *x* was changed.

When grouped together, commands within are useful to perform one task quickly. For example, if you want to go to a directory and do some cleanup but you do not want to remember how to come back to where you are currently, you would use the following command:

```
$ (cd /your-directory; doCleanUp)
```

After the command has executed, you will find yourself in the same directory that you started in. As an illustration, look at this example.

Input Output

```
$ pwd
/home/kamran
$ (cd faq; pwd; ls -CF)
/home/kamran/faq
index          p1.txt    p3.txt          p5.txt     p7.txt     shcmp.z
mksmall*  p2.txt    p4.txt          p6.txt      referenc.z     tips.z
$ pwd
/home/kamran
```

Analysis

Notice how the command (`cd faq; pwd; ls -CF`) took me to the `faq` directory, told me where it was, and then gave me a listing of this directory. Then, after the command was over, I found myself back where I started.

If I had executed this sequence without the `()` braces, thus:

```
$ cd faq; pwd; ls -CF
$ pwd
/home/kamran/faq
```

I would have found myself in the `faq` directory when I was done. Similarly, I would find myself in the `faq` directory if I had used the `{}` braces around the command:

```
$ {cd faq; pwd; ls -CF;}
$ pwd
/home/kamran/faq
```

Remember to add last semicolon before the last curly brace.

DO	DON'T
DO remember to put a semicolon before the last `}` brace in a group command. You do not have to put a semicolon before the last `)` parenthesis.	

There is one more special case you should know about. It concerns the persistence of values in shell variables.

Input
Output

```
$ x=50; st1
x at start=
x at end= 100
st2:in x:
st2:out x: 50
$ x=50  st1
x at start= 50
x at end= 100

st2:in x: 100
st2:out x: 50
$ echo $x
50
```

Analysis

In the first command, (`x=50; st1`), the semicolon separated the `x=50` statement from the `st1` shell script.

In the second command, *x* was set to 50 in the parent shell *and* was exported to the shell script `st1`.

The significance of this command sequence is that in just one line, when you did not use the semicolon, you were able to assign a value to a variable and then export it to all subshells. If you did use a semicolon, the value of *x* was not exported to the `st1` command.

UNIX Commands Learned Today

- `type` A command to determine the type of a command
- `which` A less common version of the `type` command
- `set` Shows the current environment variables
- `(...)` Executes in a subshell
- `.` Executes a shell script
- `{...;}` Executes a current shell
- `date` Used to print or set the date
- `bc` Infix calculator
- `dc` Postfix calculator
- `cal` The calendar

Summary

In this chapter, you learned the following:

- Your environment variables are those in which the shell keeps information about your login session.
- Your login shell assigns values to your `HOME`, `PATH`, and other environment variables by running the `/etc profile` and `$HOME/profile` scripts. Some environment variables are actually set by binary files. (For example, `LOGNAME` is set by `login`.)
- The `$HOME/profile` script can be used to override the values set in the `/etc/profile` script.
- You can execute shell scripts with `.` , the *period* command.

- Subshells are shells started by the current shell to execute a command. The current shell then becomes the parent shell of this subshell.
- Local variables in subshells are not returned to the parent shell.
- You can pass variables from the parent shell to subshells by exporting the variables.
- Local or exported variables in the parent shell are not modified by a subshell.
- You can group together commands within `()` and execute them in a subshell.
- You can group together commands within `{}` and execute them in the current shell.

What's Next?

Tomorrow, you will learn all about file and I/O redirection.

Q&A

Q What's an environment?

A The set of variables that the shell tracks for your login session is your environment.

Q What are three important shell environment variables?

A `HOME`, `PATH`, and `LOGNAME` (or `CDPATH`).

Q What's the `.profile` file?

A The script in your `HOME` directory that is automatically executed when you first log in.

Q What is the `dot` command?

A The dot `$ .` shell script command executes a shell script.

Q How do you convert a text file into a subscript?

A Set the execute bit to `ON` for the file with the `chmod tx` command.

Workshop

The Workshop provides quiz questions to help you solidify your understanding of the material covered. Some Workshop sections of this book also contain exercises to provide you with experience in using what you've learned. Try to understand the quiz and exercise answers before continuing on to the next chapter. Answers are provided in Appendix D, "Answers."

Quiz

1. What are the desktop utilities for calculators in UNIX for your shell?
2. How can you get the current time on the UNIX system? What about the day?
3. What's the difference between local variables and exported variables?
4. What's a subshell? Must you have a shell script to run under a subshell?
5. What's the difference between grouping commands at your shell and grouping in the subshell?
6. What's wrong with this statement:

   ```
   {ls -s ¦ sort -n ¦ lpr}
   ```

Exercises

1. Modify the `.profile` command so that you are given a calendar of today's month every time you log in.
2. Add a command in your `.profile` file to tell you what day it is when you log in. (See the section on `date` in this chapter.)
3. Convert the following postfix line into prefix notation:

   ```
   3  3 * 3.141 * 3.141 3 *  -
   ```

   What is the result of this expression in `dc` and the prefix in `bc`?
4. Use the `bc` calculator to calculate the area of a cylinder for which the radius is 4 and height is 5, given the formula:

   ```
   Area = (pi * r * 2 * ht) +  (pi * r * r * 2 )
   ```

   Hint: Reduce the formula to get the lowest number of keystrokes.

5. Save your home variable in another variable and then change your `HOME` path variable to some other path. Do all your UNIX commands still work? How can you restore your `HOME` to its original value?

WEEK 1

7

File Input/Output

Today's lesson introduces input and output redirection, which is a very powerful feature of UNIX. Throughout your interaction with UNIX, you will be redirecting input or output somewhere.

Today you will learn about the following:

- Introduction to file descriptors
- Redirection, pipes, and filters
- Input redirection
- Output redirection
- Using file descriptors
- Using pipelines
- The `tee` command
- Another way to do multiple commands on one line

Introduction to File Descriptors

When working with UNIX shells, you will usually type in commands from the keyboard and see the output presented at your terminal.

The keyboard is normally the `standard input` and the terminal is usually the `standard output` in this case. Error messages are sent through another route, called `standard error`, that normally ends at your terminal.

In UNIX, everything that can be written to or read from is a *file*. Your keyboard is a read-only file, and your terminal is a write-only file. This approach is a bit simplistic and stretches reality a bit, but you should get the analogy. In any event, UNIX refers to these files with integers called *file descriptors*.

These standard file descriptors are assigned numbers, which stand for the following:

0	The standard input
1	The standard output
2	The standard error

> **Note:** When you work with programmers, you will come across the words *stdin* (pronounced ess-tee-dee-in), which stands for standard input, *stdout* (pronounced ess-tee-dee-out), which stands for standard output, and *stderr* pronounced (ess-tee-dee-err), which stands for standard error. The roots of these words lie in the C language in which the shell and UNIX was developed.

When you open files within the UNIX shell environment, the files are assigned numbers increasing from the last open file descriptor numbers. Usually, the shell opens file descriptors 0 through 4 for you and reserves them for its own use. You will deal with these descriptors later today when you use these integers to direct input to and from the standard input and output.

Input/Output Redirection

Recall that on Day 1 you created a file `newfile` by typing the command

```
$ cat > newfile
```

Then, whatever you typed at the keyboard was written to a file called `newfile` until you typed Ctrl+d. The Ctrl+d signals an end-of-file to the shell, which in turn closes the file.

The greater-than symbol (>) is known to the shell as the output redirection symbol. This symbol redirects the output of a program into a file called `newfile`, instead of the output going to the standard output.

Normally, the `cat` command writes its output to your terminal. In other words, the output goes to standard output. By using the > symbol, you can redirect the output to a file or device. For example:

```
$ who
```

prints, on your terminal, a list of the users on the system.

```
$ who > wlist
```

prints a list of the users into a file called `wlist`.

```
$ cat wlist
```

will show you the result of the `who` command, which was stored in `wlist`. Since the contents of `wlist` were the results of the `who` command, you will see this output on your terminal.

Now look at the next listing, in which you twice concatenate the standard output to a file.

Input/Output

```
$ cat > newfile
Line 1
ctrl-d
$
$ cat newfile
Line 1
$
$ cat > newfile
Line 2
ctrl-d
$
$ cat newfile
Line 2
$
```

Analysis What happened to the text `Line 1`? It was destroyed by the second output redirection command. When output is redirected using the > operator, the shell overwrites the contents of the file to which the output is going. The contents previously in that file are destroyed.

What if you want the previous line to be overwritten by the output? To preserve the line, you would use the >> symbol to redirect the standard output. This symbol means to append the file rather than overwrite it.

- > means to write to a file from the start of the file (that is, replace the contents)
- >> means to write to a file from the end of the file (that is, append the contents)

To see how this works, look at the following example.

Input/Output

```
$ cat > newfile
Line 1
ctrl-d
$ cat newfile
Line 1
$ cat >> newfile
Line 2
ctrl-d
$ cat newfile
Line 1
Line 2
$
```

Analysis

The contents of `newfile` were not overwritten this time because of the >> operator. The operator appended the new text to the existing contents of the file `newfile`.

You can concatenate several text files into one file with the command

```
$ cat f1 f2 > f3
```

which concatenates `f1` and `f2` and places them into `f3`. Any previous contents of `f3` will be destroyed. If you want to preserve the contents of the file `f3`, use the following command:

```
$ cat f1 f2 >> f3
```

which will concatenate `f1` and `f2` and append them to `f3`. If `f3` did not exist, the execution of this command will create it for you.

Input Output

```
$ cat n1
line 1
$ cat n2
line n2
$ cat n3
line n3
$ cat n1 n2 n3 > n4
$ cat n4
line 1
line n2
line n3
$ cat n1 n2 n3 >> n4
$ cat n4
line 1
line n2
line n3
line 1
line n2
line n3
$ cat -n n4
     1    line 1
     2    line n2
     3    line n3
     4    line 1
     5    line n2
     6    line n3
```

Analysis

The output from the previous example is summarized here:

`cat f1`	Display `f1`
`cat > f1`	Enter data typed in keyboard to `f1`
`cat >> f1`	Append data typed in keyboard to `f1`
`cat f1 f2 > f3`	Concatenate `f1` and `f2` and place into `f3`
`cat f1 f2 >> f3`	Concatenate `f1` and `f2` and append to `f3`

Note: The new option shown in this example is the `-n` option to the `cat` command. This option will number all the lines in the file you are viewing.

On some systems, you have an additional command, `nl`, which will number all the lines in a file. An example follows.

```
$ nl n1 n2
  1   line 1
     2   line n2
$ cat -n n1; cat -n n2
     1   line 1
     1   line n2
```

As you can see, there is no indication given of where the first file ends and where the next one begins. It is sometimes helpful to put many outputs together to give the impression of a long numbered file. If you want separate lines, use a separate command for each file.

Input Redirection

Input redirection works in a manner similar to that of output redirection. Normally, whatever you type in from the keyboard is considered standard input to a program. However, you can redirect the input into a program from a file instead of the keyboard.

Consider the `sort` program in UNIX. It reads in the standard input if no file is specified.

Input Output

```
$ sort
f1
f2
e3
d4
ctrl-d
d4
e3
f1
f2
$
```

Analysis

The `sort` command takes its input from standard input and writes its output to standard output. The `ctrl-d` ended the input into `sort`, which then printed out its sorted input buffer.

Note: Generally, if a UNIX program expects a text file as one of its arguments as a source of input but finds none, it defaults to reading from the standard input instead.

What if you had a file with a sorted list of names in it? As an example, start with a list of names of people you know, in a file called `name1`.

Input/Output

```
$ cat name1
Robert Davis
Guy McClain
James Ellis
Charles Everett
H D Garrett
Leroy Watson
James Davidson
Darryl Katz
Herbert Gengler
Roger King
$ sort name1
Charles Everett
Darryl Katz
Guy McClain
H D Garrett
Herbert Gengler
James Davidson
James Ellis
Leroy Watson
Robert Davis
Roger King
```

Analysis

Note how the `sort` program sorted on the first character of each name. Unlike the previous example, the sort program did not expect you to type the list in because the filename was specified.

You also can type in the command to send `sort` input from the file by redirecting its input from the file `name1` by using the command

```
$ sort < name1
```

Input/Output

```
$ sort < name1
Charles Everett
Darryl Katz
Guy McClain
H D Garrett
Herbert Gengler
James Davidson
James Ellis
Leroy Watson
Robert Davis
Roger King
```

Analysis

This is equivalent to the command `sort name1`, except that now you are sending the input from the file `name1` into the sort program via the shell instead of the shell opening the file `name1` and reading from it.

When you are dealing with large files, it may be to your benefit to let the program open the file for you rather than do it through the shell. The program may use a faster method of accessing the disk than the sequential one used by the shell. Of course, you can redirect the flow of data both at the input and output of a command.

Input Output

```
$ sort < name1 > name2
$
$ cat name2
Charles Everett
Darryl Katz
Guy McClain
H D Garrett
Herbert Gengler
James Davidson
James Ellis
Leroy Watson
Robert Davis
Roger King
```

Analysis

Note how the shell gave no indication that the command had completed. This command, the `sort < name1 > name2`, redirects the input from the `name1` file and redirects the output to the `name2` file.

Input redirection is also helpful if you want to read input from a file up to a certain line. The command sequence

```
cat name1 <<  "James Ellis"
```

will read its input until a line with the words `"James Ellis"` is found. Remember that there should be no spaces on either side of the words because the match must be exact.

Input Output

```
$ cat << END > anotherFile
I am typing here
till the word END
appears at the end of
a line by itself
END
$ cat anotherFile
I am typing here
till the word END
appears at the end of
a line by itself
```

Analysis

The shell continued to read input from the keyboard until it saw the word `END` on a line by itself. It stopped reading input as if the end of the file were read. You could have gotten the same results using another file instead of using the keyboard. See the section titled "Shell Archives and I/O," later today.

Pipes

When using the disk, you use an extra resource (such as a file) and add a clutter of files on disk. You can use a *pipe* to direct the standard output of one program into the standard input of another and avoid creating unnecessary temporary files. (See Figure 7.1.)

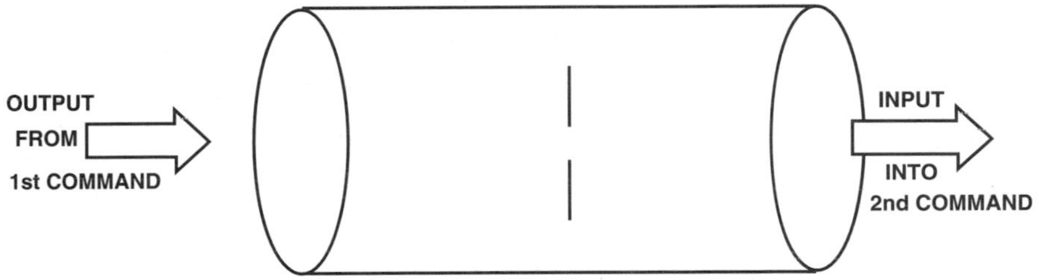

Figure 7.1. *The pipe data flow.*

Suppose you wanted to count the size of all the files in your directory. The `ls -s` command will list all the blocks used by each file. To sort the output of the list numerically, you can use the `sort -n` flag, in one of two ways.

- Use `ls -s` and redirect the output to a temporary file. Then use the `sort -n` command to sort this temporary file.

  or

- Use the pipe (¦) character to tie the output of the `ls -s` command to the input of the `sort` command.

Input Output

```
$ # this is the first method
$ ls -s > temporary file
$ sort -n temporary gile
$ # this is the second method
$ ls -s  ¦ sort -n
total 916
   1 index
   1 name1
   1 rpt3
   2 discmort.txt
   2 getit
   2 rpt1
   2 rpt2
   2 ss
   3 small
   7 may29_77.txt
 893 names
```

Analysis

The first method is shown as a comment with a # as the first method and will not be executed. After redirecting the output from the `ls  -s` command to the temporary file, you have to execute the `sort` command on this file as a separate command. You also have to remember to delete this temporary file because it now exists on your disk—and it's your responsibility.

The second method is not as clumsy as the first method. The first method would create unnecessary temporary files in your working directory, which you would have to remove yourself later. Using pipes removes the burden of tracking these temporary files from you, the user, because any temporary files created are not created by you, and are removed by UNIX, not you.

The *tee* Command

The `tee` command is used to tee the output to a file and to standard output. Using this command lets you not only look at the output of the command, but also send the output into a file. (See Figure 7.2.)

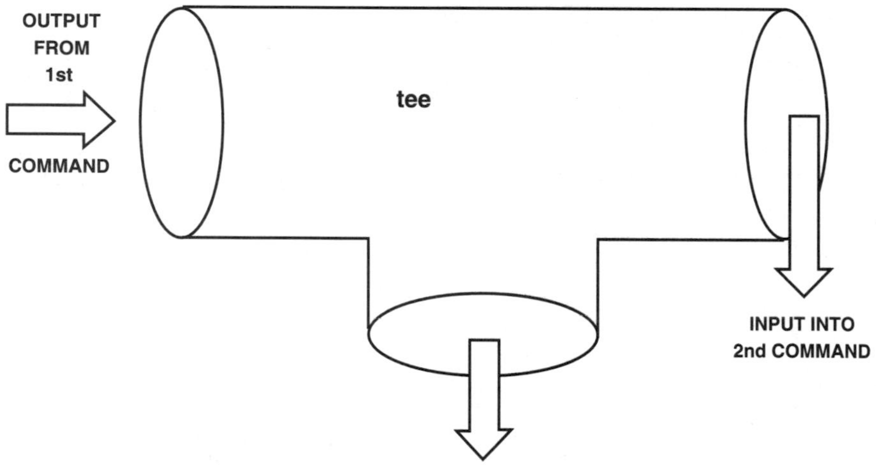

Figure 7.2. *The pipe command.*

Input Output

```
$ ls -s ¦ sort -nr ¦ tee name2
 893 names
   7 may29_77.txt
   3 small
   2 ss
   2 rpt2
   2 rpt1
```

```
    2 getit
    2 discmort.txt
    1 rpt3
    1 name3
    1 name1
    1 index
total 917
$ cat name2
 893 names
    7 may29_77.txt
    3 small
    2 ss
    2 rpt2
    2 rpt1
    2 getit
    2 discmort.txt
    1 rpt3
    1 name3
    1 name1
    1 index
total 917
```

Analysis Note how the output from the `sort` command was sent to the file `name2`, as well as being sent to the terminal for you to review. This is very helpful when you are debugging programs (since you can see what output is being generated).

Redirecting Using File Descriptors

The < and > directives enable you to redirect the standard input and output from and to another location, respectively. These directives work with file descriptors to give you more control over the redirection of output. UNIX file descriptors enable you to move the output from the standard input and output, as well as other files you may have open at that time.

You can redirect the output from a file descriptor directly to a file with the command

```
file-descriptor>filename
```

To redirect the standard error output to a file named `errors`, use the following at the end of the command:

```
$ gcc *.c 2>errors
```

All the error messages that would have gone to the terminal will now go to the file named `errors`. Note that there are no spaces between the `2`, the `>`, and the string `errors`.

In most cases, simply redirecting the output of a program to a file is sufficient to record that output. Sometimes, however, a program will send output to both the standard error (`stderr`) and standard output (`stdout`), so redirecting the output only saves the `stdout`, and not the `stderr`. To save the `stderr`, you have to be able to either save it in a separate file using `2>file` or redirect it to the same location as `stdout`. The following is an example of how to do this:

```
from>&destination
```

Note: To see an error message, try the following example:

```
$ ls -l /badplace
ls: /badplace: No such file or directory
$ ls -l /badplace >somefile 2>&1
$cat somefile
ls: /badplace :No such file or directory
```

This directive will redirect all the output from file descriptor `from` to where the output of file descriptor `destination` is going. The ampersand (`&`) is required to indicate that the `destination` is a file descriptor. If the ampersand is not specified use

```
2>1
```

The output from `2` will be redirected to a file called `1`. For example, to redirect the output from the `stderr` to `stdout`, you can force the output of `2` to `1` using the command `2>&1`.

Background Processing

When you are logged in to a terminal, a process that takes a long time to execute can tie up your terminal for a while, thus preventing you from using the terminal. In this situation, it's helpful to place the command in the background to free up your terminal to do other things. To put a process in the background, you use the ampersand (`&`) at the end of the command used to invoke the process. UNIX will then respond back with the process id of the command that will handle the output for you.

For example, if you have a large file to sort into a file named

```
../ml/names
```

you would use the command `sort ../ml/names  > long &`.

Input
Output

```
$ sort ../ml/names  > long &
[736]
$ ps  ax
  PID TTY STAT  TIME COMMAND
    1  ?  S     0:01 init auto
   37 v01 S     0:02 -bash
  301 v02 S     0:02 -bash
   24  ?  S     0:00 /usr/sbin/syslogd
   20  ?  S     0:22 /sbin/update
   26  ?  S     0:00 /usr/sbin/klogd
  677 v03 S     0:00 /sbin/agetty 38400 tty3
  591 v01 S     0:44 vi ch07
   31  ?  S     0:00 /usr/sbin/crond
   40 v04 SW    0:00 (agetty)
   41 v05 SW    0:00 (agetty)
   42 v06 SW    0:00 (agetty)
  139  ?  S     0:00 lpd
  736 v02 R     0:04 sort ../ml/names > long
  737 v01 R     0:00 ps ax
```

Analysis

The [736] at the beginning of the listing signifies the process id of the command being executed in the background. You will be returned to the prompt while this command executes. All output that would have otherwise gone to your terminal will be sent to the file `long`. The standard input of this program will be closed as if a Ctrl+d had been typed at its input. Therefore, it will not be able to read anything from its standard input while it's running.

The `ps` command gives a snapshot of the current processes being executed on the system. You have several options available to list all the processes you want listed. The most common options are `-ax`:

- `a` shows all other processes besides your own.
- `x` shows processes without a controlling terminal (for example, the processes running in the background).

If you had not redirected the output from this command to a file, the output would come straight to your terminal. This would have made working just as difficult as if the command was running in the foreground, even though the prompt was available to you.

Also, note that the `ps` command makes no provisions for the redirection of the standard error output. If there are any errors, they will not be logged to the file, but will be sent to the terminal.

To use what you learned yesterday, use the command directive `2>&1` to redirect all the output from file descriptor `2` to where the output of file descriptor `1` is going.

Sometimes, you have to wait until a process is finished before proceeding. You can wait on these commands via the `wait` command. The syntax for this command is

```
wait process-id
```

Therefore, to wait on the command in the previous example to finish before proceeding, specify the process id of the background process. The command

```
$ wait 833
```

will cause the shell to stop until process `833` is terminated.

DO | **DON'T**

DO confirm that there are spaces in between the file descriptor number and the greater than (>) symbol, as well as no spaces between the `>`, the `&`, and the other descriptor. Thus, `2>&1` is okay, but `2> &1` is not.

DON'T assume that standard output and standard error always go to the terminal via the same route.

DON'T put an ampersand at the end of a command that is by itself unless you want the command to run in the background.

DON'T leave the ampersand out in an I/O redirection command where you are redirecting one file descriptor's output to another.

Grouping Commands and Redirection

Yesterday, you learned about grouping commands to run in subshells. In this section, you will learn how to run the program's grouped commands in the background. For example:

```
$ (grep 77074 names ¦ sort > file1; wc -l file1) &
```

will execute everything in braces into one subshell and execute it in the background. The parentheses are required to send the entire job in the background. If you do not place the entire command in parentheses, only the `wc` command will be run in the background.

This example is a bit of an exaggeration because the entire chain of commands could be written by using pipes and not executed within a subshell:

```
$ grep 77074 names ¦ sort ¦ wc -l  &
```

You also might want to send entire groups to the background for processing when you are doing such things as compiling large programs. This way, you can continue to do your work while the command executes in the background:

```
$ (touch *.c; make embed.x86 ; cp embed.x86 ../bin/realtime) &
```

In this code, all the files are `touch`ed to have the current date and time, the `make` file is called to create `embed.x86`, and finally the output is copied to the `../bin/realtime` directory. These three steps are grouped together to simplify a rebuild.

> **Note:** The `touch` command simply sets the last modified date for the files specified in its arguments list to the current date. The `make` file creates and compiles all the files that have a modification date later than `embed.x86` and are required to create the `embed.x86` file. The authenticity of `embed.x86` is said to depend on these files, and the list of dependencies is kept in a file called `makefile`. As you delve into UNIX further, you will come across more and more makefiles.

In the next example, you can also redirect the `stderr` of all the programs to one location. Use the command

```
(prog1; prog2; prog3) 2>errors
```

If you were not allowed this luxury, you would have to create three separate temporary files to log these errors. That would make the command look like the following:

```
(prog1 2>error1 ; prog2 2>error2 ; prog3 2>error3) &
```

Now you have three files from which to sift the output. This is not quite as elegant as the previous method, but may have its merits if you want to store the outputs from each program to separate files.

Finally, using the grouping commands, you can effectively do powerful tasks at the command line. Perhaps you want to send output to a heavily used printer but want to append a message to the person handling the printer. The problem is that you don't know how to prevent another file from being sandwiched between your header and the file. The commands

```
$ echo "Please forward to R.R. office!" ¦ lp
$ cat mfile ¦ lp
```

will not guarantee that some other output won't be squeezed between your two output files. So to group these commands, use the pipe symbol.

```
$ {echo "Please forward to R.R. office!"; cat mfile; } ¦ lp
```

Now the two outputs are grouped together before they are sent to the printer. Note how the `{..;}` is used to group the commands together. (See Day 6.) This construct requires the semicolon before the end `}`.

Shell Archives and I/O

One of the best uses for input redirection is for shell archives. With shell archives, one or more shell scripts or other text files can be placed in a single file and then sent to another user via the `mail` command. The receiver can then restore the files by running as a shell script with the command `$ sh..archive`.

The input redirection command has two special cases.

Input
Output

```
$ cat <<HELLO
> $HOME
> *
> `date`
> \$HOME
> HELLO
/home/kamran
*
Mon Jul  4 06:28:40 CDT 1994
$HOME
$
```

Analysis

Note how the program reads from the keyboard until the word `HELLO`. The shell does substitution for the `$` and back quotes but does not do filename expansion on the asterisk. The backslash is used to ignore the $ to print the word `$HOME`.

If you wanted the shell to completely ignore all the special characters from the shell and prevent them from being expanded, you can precede the word `HELLO` with a backslash (`\`).

Input
Output

```
$ cat <<\HELLO
> $HOME
>    *
> `date`
> \$HOME
> HELLO
$HOME
    *
`date`
\$HOME
$
```

Analysis

All the special characters are safely ignored by the shell. Note how the `$HOME` is not interpreted, the backslash is printed, and the backquotes are ignored. The whitespaces before the `*` are also preserved.

This feature of completely ignoring everything up to the special termination character is especially useful in creating shell archives. As long as you can guarantee that the special termination word does not appear in your text anywhere, you are safe. Good words to use for such end-of-archive terminators are those that are weird enough not to appear in your text anywhere—for example, `ELVIS_LIVES`, `_RUSH_IS_FAR_RIGHT_`, `_END_OF_DATA_`, or even `AN_END_OF_FILE_HERE`.

Creating the Archive

So how do you create a shell archive?

The following is an example of two source files (one C file and one makefile) that already exist on my system. I have to create an archive for these programs called `tosend`. The following are the steps I have to take to create this archive called `tosend`.

Input
Output

```
1    echo "# to restore type: sh tosend" > tosend
2    echo "echo Extracting hello.c" >> tosend
3    echo 'cat >hello.c <<\END_OF_DATA'  >> tosend
4    cat hello.c  >> tosend
5    echo "END_OF_DATA" >> tosend
6    echo "echo Extracting makefile" >> tosend
7    echo 'cat >makefile <<\END_OF_DATA'  >> tosend
8    cat makefile >> tosend
9    echo "END_OF_DATA" >> tosend
```

Analysis

I have numbered these command lines for reference. The numbers should not be typed in.

Line 1 creates a new file `tosend`. The first line in the `tosend` file is a message telling the user how to extract files from this archive.

Line 2 creates a message that will tell the user what `tosend` will do when it's extracting a file.

Line 3 creates the line that will create a file `hello.c` when extracted from all lines up to, but not including, a line with the word `END_OF_DATA`.

Note: Note how the `E` in `END_OF_DATA` is escaped with a backslash. This escape character tells the shell to leave all the lines untouched and not parse any lines with backquotes and other backslashes when extracting files from this archive.

Line 4 appends the file `hello.c` to the `tosend` file.

Line 5 appends the end-of-file terminator to the `tosend` file for archiving.

Line 6 appends a new message to tell the user what the extracting shell will do next when extracting the `makefile` from the archive.

Line 7 creates the line that will create a file `makefile` when extracted from all lines up to, but not including, a line with `END_OF_DATA`.

Line 8 appends the `makefile` to the file `tosend`.

Line 9 appends the end-of-file terminator to the `tosend` file for archiving.

Note how repetitious these actions are. Tomorrow's lesson discusses ways to write a shell script that will handle files similar to the one just discussed, in order to create an archive. If you want to skip ahead, look at Day 9.

Now look at the archive.

Input Output

```
# to restore type: sh tosend
echo Extracting hello.c
cat >hello.c <<\END_OF_DATA

#include "stdio.h"

main()
{
printf("\n hello world!");
}
END_OF_DATA
echo Extracting makefile
cat >makefile <<\END_OF_DATA

CC    = gcc
INCHDRS    = #
CFLAGS     = -g
              LIBS = -lXm -lXt -lX11
              PROG       = t1
              # gcc -g -o t1  t1.c -lXm -lXt -lX11

              t1: t1.c
                   $(CC) $(CFLAGS) $#  -o t1 $(LIBS)
END_OF_DATA
```

Analysis The first line in this archive shows you how to extract the files from this archive. Note how the text of the two files is created in the body of this archive. Note also how the `makefile` contains variables that the shell may have recognized but did not expand (the `$` and `#` characters).

Also note that the number of lines in the archive is slightly larger than the sum of the lines in all the archived files put together. The increase in number is small for so great a benefit.

These archives are called shar archives for *sh*ell *ar*chives.

Extracting Files from this Archive

Let's test the archive to see if you can extract the files from `tosend`. The first line in this archive shows you how to extract the files from this archive. The recipient will also have this information embedded in `tosend`, line 1. The `tosend` archive can be tested out in another directory to see if it worked.

Input Output

```
$ mkdir test
$ cp tosend test
$ cd test
$ ls
tosend
$ sh tosend
Extracting hello.c
Extracting makefile
$ ls
hello.c makefile tosend
$ diff hello.c ../hello.c
$ diff makefile ../makefile
```

Analysis

The shell extracts all the files out from this archive correctly. It also echoes messages about what it is doing.

Note how the sh command is used to execute the archive. You could have used the period (.) operator to get the same results. An example would be

```
$ . tosend
```

See Day 6 for more information about the period operator.

The `diff` command told you that there were no differences between the archived files and the original files. You should now be able to safely send these files to your recipient.

Note: If the end-of-file terminator `END_OF_DATA` is preceded by a -, all leading tabs on all lines are removed from all the input lines.

```
$ cat <<-END
>           Hello
>     I am here
```

7

```
> END
Hello
I am here.
```

Before the end of the file terminator, this is useful for aligning maligned archived text.

Caution: When using the shell command, you will sometimes see the first line of the command with a `#!` in front of it, followed by a pathname to a shell. For example:

```
#!/bin/sh
```

or

```
#!/bin/ksh
```

This is a special case of a shell archive. The first line (`#!/bin/ksh`) is a shorthand way for the shell to request that the `/bin/sh` program be executed when extracting the archive. The `#!` in the first line is a shorthand way for the shell to recognize this request. The second line (`#!/bin/ksh`) requests that the Korn shell be used.

You can extract files by using the regular method shown previously, or you can let the archive do the extracting work itself. In the latter case, set the execute bit "on" for the archive and type its name at the prompt.

Input Output

```
$ head -2 tosend
#!/bin/sh
# to restore type: sh tosend
$
$ chmod +x tosend
$ ls -al tosend
-rwxr-xr-x   1 kamran   users        383 Jul  4 21:02 tosend
$ tosend
Extracting hello.c
Extracting makefile
$ ls
hello.c makefile tosend
```

> **Note:** The text after the `#!` is interpreted as a command without the benefit of a `PATH` search. So, a full pathname is required.

Analysis As you can see, the shell executed the file `/bin/sh` on the file `tosend` to perform the same function as `sh tosend` at the command line.

This is an effective way of explicitly specifying which shell to use when extracting the archive, because you cannot be certain that your recipient is using the Bourne shell. It's a safe bet that the Bourne shell resides in the `/bin` directory. The reader could be using some shell that may or may not work with the input redirection.

DO / **DON'T**

DO specify an explicit pathname for the executable after the `#!` because the shell does not search the path via the `PATH` environment variable when trying to execute this command.

DO copy the archive into a new subdirectory before extracting, just to be sure that no errors occur and wipe out the archive.

If the `#!` isn't supported on your system, the archive's commands may be executed by your current shell. So be careful.

DON'T assume that the `#!` will work on all systems. Give some comments or instructions to a new user.

UNIX Commands Learned Today

- `sort` Sorts the input
- `nl` Numbers the lines
- `wait` Waits for a process to finish
- `touch` Resets the modification time to now
- `ps` Shows the system process states

Summary

Today's lesson summarized what you have learned in the past few days about input and output redirection. You then went on to learn about how to work with input/output redirection with the various tools you have picked up along the way.

You were introduced to file descriptors, input and output redirection, pipes, and tees, and you learned how to use these tools with grouped commands.

You also learned the following:

- ☐ The `>` is used to redirect the output to a specific location, such as a file or device. This will overwrite any contents of the file to which it is redirected.
- ☐ The `>>` is used to redirect the output to a location and append the redirected data to the file.
- ☐ The < reads from a file until the end of the file is reached.
- ☐ The << TOKEN reads from a file until Ctrl+d or an entire line with the word TOKEN is encountered.
- ☐ The pipe symbol connects the output from one command to the input of another.
- ☐ The `tee` command is used to send the output of the file to two locations.
- ☐ The `&` at the end of a shell command puts that command in the background.
- ☐ The `1>filename` sends all output to the `filename` file.
- ☐ The `2>&1` at the end of a command redirects the output of file descriptor `2` to the same location as the output of file descriptor `1`.
- ☐ Redirecting the output from grouped commands effectively sends all the output to one location if the redirection is outside the braces.
- ☐ Other options to the `sort` command. The `-r` option handles reversed sorting, and the `-n` option sorts items numerically.
- ☐ Shell archives, shars, are a convenient way to send text files to other users via the mail system. Shars also can specify the program to use in self-extracting archives in the first line, although this feature is not supported in older systems. If this feature isn't supported, use the `sh archive` command.

What's Next

The work on shell scripts began today. Tomorrow's lesson deals with shell programming. All the information you have learned so far will come together when you use shell scripts.

Q&A

Q How can I keep a record of the times I logged in to the system?

A By adding a line to your `.profile` file to echo the date to the end of a file:

```
$ echo `date` >> ./logfile
```

Q When are pipes better than temporary files? When is the reverse true?

A Pipes are easier to use and do not necessarily have to go to disk because UNIX can use other means of communication to connect the ends of a pipe, which does not lead to clutter.

Q Why is it helpful to group commands?

A An entire group of commands can be sent for execution in the background, and the output from several programs within a group can be sent to one location.

Q When is input redirection helpful? What is the one major drawback to input redirection?

A To create shell archives, you read from a file until a known line is encountered using input redirection. The major drawback to using input redirection is that your program may hang if the exact line you are going to terminate on is not found.

Q What is a shar archive?

A This is a self-extracting shell archive, which uses the input redirection feature to store and extract text files.

Workshop

The Workshop provides quiz questions to help you solidify your understanding of the material covered. Some Workshop sections of this book also contain exercises to provide you with experience in using what you've learned. Try to understand the quiz and exercise answers before continuing on to the next chapter. Answers are provided in Appendix D, "Answers."

Quiz

1. Which of the following words are good to use as shell archive file terminators? Why?

```
help
NO_MORE_DATA
end
END_OF_DATA_HERE
GONZO_WAS_FRAMED
bye
```

2. How do you redirect the standard output to the `stderr`?
3. How would you send output to yourself and the printer from the `cal 1994` command?
4. How can you sort on numbers instead of characters?
5. How would you automate the shell archiving feature? Make a general purpose shell script. (See Day 9.)

Exercises

1. Placing the file redirection commands is very important. Which one of the following commands will work?

```
$  < file1
$  wc file <
$  nl < file
$  cat file ¦ nl
$  cat < file ¦ wc
$  wc ¦ cat
```

2. Send the contents of more than one file (`ch*`) to the printer.
3. Send a one-page header in front of a long file to the printer.
4. What's the difference between the output of the `ls -l` and `ls -s` commands?
5. Provide a numbered listing of all the files in your directory in reverse order and use `grep` to get the seventeenth file in a sorted listing.
6. Discover other ways to send binary files via the mail system. Do a man page on `uuencode` and `uudecode`. (I will cover this in Day 11.)

7. Why does this command

```
$ ls *.c ¦   tar -cvf tarfile
```

not work as a replacement for

```
$ tar -cvf tarfile `ls *.c`
```

WEEK 1 IN REVIEW

You learned a lot about the basics of UNIX on Day 1:

- ☐ How to log on to UNIX
- ☐ The concepts of UNIX users, login names, and passwords
- ☐ Using UNIX commands such as `ls` and `passwd`
- ☐ An introduction to the shell and its role under UNIX
- ☐ The types of shells and how to tell which shell you are using
- ☐ The standard syntax of commands under UNIX
- ☐ How to stop scrolling output, both temporarily and permanently
- ☐ How to change your password
- ☐ How to log off

On Day 2, you learned the following things:

- The concept of files and directories under UNIX.
- The basic tools in the UNIX system.
- The `more`, `less`, `head`, and `tail` commands for looking at small, manageable sections of large text files.
- The `file` command, which is useful to check whether a file contains ASCII text.

On Day 3, you covered shell variables and how to use them. You grasped the following concepts:

- How to customize your environment with environment variables.
- What the important environment variables are and how to see what they are with the `set` command.
- How to shorten commands with simple names for extensive commands.

Day 4's text got more technical as it covered metacharacters in the shell. You learned the following:

- Metacharacters—characters that carry a special meaning to the shell.
- That the shell uses filename substitution to expand the value of a shell variable into file or directory names.
- How to use special characters in file and directory names by using the quoting mechanisms in UNIX.
- When using double quotes, the `$`, `\`, and `'` are interpreted as metacharacters. With single quotes, the `$`, `\`, and `'` are not interpreted as metacharacters.
- About the backslash (`\`), a unary operator (not paired), which works on one character only.
- That the shell does not preserve any newlines with the backslash character. It does preserve them with the paired quotes.
- How to use the `grep` command to extract strings from a file.

Day 5 was a milestone of sorts, when you discovered the power of regular expressions and how to use them. Regular expressions are used to describe complex strings. Some of the important regular expressions are listed here. Please refer to the inside back cover for a full list of all these expressions. On Day 5, you learned the following:

- ☐ How the UNIX `grep` utility is used to specify these search patterns.
- ☐ That the asterisk (`*`) matches zero or more occurrences of a preceding pattern.
- ☐ That the `?` matches zero or one occurrence of a preceding pattern.
- ☐ That the `+` matches one or more occurrences of a preceding pattern.
- ☐ That special characters can be escaped with the `\` character.
- ☐ That the `[]` brackets offer a way of specifying a set of characters from which to choose.
- ☐ That the `-` operator between characters within `[]` specifies the range of ASCII letters between the characters.
- ☐ That the `^` (caret) matches the start of a line when it's used outside the `[` and `]`. It negates the list following itself when it's used within the `[` and `]`.
- ☐ That the `$` signifies the end of line.
- ☐ That empty lines are specified by using the expression `"^$"`.
- ☐ That blank lines are specified by using the expression `"^ *$"`.
- ☐ That the `grep` command uses regular expressions to search for types of strings. It has two other versions: `fgrep` and `egrep`.
- ☐ That the `fgrep` utility offers more features than the standard `grep` command, including the feature to specify more than one pattern in a file.
- ☐ That a closure specifies the number of times a pattern may be repeated. User-defined closures are not supported by the standard `grep` command or by `fgrep`.
- ☐ That the `egrep` utility offers the support for closures in addition to those features offered by `fgrep`.
- ☐ That on DOS machines, the `grep` command may call a special command called `glob.exe` to do the regular expression parsing. If things do not work right on the DOS version of the shell, check the manual for that shell to see if you need `glob.exe` installed from the vendor.

On Day 6, you learned the following about important environment variables:

- That your environment variables are those that the shell keeps information about during your login session.
- That your login shell assigns values to your `HOME`, `PATH`, and other environment variables by running the `/etc/profile` and `$HOME/profile` scripts.
- That the `$HOME/profile` script can be used to override the values set in the `/etc/profile` script.
- That you can execute shell scripts with the `.` command.
- That subshells are shells started by the current shell to execute a command. The current shell then becomes the parent shell of that subshell.
- That local variables in subshells are not returned back to the parent shell.
- How you can pass variables from the parent shell to subshells by exporting them.
- How local or exported variables in the parent shell are not modified in any way by a subshell.
- How you can group together and execute commands within parentheses `()` and execute them in a subshell.
- How to use the UNIX calendar utility, `cal`, and desktop calendars, `dc` and `bc`, as desktop tool alternatives.
- That you can group together and execute commands within `{}` and execute them in the current shell's environment.

Day 7 capped the week off with details about I/O redirection. You then went on to learn about how to work with I/O redirection with the various tools you have picked up along the way. Today, you were introduced to file descriptors, pipes, tees, and how to use them with grouped commands. Day 7 also covered the following:

- That the `>` is used to redirect the output to a location.
- That the `>>` is used to redirect the output to a location and append output to the file.
- How `<` will read from a file.
- That the `<< TOKEN` will read from a file until Ctrl+d or an entire line with the `TOKEN` is encountered.

- How the pipe symbol (¦) connects the output from one command to the input of another.
- How the `tee` command is used to send the output of the file to two locations.
- That the `&` at the end of a shell command will put that command in the background.
- How the `1>`*`filename`* will send all output to the file.
- How the `2>&1` at the end of a command will redirect the output of file descriptor 2 to the same location as output of file descriptor 1.
- That redirecting the output from grouped commands will effectively send all the output to one location if the redirection is outside the braces.
- How to use options to the `sort` command to handle reversed sorting with the `-r` and `-n` options to sort items numerically.

You should now have enough UNIX tool experience to write your own shell scripts. You will start that process next week.

WEEK 2 AT A GLANCE

8 9 10 11 12 13 14

The first week was probably not as rough as you imagined. You've made it so far, and it will get easier.

This week, you will build upon what you know to create shell scripts that actually do something useful. You will be experienced in shell programming by the time the week is over.

On Day 8, you will write your first shell script. On Day 9, you will learn about looping constructs and decision making when using shell scripts. Day 10 covers how to handle user input and other related topics. In Day 11, you will use what you have learned about shells and tools to create a `todo` application.

On Day 12, you will learn about another tool called `awk`, which when used with the shell is a powerful UNIX tool for special purpose programming.

On Day 13, you will get a quick introduction to the next generation shell, called the Korn shell. This is a shell with which you can use all your Bourne shell knowledge.

Day 14 is a fun day. It covers the oddities of the Bourne and Korn shells, as well as teaching tricks about the file and mail systems—and other items that did not fall into any previous days' text. Day 14 wraps up shell programming and provides the spring board for your own learning experiences.

8

WEEK 2

Introduction to Shell Scripts

Today's lesson introduces the basics of shell programming. You will use the knowledge you gained in the past seven days to create shell scripts and work with the following topics:

- More details on writing your first shell script
- How to create a shell script
- Different ways to execute a shell script
- Command-line processing
- How to handle arguments to a shell script
- Integer arithmetic
- How to debug shell scripts

Shell Programming, Part 1

Today's lesson is the core of the book. You will learn about shell scripts in this and following days. You will build on all the concepts, work, and learning of the past seven days to put together powerful shell scripts.

For today's text and for all the rest of the book, you must be comfortable with using a text editor under UNIX. The editor you are using must be capable of writing ASCII (text) files to disk.

So, what is a shell script anyway?

If you have a set of commands that have to be executed in a certain order, it is simpler to place them in a shell script and execute it rather than type the commands in every time for that task.

Note: Shell scripts are to UNIX what batch files are to DOS. The difference is that shell scripts are a whole lot more powerful and flexible.

Your First Shell Script

You have already created shell scripts, or at least worked with them by now. You wrote your first shell script when you wrote the `.profile` file. There are several steps you need to take to create a shell script.

- Create a text file and add shell commands to it in the order that they will be read from the file. Usually, you fire up your favorite editor to write out a text file.
- Give the text file execute permissions. You do this by executing the chmod +x filename command.

Note: If you do not know how to use any of the UNIX editors by now, I would recommend learning either `vi` or `emacs`. These are the most prevalent and common editors in the UNIX operating systems.

If you are not familiar with the UNIX editors or want to create a small uncomplicated shell script, you can use the command:

```
$ cat > scriptname
```

Continue typing until the end of the input file and press Ctrl+d to end the text. This command will direct all your keystrokes to the scriptname.

This method is quick, but is rather crude. You cannot back up to correct previous lines, and you have to start all over again to write a completely new shell script.

The following code will create a shell script that prints a big `hello` for you. You will use the file indirection in this example, but if you are familiar with a UNIX editor, you can use the editor instead.

Input
Output

```
$ cat > hello
banner -w80 Hello
ctrl-d
$ chmod u+x hello
$ hello
```

(You will see a big `Hello` on your screen.)

Analysis

The `-w80` option is used to specify a width of 80 characters. Normally, the banner output defaults to a line printer width of 132 characters. This `-w` flag gives a scrunched output with 80 columns, but it's easier to see on an 80-column printer. The -w option may not be available on your system and isn't a standard.

> **Note:** On my Sun and AIX systems, the banner output is horizontal, 10-characters wide. This output is most common. Your output may look different, though, depending on your system. On Linnux, for example, the output is rotated 90 degrees and defaults to 132-characters wide.

Comments in Shell Scripts

It's always a good idea to annotate your shell scripts with comments. The # in a command line causes all the characters in a shell script, up to the end of the line, to be ignored. If the # is quoted out, it is ignored and all the characters are read. See Days 3 and 4 for more information on quoting. A typical comment would be

```
#
# A script to print a  file with all it's lines numbered.
#
```

DO | **DON'T**

DO comment your shell scripts, except in the most obvious cases. A year from now, you may not have any idea what your "obvious" script does. When in doubt, comment some lines in the script.

DON'T overcomment. Be precise. The shell will still read these lines as it interprets your commands. Think twice about whether you need to write a page of comments for a two-line shell script. I have seen an outrageous 44-line heading for a two-line shell script that simply prints the count of all the words in a list of files. The company's "standard header" had to be used on all programs and was 44 lines long! Use your own judgment when commenting.

Command-Line Processing

Next, you are going to create a shell script that handles command-line arguments. Create a file called scr1 with the following lines.

Input Output

```
$ cat scr1
1. echo I am in scr1
2. echo The arguments are
3. echo $1
4. echo $2 $3
```

Analysis

(As before, the line numbers do *not* exist in the shell script; they are only there for clarity.) Lines 1 and 2 echo the fact that you are in the script `scr1`. Line 3 prints the first argument to the shell script on one line. Line 4 prints the second and third arguments to this shell script.

Now, give the script execute permissions, using the following line of code:

```
$ chmod +x scr1
```

Or you can be explicit with the flags:

```
$ chmod 755 scr1
```

As a third alternative, you can use the preferred version using the `u` keyword:

```
$ chmod u+x scr1
```

This limits execution to the owner of the script file. The group and other permissions remain unchanged.

Now you can execute your shell script.

Input Output

```
$ scr1 Your Name Here
I am in scr1
The arguments are
Your
Name Here
$
```

Analysis

The arguments to this shell script are `Your`, `Name`, and `Here`. They are addressed through the variables `$1`, `$2`, and `$3`, respectively. The `echo` commands work as faithfully as before.

You do have to give a shell script execute permission before using it. If you do not do this, you will get a "Permission Denied" message. You only have to give the execute permission once. From then on, any changes you make to the contents of the file itself do not turn the `x` bit off.

There are several ways you can execute a shell script without giving it execute permissions. The following are some common ways:

- Use the dot (.) command at the prompt.
- Use an explicit shell command at the prompt (for example, the `sh` command).

- ☐ Use the `#!` command in the shell script itself (remember shell archives?), in addition to giving it execute permissions.

The end result for the first two items is the same—the script gets executed by a shell program via the command line. The period will run the current version of whatever shell you are running, and `sh` will run the Bourne shell on the script regardless of your current shell.

Now, let's work with the following shell script. Don't worry if you don't understand how it works. You'll learn more later today in the section titled, "Integer Arithmetic." The script is called `add1`.

Input
Output

```
$cat add1
echo $1 $2
echo $1 + $2 = `expr $1 + $2`
echo $1 - $2 = `expr $1 - $2`
$ chmod -x add1
$ ls -l add1
-rw-r--r--   1 kamran   users          72 Jul  9 06:55 add1
$ add1 12 45
sh: ./add1: Permission denied
$ sh add1 12 45
12 45
12 + 45 = 57
12 - 45 = -33
$ . add1 12 45
12 45
12 + 45 = 57
12 - 45 = -33
```

Analysis

The end result of the commands were the same; a shell executed the script regardless of the permission.

Yesterday, you learned about the `#!/bin/sh` comment line when dealing with shell archives.

Later versions of the shell support this `#!` syntax. Test your shell scripts first. The feature enables the first commented line of a shell script to be a shell command line if it has a `#!` in front of it followed by a path name to a shell. For example:

```
#!/bin/sh
```

requests an execution of the Bourne shell, or

```
#!/bin/csh
```

requests an execution of the C shell.

The `#!` in the first line is a simple way to confirm that your script will run under a specific shell. I use this a lot with shell scripts and archives because of its simplicity. Also, because some of my shell scripts have to run across a network on different machines and accounts, a . command might not invoke the Bourne shell (since the end user may be running a shell other than the Bourne shell). Using #!/bin/sh almost ensures that the Bourne shell will be used to execute this script. In such cases, the #! command will still enable the script to execute correctly. Unfortunately, I still come across systems that do not support this command syntax. I use it unless forced to do otherwise.

DO | **DON'T**

DO use the #! command with the understanding that your script may not be supported on some systems.

DON'T use the #!/bin/csh if you can use the #!/bin/sh and write it is a Bourne shell script. The C shell is not as widely distributed as the Bourne shell; consequently the system on which your script executes may not have the #!/bin/csh executable. (See the following note for the special case of the shell.)

Note: In some shell scripts, you will see the colon as the first line in the shell script. The colon command is a null command. It is prevalent in shell scripts that are written for the Bourne shell but are also executed in C shell environments.

When the C shell sees a # as the first line (without the !), it executes a C shell on it. If it does not see the #, it passes the script to the Bourne shell for execution. It's simple to leave the first line blank but it's also easy to delete a blank line. So a null command is a safe way to force a blank line and also force the C shell to pass the script to the Bourne shell.

Quoting Revisited

Try the scr2 command in your script's directory to see how arguments are handled in shell scripts.

Input/Output

```
$ cat scr2
echo $1
echo $2
$
$ scr2 "This is One" "This is Two"
This is One
This is Two
```

Analysis

Note that the double quotes have passed a quoted string to the shell script.

A shell running a script accesses its arguments much the same way it handles shell variables. For example, `$1` is the first argument, `$2` is the second, and so forth, until the ninth argument `$9`. The `$0` is the pathname of the shell script being run.

The shell sets two special variables in every script to identify these arguments:

`$#` is the total number of arguments to the variable
`$*` is the entire argument list

You can write a simple shell script to show how these two work.

Input
Output

```
1. $ cat arg
echo $# arguments
echo arg1=:$1:
echo arg2=:$2:
echo arg3=:$3:
echo All of them are $*
2. $ arg a b c
3 arguments
arg1=:a:
arg2=:b:
arg3=:c:
All of them are a b c
3. $ arg "a b" "Hello I am the second one" " fresh     "
3 arguments
arg1=:a b:
arg2=:Hello I am the second one:
arg3=: fresh    :
All of them are a b Hello I am the second one fresh
```

Analysis

In the third command, the spaces around the word `fresh` were shown correctly with the `$3` variable. However, in the `$*` expansion these spaces were removed. The `$*` variable in the script expands to the entire list of arguments, with surrounding white spaces removed.

No arguments specified at a location are assigned the `NULL` value. Nothing is defined here. To check this out, try the following.

Input
Output

```
$ arg
0 arguments
arg1=::
arg2=::
arg3=::
All of them are
```

Analysis

As you can see, there are no arguments to the script. Nothing is printed in place of `$1`, `$2`, `$3`, and `$*`.

The shell also does its command-line processing before sending the arguments to the script. Thus, use the listing of `n*` in the shell command.

```
$ ls n*
n n2 n4 name2 numlines
n1 n3 name1 newkorn.asc
$ arg n*
9 arguments
arg1=:n:
arg2=:n1:
arg3=:n2:
All of them are n n1 n2 n3 n4 name1 name2 newkorn.asc numlines
$ arg n?
4 arguments
arg1=:n1:
arg2=:n2:
arg3=:n3:
All of them are n1 n2 n3 n4
```

The filename expansion is done before the `arg` script gets the arguments. If you try the `$ arg n?` command (as far as the script is concerned), the command could have been

```
$ arg n1 n2 n3 n4
```

Because you know that the filename expansion is done by the parent shell when calling this script, you can take advantage of all the quoting mechanisms learned about in the previous days. For example, you know that you can expand filenames before you call a script rather than type a long list. See the following example.

```
$ arg  "n?" "n\?" 'n\?'
3 arguments
arg1=:n?:
arg2=:n\?:
arg3=:n\?:
All of them are n1 n2 n3 n4 n\? n\?
$ arg \$ \? \\
3 arguments
arg1=:$:
arg2=:?:
arg3=:\:
All of them are $ n \
```

All the quoting features of escaping the characters are available to you in this shell script.

Note that in the second command, `arg \$ \? \\` were expanded correctly in the individual arguments but not so in the `$*` expansion. The `\$` was expanded to `$`, and `\\` was expanded to `\` as expected. Why was `n` (the output from filename expansion) printed instead of a question mark? The `$*` does filename expansion too.

The backquote features are also available to you, as shown in the following example.

Input
Output

```
$ who
kamran   tty1     Jul  9 05:31
kamran   tty2     Jul  9 05:38
$ arg `who`
10 arguments
arg1=:kamran:
arg2=:tty1:
arg3=:Jul:
All of them are kamran tty1 Jul 9 05:31 kamran tty2 Jul 9 05:38
```

Analysis

All the lines in the `who` command are concatenated together into one long line. All newlines and whitespaces are completely removed in the `$*` expansion.

The result of this is that you can have a long list of filenames, giving you an argument list greater than 9. Next, modify the `arg` script to get `arg2`.

Input
Output

```
$ cat arg2
echo $# arguments
echo arg1=:$10:
echo arg2=:$0:
echo arg3=:$1:
echo All of them are $*
$ arg2 n*
10 arguments
arg1=:n0:
arg2=:./arg2:
arg3=:n:
All of them are n n1 n2 n3 n4 name1 name2 name3 newkorn.asc numlines
```

Analysis

The first argument is expanded by looking at `$10` as two distinct components, `$1` and `0`. The first argument, `$1`, is `n`, so the string becomes `n0`. The variable `$0` expands to `./arg2` (the current script being run), and the variable `$1` expands to `n`.

So how do you get the tenth argument? The answer is that you cannot get to it directly. You have to shift all the arguments left one at a time to get to the argument. The command to do this is the `shift` command:

```
shift [number]
```

The number is optional. If you do not specify it, it is defaulted to 1. Look at the shell script `arg3`.

Input
Output

```
$ cat arg3
echo :$#: $*
shift
echo :$#: $*
shift 2
echo :$#: $*
shift
echo :$#: $*
shift 4
```

```
echo :$#: $*
shift
$ arg3 1 2 3 4 5 6 7 8 9 10 11 12 13 14 15
:15: 1 2 3 4 5 6 7 8 9 10 11 12 13 14 15
:14: 2 3 4 5 6 7 8 9 10 11 12 13 14 15
:12: 4 5 6 7 8 9 10 11 12 13 14 15
:11: 5 6 7 8 9 10 11 12 13 14 15
:7: 9 10 11 12 13 14 15
```

Analysis The shell script demonstrates the power of the `shift` command. The `shift` command moves all the arguments to the left. After they are shifted left, the ones that fall off the left are gone forever, because the shifted ones overwrite their places. Note how the number of arguments is changed to reflect this loss. Now try the `shift` command with no arguments.

Input/Output

```
$ arg3
:0:
:0:
:0:
:0:
:0:
```

Analysis No error messages were printed in this shell. In some shells, you will see a message similar to `./arg3:cannot shift when $# is zero.`

So how do you keep the first argument from falling off into the great bit bucket? Assign its value to a known shell variable before doing the shift:

```
arg1=$1
shift
arg10=$9
```

Integer Arithmetic

The shell can count and process variables to do integer arithmetic. Do not forget the `expr` command you learned about in Day 3. You will work with it through the end of the book. Use the `expr` command to create the shell script `add1`.

Input/Output

```
$ cat add1
echo $1 $2
echo $1 + $2 = `expr $1 + $2`
echo $1 - $2 = `expr $1 - $2`
$ add1 32 15
32 15
32 + 15 = 47
32 - 15 = 17
```

It was quite easy to get a simple calculator that works with two numbers. Of course, the `expr` command expects numbers as its arguments. Therefore, the command

```
$ add1 r 3
```

will give you an error message or two because the `r` is not an integer.

```
$ add1 r 3
r 3
expr: non-numeric argument
r + 3 =
expr: non-numeric argument
r - 3 =
$
```

This output does not illustrate a graceful way of handling errors. You will deal with the methods of catching errors in Day 10.

Now try another shell script, called `mul1`, to multiply and divide these numbers.

```
$ mul1
echo $1 $2
echo $1 * $2 = `expr $1 * $2`
echo $1 % $2 = `expr $1 % $2`
echo $1 / $2 = `expr $1 / $2`
```

The `*` will multiply the two numbers, `/` will divide them, and `%` will give the remainder of the division of `$1` by `$2`.

```
$ sh mul1 25 12
25 12
expr: syntax error
25 333 a.out add1 add2 arg arg2 arg3 ch01 ch02  ... <all files>..
25 % 12 = 1
25 / 12 = 2
```

Gadzooks! The * (multiplication) has become the list of filenames. Plus, you got an `expr` syntax error. Something is not right here. It's apparent that this example is contrived to get you into the mood of debugging a shell script.

DO	DON'T

DO use the `dc` or `bc` desk calculators instead of relying on the shell's mathematical capabilities.

DON'T expect to do extensive arithmetic with the `expr` command. It's limited to integer arithmetic only.

Debugging Scripts

You will find yourself debugging shell scripts at one time or another. The easiest way to find out the values of shell variables is to use the `echo` statement. However, in the final version of the shell program, after debugging, you will have to go back and remove all the `echo` commands.

The shell offers a debug flag, `-v`, which displays the current line being executed and the values of the shell variables at the time of execution. The shell also shows the values of all shell variables that are affected before and after the execution of every line in the script file. Take a look at the following output of the command `add1`.

Input
Output

```
$ cat add1
echo $1 $2
echo $1 + $2 = `expr $1 + $2`
echo $1 - $2 = `expr $1 - $2`
$ add1 4 2
4 2
4 + 2 = 6
4 - 2 = 2
$ sh -v add1 4 2
echo $1 $2
4 2
echo $1 + $2 = `expr $1 + $2`
expr $1 + $2
4 + 2 = 6
echo $1 - $2 = `expr $1 - $2`
expr $1 - $2
4 - 2 = 2
```

Analysis

The `-v` option gave you the output of each line as it was being executed. You may want to redirect the output to another file if the output is very long. Note also that your output may be different than the one shown here. This would be due to different versions.

The only problem with this command is that it's hard to differentiate between the `echo` command in the script and its execution `debug` statement. For example, the line

```
echo $1 + $2 = `expr $1 + $2`
```

has been executed in two steps because of the backward quotes around the `expr` command:

```
expr $1 + $2
4 + 2 = 6
```

It's not very obvious what the command is and what the debug output is at this stage.

A better option to use when you want a clearer, though more verbose, debug output is the -x option. This option does not, however, print the line in the script file. It prints the line after variable substitution.

Input/Output

```
$ sh -x add1 4 2
+ echo 4 2
4 2
+ expr 4 + 2
+ echo 4 + 2 = 6
4 + 2 = 6
+ expr 4 - 2
+ echo 4 - 2 = 2
4 - 2 = 2
```

Analysis

The + indicates the shell level at which the command is being executed. The values of any variables used in the command are shown. (In some shells, this + can be changed via the environment variable PS4.)

You use the -x and -v options together. Use -xv or vx, but not -x and -v separately. However, some shells do take -x and -v commands as separate arguments.

Input/Output

```
$ sh -xv add1 11 23
echo $1 $2
+ echo 11 23
11 23
echo $1 + $2 = `expr $1 + $2`
+ expr 11 + 23
+ echo 11 + 23 = 34
11 + 23 = 34
echo $1 - $2 = `expr $1 - $2`
+ expr 11 - 23
+ echo 11 - 23 = -12
11 - 23 = -12
```

Analysis

You used the two options -v and -x together to get an even more detailed output. In most shell scripts, you would want to catenate the output to a text file.

Debug the mul1 script used earlier to see if you can figure out what's going on.

Input/Output

```
$ sh -xv mul1 25 12
echo $1 $2
+ echo 25 12
25 12
echo $1 * $2 = `expr $1 * $2`
expr $1 * $2
++ expr 25 333 a.out add1 add2 arg arg2 arg3 ch01 ch02 ...
expr: syntax error
+ echo 25 333 a.out add1 add2 arg arg2 arg3 ch01 ch02 ...
25 333 a.out add1 add2 arg arg2 arg3 ch01 ch02 ...
echo $1 % $2 = `expr $1 % $2`
expr $1 % $2
++ expr 25 % 12
```

```
+ echo 25 % 12 = 1
25 % 12 = 1
echo $1 / $2 = `expr $1 / $2`
expr $1 / $2
++ expr 25 / 12
+ echo 25 / 12 = 2
25 / 12 = 2
```

Analysis In the line `expr $1 * $2`, you can see that the `*` has expanded to the list of filenames. Thus, the probable solution is to quote the asterisk out with single quotes in this line. Try it now on another file, called `mul2`.

Input Output

```
$ cat mul2
echo $1 $2
echo $1 '*' $2 = `expr $1 '*' $2`
echo $1 % $2 = `expr $1 % $2`
echo $1 / $2 = `expr $1 / $2`
$ sh -xv mul2 25 12
echo $1 $2
+ echo 25 12
25 12
echo $1 '*' $2 = `expr $1 '*' $2`
expr $1 '*' $2
+ expr 25 * 12
+ echo 25 * 12 = 300
25 * 12 = 300
echo $1 % $2 = `expr $1 % $2`
expr $1 % $2
+ expr 25 % 12
+ echo 25 % 12 = 1
25 % 12 = 1
echo $1 / $2 = `expr $1 / $2`
expr $1 / $2
+ expr 25 / 12
+ echo 25 / 12 = 2
25 / 12 = 2
```

Analysis The results are what you would expect from the multiplication command.

Summary

Today, you learned the following:

- ☐ Shell scripts are handy when you put UNIX tools together to create your own complex commands.
- ☐ The colon (`:`) command is a null command used to force a C shell to run the Bourne shell on a command when the colon is used as the first line in a file.
- ☐ The `$#` variable in a script is the number of arguments specified at the command line.

- The `$*` variable in a script expands to the list of arguments with surrounding whitespaces removed.
- The `shift` command shifts all the arguments left once. The `shift n` command shifts all the arguments left `n` times. The `$#` is changed to reflect this change.
- The `expr` command is very useful when you are doing shell integer arithmetic.
- You can debug your shell script by using the `-v` and `-x` options.

What's Next?

Tomorrow's text discusses the looping and decision-making commands in shell scripts. This will enable you to make decisions on how and what to execute based on values of shell variables, types of files, and so on.

UNIX Tools Learned Today

`sh`	Bourne shell command to execute shell scripts
`.`	Dot command to execute shell scripts with your current shell
`#!/bin/sh construct`	Syntax
`banner`	Prints text with big characters
`expr`	Evaluates math expressions

Q&A

Q What is a shell script?

A A shell script is a text file containing commands for the shell to execute.

Q Can I execute a Bourne shell script if I am in another shell?

A Yes, use the `sh` script command. Type a colon as the first line in the file.

Q Can one shell script call another? How can I debug this?

A Use the `-x` option on the shell command-line invocation.

Q Can a shell script work on every word in a text file?

A Yes, you can cat the file to shell script within backquotes. The `$*` will contain all the words. The drawback to this approach is that you may be limited in memory if you are working with large files. Also, all whitespaces and linefeeds are removed. Handling data and large files is covered in Days 10 and 11.

Q What are the limitations with arithmetic operations in the shell?

A It's clumsy at best, slow, and works only with integers.

Workshop

The Workshop provides quiz questions to help you solidify your understanding of the material covered. Some Workshop sections of this book also contain exercises to provide you with experience in using what you've learned. Try to understand the quiz and exercise answers before continuing on to the next chapter. Answers are provided in Appendix D, "Answers."

Quiz

1. What are three ways of executing a shell script?
2. What are the two steps in creating a shell script?
3. How do you handle more than 10 arguments?
4. When do you have to suppress filename expansion with double quotes?
5. What happens when you shift with a negative number?
6. What is wrong with the following script:

```
:#!/bin/sh
echo $1
shift -3
echo    'This is a long list of the file $1in the directory'
ls -l $1
wc -l $1
```

7. You wrote a shell script to see if a user you named is logged into the system. It's catching `ann` in addition to `joanne`, and `rob` in addition to `robbie`, `betty`, and `tty`.

   The script is

```
who ¦ grep "$1"
```

Modify the shell script to catch `name`.

Exercises

1. Write a shell script to write your user name as a banner to the front of a file being sent to the printer.
2. Write a shell script to print the first five arguments in reverse order.
3. Write a shell script to count to 10. (If you have skipped ahead, write one that prints out the lowercase alphabet a through h.)
4. Write a shell script to append a line to a file. Both the filename and line have to be specified to the script at the command line. Ensure that it runs the `sh` shell script. Print the number of lines in the file after you are done.

9

WEEK 2

Decision Making in Shell Scripts

Today's lesson consists of the second part of shell programming and introduces the following concepts:

- `if-then-else-fi` and `case` statements
- What an exit status is
- Conditional test for decision making
- Loops and conditionals covering `for`, `while`, and `until` loops
- How to break out of loops

You will also learn how to process options to commands and how to process work in the background.

Shell Programming, Part 2

This is the second section on shell programming. Today, you will work with loops to perform repetitive tasks and recognize conditions with shell scripts to do decision making. For example, a condition to test at the beginning of a shell script would be to test if the input file existed at all before going any further.

Loops are used to perform a task repeatedly until a condition is true or false. To test for these conditions, you use conditional operators such as `x less than 10` and `no more files`. Loops and conditional testing go hand in hand. You will learn about both of these items simultaneously. As you work with UNIX, you will constantly use loops to perform tasks such as counting the number of directories in the present working directory, waiting until a certain user logs in, and so forth.

if-then-else Constructs

The `if` command enables you to test if a condition exists and then change execution based on the results of the test. The shell's syntax for this test is

```
if condition
then
     command if exit status of condition is 0
     ...
fi
```

When the condition is tested, its exit status is tested. If the exit status is `0`, the commands between the `then` and `fi` statements are executed. (See Figure 9.1.)

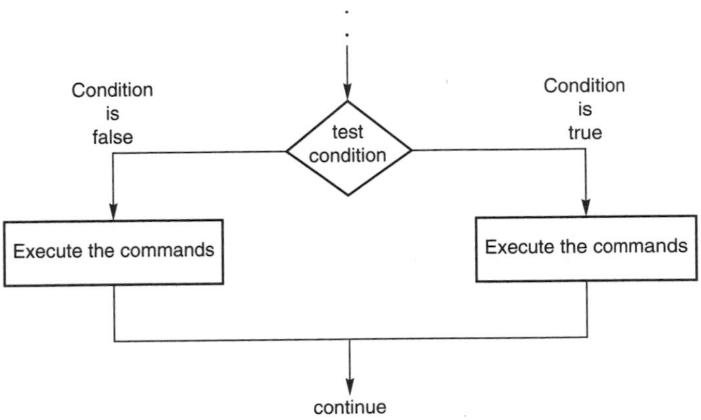

Figure 9.1. *An `if-then-else` construct.*

Exit Status

By convention, UNIX commands return a status of 0 when successful and a number other than 0 when they are unsuccessful. The value returned by the command is placed in a shell variable called `$?`. Because `$?` is changed on a per-command basis, it is set to the last command executed. In the case of a pipeline, this is the last command in the pipe.

Input/Output

```
$ rm badfile
rm: badfile: no such file or directory
$ echo $?
1
$ echo $?
0
```

Analysis

The first `$?` gave the status of the `rm` command as non-zero, or failed. The second `$?` gave the "completed without errors" status of the last `echo` command.

The `grep` command can now be used to find if a user exists on a system.

Input/Output

```
$ grep Dave /etc/passwd
dbarry:Fpevq40U4ILJc:503:100:Dave B. Arry:/home/dbarry:/bin/bash
$ echo $?
0
```

Analysis

The `grep` command returns `0` when successful. This can then be used directly in the `if` condition.

Write the script out in a file called add2.

```
if grep $1 /etc/passwd
then
     echo "Found $1"
fi
```

Now run it.

Input Output

```
$ add2 Dave
dbarry:Fpevq40U4ILJc:503:100:Dave B. Arry:/home/dbarry:/bin/bash
Found Dave
```

Analysis

The command seemed to test everything out okay, but the output of the passwd line from the grep command is quite unsightly. You can get rid of this line by redirecting the output of the grep command to /dev/null. Modify the shell script to read:

```
if grep $1 /etc/passwd > /dev/null
then
     echo "Found $1"
fi
```

Note: There is a special file in UNIX called /dev/null, which is used for unwanted output. This is a place where nothing will be printed and is usually a "bit bucket." Use it for all unwanted output.

Now run add2 again.

Input Output

```
$ add2 Dave
Found Dave
$
```

Analysis

This is much better, because the unsightly output from the grep command is not shown.

What Are Tests?

So far in your use of the if clause, you have only been testing the input from the command to see if it returned a 0 or not. There is a built-in command, called test, which does this for you. What test does is that it tests to see if an expression is true, and if it is true it returns 0. Otherwise, it returns a non-zero number, indicating a false condition.

The syntax for the test command is

```
test condition
```

where condition is the expression being tested.

For example, if you write a shell script that requires one argument for execution, you have to be able to see if the argument is missing very early on in the shell's execution. Your shell script would look like the following.

Input
Output

```
$cat sample
if  test $# -eq 0
then
     echo "$0:You must supply a destination file name" >&2
     exit 1
fi
touch $*
```

Analysis

This example has several key points to note, and I will discuss these one line at a time.

The line test $# -eq 0 tests to see if the number of arguments is equal to 0. The $# is the number of arguments, and -eq is the equate symbol (more on that in a moment).

The echo line has the >&2 at the end, forcing the output to stderr. This way, you are forcing the output to the terminal even if you are in a pipe. (This is with the assumption that the parent shell has not redirected the output either.) The $0 is your shell script name.

The exit command returns a 1 to show an error condition. Note that there is no exit at the end of the shell script. It defaults to exit 0, but there is no harm in executing an exit 0 statement as the last line of the file.

So where did this -eq come from? This operator is used to equate two integers together. The other related operators are:

Operator	Returns true if
int1 -eq int2	int1 is equal to int2
int1 -ne int2	int1 is not equal to int2
int1 -lt int2	int1 is less than int2
int1 -le int2	int1 is less than or equal to int2
int1 -gt int2	int1 is greater than int2
int1 -ge int2	int1 is greater than or equal to int2

As with anything else in UNIX, there is an alternative method of doing comparisons. You also can place brackets ([) around the expression. Instead of

```
test expression
```

you can write

```
[ expression ]
```

This is the `test` command in disguise. It's clearer to read and is the preferred way of annotating conditionals in this text. Spaces are required around the `[` and `]`. Therefore, in the previous example, the same test could be written as

```
if [ $# -eq 0 ]
```

Also, note that you must supply the right bracket (`]`) if you supply the left bracket (`[`); otherwise, you will get an error.

This `test` command works with three types of comparisons:

- Integer
- File types
- Character strings

Integer Comparisons

Try this method of comparing integers with a shell script.

Input Output

```
$ cat comp
#!/bin/sh
# comp #
# This shell script compares two arguments passed in at
# the command line. It's used to illustrate the many ways
# of comparing integers in the shell.
#
arg1=$1
arg2=$2
if [ $# -ne 2 ]
then
     echo "$0: You must supply two integers" >&2
     exit 1
fi
if [ $arg1 -eq 0 ]
then
     echo "arg1 equals 0"
fi
if [ $arg1 -lt $arg2 ]
then
     echo "$arg1 is less than $arg2"
fi
if [ $arg1 -le $arg2 ]
then
     echo "$arg1 is less than or equal to $arg2"
fi
if [ $arg1 -ge $arg2 ]
```

```
27    then
28          echo "$arg1 is greater than or equal to $arg2"
29    fi
30    if [ $arg1 -gt $arg2 ]
31    then
32          echo "$arg1 is greater than $arg2"
33    fi
```

```
$ comp 0 1
arg1 equals 0
0 is less than 1
0 is less than or equal to 1
$ comp 8 8
8 is less than or equal to 8
8 is greater than or equal to 8
```

Analysis Line 1 is the request to run the Bourne Shell. Lines 2 to 6 are comments.

Lines 7 and 8 set up two local shell variables, arg1 and arg2.

Lines 9 to 13 check and display the message if arg1 is zero.

Lines 14 to 17 check if arg1 is equal to zero.

Lines 18 to 21 check if arg1 is less than arg2. Lines 22 to 25 check if arg1 is less than or equal to arg2.

Lines 26 to 29 check if arg1 is greater than or equal to arg2.

Lines 30 to 33 check if arg1 is greater than arg2.

The *else* and *elif* Statements

The output from the previous command can be improved a little bit. Instead of getting two or three messages after comparisons, I want to give one message only: either `arg1` is equal to, greater than, or less than `arg2`. Use the `else` statement for this.

The `else` statement is a part of the `if` statement and cannot be used on its own. (Refer back to Figure 9.1.) The syntax is

```
if condition
then
     condition is true (0)
     execute all these commands up to the else statement
else
     condition is false (not 0)
     execute all these commands up to the fi statement
fi
```

If you wanted to create multilevel `if-then-else` statements, you can use the `elif` statement. (See Figure 9.2.) The syntax for this statement is

```
if condition
then
     condition is true (0)
     execute all these commands up to the elif statement
elif another condition1
     condition1 is true (not 0)
     execute all these commands up to the elif statement
elif another condition2
     condition2 is true (not 0)
     execute all these commands up to the elif statement
else
     nothing else is true.
     execute all these commands up to the fi statement
fi
```

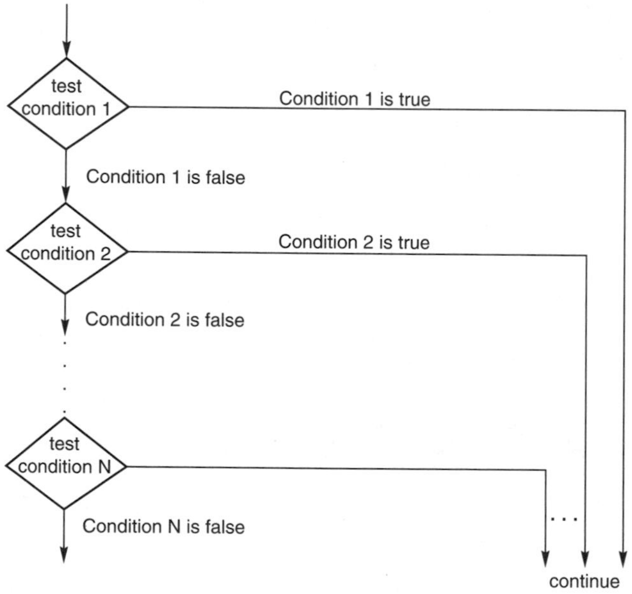

Figure 9.2. *The* `if-then-elif-else-fi` *construct.*

The new improved shell script looks like the following.

```
$ cat comp
     #!/bin/sh
     #
     # This shell script compares two arguments passed in at
     # the command line. It's another way to use the else
     # statement.
     #
     arg1=$1
     arg2=$2
     if [ $# -ne 2 ]
```

```
10    then
11         echo "$0: You must supply two integers" >&2
12         exit 1
13    fi
14    if [ $arg1 -eq $arg2 ]
15    then
16         echo "arg1 equals arg2"
17    elif [ $arg1 -lt $arg2 ]
18    then
19         echo "$arg1 is less than $arg2"
20    else
21         echo "$arg1 is greater than $arg2"
22    fi
```

```
$ comp1 11 31
11 is less than 31
$ comp1 21 09
21 is greater than 09
$ comp1 17 17
arg1 equals arg2
```

Analysis

On line 20, you see the `else` statement. What's also interesting is the `elif` statement on line 17. This is a combination of the `else` and `if` put together to do selective conditions.

String Comparisons

The shell can also test for the same length and content of strings. The list of comparisons are as follows:

Operator	Returns true if
`str1 = str2`	`str1` is equal to `str2`
`str1 != str2`	`str1` is not equal to `str2`
`str1`	`str1` is not NULL
`-n str1`	`str1` is not NULL and does exist
`-z str1`	`str1` is NULL and does exist

A few examples will illustrate this point.

Input Output

```
$ h1=hello
$ [ $h1 = hello  ]
$ echo $?
0
$ h1='hello'
$ [ $h1 = hello  ]
$ echo $?
0
$ h1=hello
$ [ "$h1" = hello  ]
$ echo $?
```

```
1
$ [ "$h1" ]
$ echo $?
0
$ test "$h1"
$ echo $?
0
$ test -z $h1
echo$?
1
$ [ -z $h1 ]
echo $?
1
$ [ -n $h1 ]
$?
0
```

Analysis In the first case, the `h1` is equal to `hello` because spaces are eaten up by the shell. In the next case, `h1` is equal to `hello` even though the extra space after `hello` was quoted, because you did not quote `h1` during the comparison.

When you did quote `h1`, you preserved the extra space and the match failed with a return of `$?` instead of `1`.

To test if the string itself is not NULL, the test commands `[$h1]` and `"test $h1` were used to get `0`.

The `-z` flag for the test command returned `1` because the `h1` string is not NULL. The `-n` flag returned a `0` for the same reason.

This area is perhaps the most important one to remember with strings. Misquoting is the cause of many shell programming errors. Understand the quoting concept correctly, and you will be at ease with the shell. At times, you may have to work with strings that consist of valid symbols for the shell. The = sign is a good example. In this case, it's safer to use the construct:

```
test X"$symbol" = X
```

which prevents the symbol from being expanded into an equal sign by itself for the `test` command. It then proceeds to test `X=` to the string `X` instead and returns a `1`, indicating failure.

Note: If you are C programmer, you will note the exact reversal of the concept of true and false in the shell. In C, a 0 value implies a false condition to a conditional, and a non-zero value as true.

Always remember to use double quotes when you are comparing strings. This will enable variable expansion within the quotes for a comparison. Look at the following example.

Input Output

```
$ fruit=tomato
$ vegetable=tomato
$
$ [ "$fruit" = "$vegetable" ]
$ echo $?
0
$ [ '$fruit' = '$vegetable' ]
$ echo $?
1
```

Analysis

In the first comparison, the two variables were expanded and came to be `tomato`. The second test attempted to compare `$fruit` to the word `$vegetable`.

DO | **DON'T**

DO remember to use double quotes when comparing strings.

DO remember that you can concatenate two variables together to compare a non-existent argument.

DON'T execute another statement before checking the value of `$?`, because `$?` is set to a value by the shell after the shell executes a command.

File Types

The shell also can test for types of files and directories. The syntax for this command is

```
[ -type name ]
```

The `-type` is set to one of the following types to test for the existence of `name`.

Test	True if
`-s`	A non-empty file
`-f`	A file and not a directory
`-d`	A directory and not a file
`-w`	Is writeable
`-r`	Is readable

Some test examples include the following ones.

Input/Output

```
$ test -f /etc ; echo $?
1
$
$ test -d /etc ; echo $?
0
```

Analysis

The first command tested if `/etc` was a file or a directory. In the `-f` case, the condition was false because it returned a `1`. In the `-d` case, the shell correctly tested the `/etc` directory and set `$?` to `0`.

Combining File Conditionals

You can combine several test conditions together with the `-o` and `-a` operators. The `-o` is the Boolean OR operator and `-a` is the Boolean AND operator. For example, the condition

```
[ -f "$arg1" -a -r "$arg1" ]
```

returns true if the file specified in the variable `arg1` is a file and is readable by you. As another example, you may want to test if a file exists before appending another file to it with the test

```
[ -r "$arg1" -a -w "$arg2" ]
```

This will confirm that you can read from `arg1` and write to `arg2`. A sample script would be this:

```
#
# append arg1 to arg2
#
if [ -r $1 -a -w $2 ]
then
     cat $1 >> $2
else
     echo "$1 must be readable, $2 must be writeable"
fi
```

The logical OR operator has a lower precedence than the `-a` operator. Therefore, the expression

```
[ $a -ge 0 -a $b -lt 100 -o $b -gt 10 ]
```

will be evaluated as

```
(  $a -ge 0 -a $b -lt 100 ) -o ( $b -gt 10 )
```

To get the expression evaluated as

```
( $a -ge 0 ) -a ( $b -lt 100  -o  $b -gt 10 )
```

you can use parentheses if you have to by escaping them with the `\(` and `\)` statements.

```
\( $a -ge 0 \) -a \( $b -lt 100  -o  $b -gt 10 \)
```

DO	DON'T

DO remember to match the number of open braces with closed braces. If you use `vi`, you can use the percent sign (`%`) to match braces. `emacs` users can enable automatic brace matching.

DON'T use integers greater than 2 to the power of 32 to be safe. Integers are limited to 32 bits on most UNIX platforms, but this is not a guarantee. For higher math functions, use a calculator such as `dc` or `bc`.

Sometimes, working with negative numbers causes the number to be interpreted as an option to another command. Be prepared for such errors by not allowing such commands to go through. Send a message to the user, such as the one in the following command:

```
if [ "$t" -lt 0 ]
then
    echo  "$t is less than 0, may cause grief"
    exit 1
fi
```

Negative Operators

The negation operator is the bang (`!`) sign. Both of the following statements will be false when `$x1` is equal to `$x2`:

```
[ ! x1 = x2 ]
```

since the `!` negates the response from the comparison, and

```
[ x1 ! = x2 ]
```

uses the not-equal-to (`!=`) symbol.

Other Test Operators

The following shows some of the test conditions available to you in shell scripts:

File operations	
`-b` file	Block device
`-c` file	Character device
`-d` file	Directory
`-f` file	Ordinary file
`-g` file	Sticky bit set, always resides in memory
`-p` file	Named pipe
`-r` file	Read only by this shell
`-t` file	File descriptor for standard output
`-u` file	The file has root privileges
`-w` file	Writeable by this shell
`-x` file	Executeable
String operations	
string	String is not NULL or not defined
`-n` string	String is not NULL and is defined
`-z` string	String is NULL and is defined
`str1 = str2`	`str1` is identical to `str2`
`str1 != str2`	`str1` is not identical to `str2`
Integer operations	
`int1 -eq int2`	`int1` is equal to `int2`
`int1 -ne int2`	`int1` is not equal to `int2`
`int1 -lt int2`	`int1` is less than `int2`
`int1 -le int2`	`int1` is less than or equal to `int2`
`int1 -gt int2`	`int1` is greater than `int2`
`int1 -ge int2`	`int1` is greater than or equal to `int2`
Boolean operations	
`! exp`	`exp` expression is negated
`exp1 -a exp2`	If `exp1` AND `exp2` are both true, this is true otherwise it is false.
`exp1 -o exp2`	If either `exp1` OR `exp2` is true, this is true otherwise it is false.

The *case* Statement

The `case` statement is a better organizational tool than a multilevel `if-then-else-fi` condition. The `case` statement will enable you to match several values against one variable. The syntax for the `case` statement is as follows:

```
case value in
     pattern1) command
            ...
            command ;;
     pattern2) command
            ...
            command ;;

     ...
     patternN) command
            ...
            command ;;
     *)
          command
          ...
          command;;
esac
```

The word value is compared against the patterns until a match is found. The shell then executes all the statements up to the two semicolons that are next to each other.

The `*)` is not required. Its purpose is to catch anything that has not been matched up to that point. The `*)` is usually placed at the end of the case statement, just before the esac statement.

The following example uses the case statement.

Input
Output

```
$ cat rental
rental=$1
case $rental in
     "car" ¦ "vehicle" ¦ "automobile" )
          echo " Thank you, Let me get your ";;
     "subcompact")
          echo " Wait here while I get  " ;;
     "tiny")
          echo " How do plan to sit in this " ;;
     "scooter")
          echo "  We charge extra to put gas in ";;
     "bicycle")
          echo " Of course, the deodorant comes with the ";;
     "Unicycle")
          echo " Do you want me to reserve "
          echo " your clown costume with ";;
     *)
          echo "I cannot get a ";;
esac
echo " $rental for you"
$
$
$ rental scooter
 Do you want us to put gas in
 scooter for you
$ rental car
 Thank you, Let me get your
 car for you
```

```
$ rental aircraft
I cannot get a
 aircraft for you
```

Analysis

Note how the `car`, `vehicle`, and `automobile` selections were combined into one statement using the pipe (¦) operator. The ¦ operator is the OR operator you saw in regular expressions. Speaking of regular expressions, you can even include regular expression in the conditional matches for `case` statements.

Consider this example of using regular expressions in `case` statements:

Input/Output

```
$ cat reg1
#!/bin/sh
#
#     Test if this is a valid shell variable name.
#
if [ $# -ne 1 ]
then
     echo "Usage: $0 variable"
     exit 1
fi

var="$1"

case $var in
     [0-9] ¦ [0-9][0-9]*) echo "This is a number";;
     [a-zA-Z_][a-zA-Z_0-9]*) echo "Valid variable";;
     *) echo " I do not think this is valid";;
esac
$
$ reg1 34
This is a number
$ reg1 _d42
Valid variable
$ reg1 Idontknow
Valid variable
$ reg1 I_dont_know
Valid variable
$ reg1 2_4
 I do not think this is valid
```

Analysis

This script tests whether a name passed in `variable` is valid or not. The first match

```
[0-9] ¦ [0-9][0-9]*
```

checks whether the value passed in to the `case` is a single digit `[0-9]`, or a single digit followed by one or more digits.

The next match

```
[a-zA-Z_][a-zA-Z_0-9]*
```

checks for variables beginning with a lowercase or uppercase letter of the alphabet or an underscore, followed by zero or more occurrences of a letter, underscore, or number.

The last line is the catch-all phrase to get anything that does not fall in either of the two categories shown previously. In which case, we give up and print out a message that we do not know.

The *for* Loop

The past few shells were great for handling a small number of arguments, but what if you have to process many arguments at one time? In this case, you would execute a shell script several times for all the files in a list. The command to do this is called the `for` command. The syntax for this command is as follows:

```
for variable in list
do
     execute one for each item in the list until the
     list is exhausted.
done
```

The first line defines the variable. This variable is assigned a value from the list. Then all the statements between the `do` and `done` are executed. The assigned variable does not have to be a part of these statements.

For practice, count up to 10 in a shell script loop. Try the `for` command at the prompt.

Input Output

```
$ for i in 1 2 3 4 5 6 7 8 9 0
> do
>     echo $i
> done
1
2
3
4
5
5
7
8
9
0
$
```

Analysis

The `for` loop created the variable `i` and assigned a number to `i` from the list of numbers from `1` to `10`. The shell executed the `echo` statement for each assignment of `i`. The shell printed all the numbers out one by one on each line until all the items in the list were used up.

I indent the statements between the `do` and `done` statements for readability purposes only. The shell will remove the first tab from the `echo` statement before parsing it. When in doubt, indent the code to your taste.

Next, try a shell script to print each filename passed to it. The shell script will be as shown in fs1.

Input
Output

```
$ cat fs1
#
# This shell script will print all the arguments
# passed to it one at a time
#
echo "$# arguments in all"
ctr=0
for i in $*
do
   ctr='expr $ctr + 1'
   echo $ctr " " $i
done


$ fs1 n*
10 arguments in all
1   n
2   n1
3   n2
4   n3
5   n4
6   name1
7   name2
8   name3
9   newkorn.asc
10   numlines
$ cat n4
line 1
line n2
line n3
line 1
line n2
line n3
line 1
$ fs1 'cat n1'
12 arguments in all
1   line
2   1
3   line
4   n2
5   line
6   n3
7   line
8   1
9   line
10   n2
11   line
12   n3
```

Analysis The first command with `n*` as its argument printed all the filenames starting with the letter `n`.

In the second command, `cat n1`, produced one line with two words. The script showed two arguments. This is because by the time the arguments get to the script, the new lines are removed, and as far as the script is concerned, the entire file is one long line with each word separated by one white space.

The `for` loop executes each set of commands in a subshell by itself. The shortcut for processing in a `for` loop for all the arguments passed to a shell is to leave out the keyword `in`. So the previous shell script could also be written as `echo "$# arguments in all"`. The `for` construct would look like this:

```
for i
do
Ctr = 'expr $ctr + 1'
echo $ctr " " $i
done
```

You can nest loops within loops. The following shell commands are shown as a means of printing numbers 1 through 30.

The `for` loop for the `i` command is nested within the `j for` loop. The shell script `freq` is executed 30 times in the previous example.

Remember not to use the same variable twice in any of the nested loops. This will not cause you to loop forever, but it will make the code unreadable. This works because each command in between the `do` and `done` is executed by a subshell. (See Day 7.) Consider the following bad example:

```
$ cat freq
echo "$# arguments in all"
ctr=0
for i in $*
do
   ctr='expr $ctr + 1'
   echo $ctr " " $i
done


$ for j in 1 2 3
> do
> for i in 0 1 2 3 4 5 6 7 8 9
>   do
>    echo $j$i
>    freq
>   done
> done
```

Input
Output

```
$ cat bad
#
# Not a good idea
#
for i in A B C
do
#
#    outer loop, "outer" i
#
          echo $i

     for i in 1 2 3
     do
#
#    inner loop , "inner" i
#
      echo $i

     done
done
$ bad
A
1
2
3
B
1
2
3
C
1
2
3
```

Analysis

The value of `i` in the inner loop is in a subshell and is independent of the value of `i` in the outer `for` loop. Therefore, even though the inner `i` is set to `1`, `2`, and `3`, the outer `i` remains at `A`, `B`, and `C` for each invocation.

Note: On Day 7, I promised you a shell script to create a `shar` archive from multiple files. Here is the script:

```
#!/bin/sh
#
#Usage: mkshar sharname file1 file2 ...
#
sharname = $1

echo "# to restore type: sh$1" > $sharname
shift
```

```
for i in $*
do
     echo "extracting $i >> $sharname
     echo "cat >$i << \END_OF_DATA" >> $sharname
     cat $i >> $sharname
     echo "END_OF_DATA" >> $sharname
done
```

To create a `shar` archive of all `*.c` files, you would use

```
$ mkshar cfileArch *.c
```

DO / **DON'T**

DO remember that each command in a `for` loop is executed by the subshell and any variables declared between the `do` and the `done` is local to the `do/done` pair. Such variables are undefined after the loop is finished.

DON'T use the same variable in a `for` loop and its nested `for` loop. It's not very readable code, even if it does work.

The *continue* Statement

There are times when you may not want to process all the files in a `for` loop if the file does not match certain criteria. For example, given a directory listing, you might want to run a script in all the files in that directory but not run it on any of its subdirectories. This is where you would want to continue on to the next item in the `for` loop.

Input/Output

```
$ cat testscript
#
# The shortcut for processing all the arguments
#
for thisFile
do

     if [ -d "$thisFile" ]
     then
          echo "Skipping directory $thisFile"
          continue
     fi
```

```
          if [ ! -r "$thisFile " ]
          then
               echo "Skipping $thisFile"
               continue
          fi

          # run your command

          yourScript $thisFile

     done
```

Analysis

The `continue` statement will cause the next item in the passed argument list to be processed without ending the loop. You could just as easily have made this into a set of `if-then-else-fi` statements, or even one statement without the warning message:

```
if [ ! -r "$thisFile "  -o  -d "$thisFile" ]
```

Sometimes it's easier to set up multiple test conditions to see if you must continue instead of using one test condition. You have to decide which solution is best for the task at hand.

Background Processing

To put the entire `for` loop in the background, put an ampersand at the end of the `done` statement:

```
for i
do
     ...
     ...
done &
```

All standard error messages can be redirected as well. To do this, put `2>errors` at the end of the `done` statement:

```
for i
do
     ...
     ...
done 2>errors
```

Loops are not restricted to one line if you use the semicolons to separate the components:

```
$ for i in 1 2 3 4 ; do ; echo $i ; done
```

With UNIX tools, you can come up with several ways of doing the same thing. This is where your experience and judgment will guide you in finding the best solution to your specific problem.

The *while* Loop

The `while` continues to loop until a condition is not true. The syntax is as follows:

```
while condition1
do
     command1
     command2
     ...
done
```

The shell executes the `condition1` command and then tests the exit code to see if it's `0`. If a `0` value is returned, the shell executes all the commands between the `do` and `done`. Then it checks the value returned from `condition1`. The process is repeated until the return code from `condition1` is false. (See Figure 9.3.)

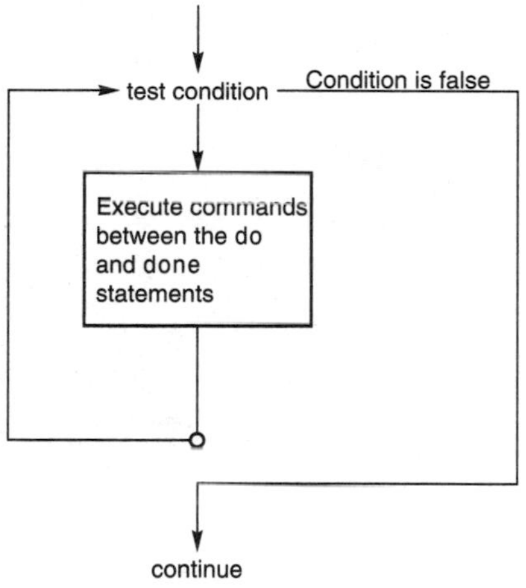

Figure 9.3. *A* `while` *construct.*

To count to 10 using a `while` loop, you can use the following script.

Input
Output

```
$ cat testWhile1
#
# set i to 1
#
i=1

while [ "$i" -le 10 ]
do
     echo $i
```

```
    i='expr $i + 1'
done
```

Analysis

In this loop, i is set (initialized) to 1 at the start of the loop. While i is less than or equal to 10, the echo and expr statements are executed. The expr statement increments the value of i by 1.

Note one important difference between this while loop and the for loop: the while loop continues until a condition is satisfied (and could possibly run forever), but a for loop processes a known list of items.

To process all the arguments to a shell script, use the following code.

Input/Output

```
$ cat testWhile2
#
# Print all the passed arguments
#
echo "$# arguments in all"
while [ $# -gt 0 ]
do
      echo $i
      shift
done
```

Analysis

In this shell script, you are checking to see if there are at least one or more arguments to process. If $# is greater than 0, this condition is true.

The number of arguments ($#) is decremented by the shift command. You continue to shift until all the arguments have been processed. When the last argument is processed, $# will be equal to 0 and the while condition will cause the while loop to stop.

The *until* Command

The until command is the inverse of the while loop. The until loop stops if the condition is non-zero, whereas the while loop stops if the condition returns zero. (See Figure 9.4.) The syntax is shown here:

```
until condition1 is not true
do
     command1
     command2
     ...
done
```

This loop is useful when waiting for a condition to occur. For example, if you want to wait for a user to log in to the system, you can set up a background process to periodically check it. The catch is knowing how long to wait. For this you can use the sleep command to check every 60 seconds.

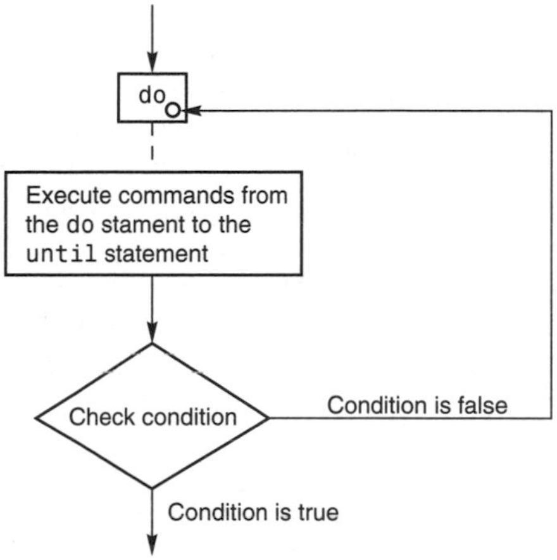

Figure 9.4. *The* `until` *loop construct.*

Input
Output

```
$ cat fs1
#
# Wait for a user to log in.
#
if [ "$#" -ne 1 ]
then
     echo "Usage: $0 username"
     exit 1
fi

lookfor=$1


until who ¦ grep "^$lookfor " > /dev/null
do
     sleep 60
done

echo "$lookfor has logged on... "


$ lookforuser hira  &
[322]
$
$ ls      (do other stuff )
..
```

Analysis The first thing the script does is confirm the existence of a username. If it cannot find a username, it bails out with an error message. Note the use of `$0` as the filename for the usage message.

The script then goes into a loop until the `grep` search for the username returns true. When that event occurs, the shell drops out of the loop and prints out the login message.

The script is run in the background. If you ran it in the foreground, you would be forced to wait until user `hira` actually logs into the system. By putting the process in the background, you are freeing your terminal to do other things.

Note: The `sleep n` command is used to wait for a known number of seconds. At the end of the interval, the shell starts up where it left off.

Breaking Out of Loops

The loops discussed so far end only when the loop condition is tested and met at the start of the loop. What if you have to break out of a loop from somewhere in the middle? In that event, you would use the `break` command.

Therefore, a forever `while` loop such as the following:

```
# The : is the command that always returns true
while :
do
     ...
     if [ some Condition ]
     then
          break;
     fi
done
```

will cause the shell to execute the statement after the `done` statement when the `some Condition` test is true. If the `done` statement is the last statement in a script (or interactively via the shell), the shell will return a prompt.

The `break` command will break out of the inner-most loop if several `while` loops are nested:

```
while :
do
     until false
     do
          if [ -z "$badMessage" ]
```

```
            then
                  break 2
            fi
      done
done
```

The `break 2` command will break out of both the `while` and `until` loop. This gets two levels deep in loops.

Note how the : always returns true, whereas the `until` loop used the built-in variable `false`.

The *getopts* Command

This command is designed to be executed in a loop and gets the options passed to a shell script. Each time through the loop, `getopts` examines the input variable with a list of valid options. If it finds a variable that matches an option, it assigns it to a variable. The syntax for this command is as follows:

```
getopts   optionsList variable
```

Options to a script are of the form `-OptionLetter`. The following are valid options:

```
-n
-t 6
-n -t 6
-t 6 -n
```

The following are not valid options:

`-t6`	No space between `t` and `6`
`-tn`	Not good enough
`-6`	Not a valid option
`-n 6`	`n` may or may not require an option

You use the `getopts` command in a `while` loop to parse the input arguments. As an example, modify the shell script that watched for a user to take both the number of seconds and the username as an argument. The time option is to be specified with a `-t` option. Otherwise, the time will default to 60 seconds.

Input/Output

```
$ cat whothere
#!/bin/sh
# ----------------------
# Wait for a user to log in.
# ----------------------

if [ "$#" -lt 1 ]
then
     echo "Usage: $0 username [-t] seconds"
```

```
     exit 1
fi

# ----------------------
# default to 60 seconds
# ----------------------
tot=60
while getopts t:q: opt
do
     case "$opt"
     in
          t)    tot="$OPTARG";
                echo  I will check every "$tot" seconds;;
          q)     a1="$OPTARG"
                 echo "This is -q's parameter $a1";;
          \?)    echo "Usage: $0 username [-t seconds]";;
     esac
done

#
# Now the OPTIND variable contains the number of arguments
# processed.
#
shcount='expr $OPTIND - 1'
shift $shcount
lookfor=$1

echo I will look for "$lookfor"

#
# now wait forever
#
until who ¦ grep "^$lookfor " > /dev/null
do
     sleep $tot
done

echo "$lookfor has logged on... "
```

Analysis The `getopts` command in this command has some special features. The colon after the `t` option is an indicator that the `t` option requires an additional variable as a parameter. If the `t` option does not require the additional parameter, do not specify the colon. Because you have another option, `q`, which requires another parameter, you used the string `t:q:` to specify the parameters to each option.

The `OPTARG` variable is a special variable that is set to the value following the option for the `:`. In the case of the `-t` option, `OPTARG` is set to the value following `t`.

The `OPTIND` variable is incremented to count the number of options and their parameters processed via the `getopts` command. `OPTIND` is a number counted from `1` up. Thus, the arguments are shifted to the script by `OPTIND` to get to the username. If no valid arguments were specified, `OPTIND` would be set to `1`, in which case the arguments would not be shifted at all and you would get the username immediately as `$1`.

Summary

Today, you were introduced to the testing and looping commands in the shell. You also learned how to use these features to get options and arguments to commands from a shell script using a standard command called `getopts`. When you use looping commands, you can process many repetitive tasks very quickly and efficiently, on many files at once.

- The `if` conditional test can check for strings and numeric comparison, as well as for the existence and type of a file or directory.
- The `[ ]` is a shortcut for the `test` command. The `test` command is usually built into the shell itself, but may also reside as a binary.
- The `else-if` clause is combined to form the `elif`.
- The `case` statement is a powerful means of selecting a value from a list of choices. You can use regular expressions to match the variable you are looking for.
- The shortcut for processing all the arguments in a `for` loop is to leave out the `in` keyword.
- The `(` and `)` parentheses in test conditions have to be escaped with a backslash.
- The `for` command processes a known number of arguments in a loop. The `while` and `until` commands run until a condition is false or true, respectively.
- The `break` command will break you out of one level of a loop. The `break n` command will break you out of *n* levels of loops.
- The ampersand at the end of a `done` statement will put the entire `for` loop in the background.
- The `sleep n` command causes your shell to wait *n* seconds.
- The `getopts` command is used to process the incoming options and arguments within a `while` loop and a `case` statement. This command provides a standard mechanism for processing shell arguments.

UNIX Commands Learned Today

- `for`
- `while`

- ☐ `until`
- ☐ `sleep`
- ☐ `getopts`

What's Next?

In the next few days, you will build further on the `getopts` and `case` commands to handle data and actually build an application to handle a rolodex file. This application will provide examples of how to read values from the command line into variables.

Q&A

Q What's the shortcut for processing all the arguments to a command line? What about arguments that can be preceded by hyphens?

A You can use the `for var` command to process each option as it's entered at the command line. Or, if you want to use generic UNIX options preceded with a dash (`-`), you can use the `getopts` command.

Q What's the best way to process script arguments? Why?

A The `getopts` method is probably the best way to process arguments because it's a standard for most UNIX shell commands.

Q Can a `case` statement also be written as an `if-then-else-fi`?

A Yes. Generally, they are interchangeable. It just takes practice to know which will be better suited to what you want to do. Ten levels of `elif` statements are not quite as readable as one `case` statement. However, for one test or two, it's easier and simpler to use the `if` statement.

Workshop

The Workshop provides quiz questions to help you solidify your understanding of the material covered. Some Workshop sections of this book also contain exercises to provide you with experience in using what you've learned. Try to understand the quiz and exercise answers before continuing on to the next chapter. Answers are provided in Appendix D, "Answers."

Quiz

1. What are the differences between a `for`, `while`, and `until` loop?
2. How do you send a `for` loop to the background? What about its output to `/dev/null`?
3. How can you compare two strings that have blanks on either side of them?
4. If you have a long string of filenames, how can you quickly determine whether a variable exists in the list?

Exercises

1. Write a shell script to execute a shell script 27 times, without having to type the numbers 1 through 9 on one line.
2. Modify the previous shell script to break out of the second shell script if the `timesNine` script returns false.
3. If the `for` loop can be written on one line, can you run the `while` statement on one line? How?
4. Write a shell script to periodically count the number of users logged in to the system. Send the number of minutes at which to check as a parameter. (Hint: modify the script that checks for a user login.)
5. Modify the `reg1` script to process more than one argument and print each variable that it processes.

10

WEEK 2

User Interface

Today you will build up an application using all the tools you have learned about so far. The application will be a `todo` list manager. Tomorrow you will formalize this application by using more tools while you write another application for an office desktop. Today you will learn the following:

- How to interact with the user
- How to use the `read` command
- How to use files and defaults in shell scripts
- How to use assignments in shell variables

By the end of the day you will have a fully functional `todo` list manager. This application will be menu-driven and will show you how to use all of the concepts just mentioned.

Interacting with the User

Up until now, you have simply been reading the command line to a script when you wanted to get input. This is definitely not going to work if you are to create interactive shell scripts, because you have to be able to read into variables from the prompt. To do this you have to use the `read` command.

```
read [variable1] [variable2] ... [variableN]
```

The square brackets indicate that more than one variable may be specified to this command. The text you type in will be broken into words, which will be assigned to all the variables one at a time. Any extra words left over will be assigned to the last variable (`variableN`).

For example, if you specified only one variable to the `read` command, `read` will assign the entire line as the value to the variable one line from the input and assign the entire line to `name`.

Input Output

```
$ cat ch10s1
echo "What is your name?"
read name
echo "Hello $name, I am so happy to meet you"
$ ch10s1
What is your name?
This is a test
echo "Hello This is a test, I am so happy to meet you"
```

Analysis

The entire line was assigned to this variable. Now try to assign the values to two variables and type in a whole line.

Input Output

```
$ cat ch11s2
echo "What are your first, last and middle names?"
read fname lname mname
echo "First Name: $fname"
echo "Last  Name: $lname"
echo "Middle Name: $mname"
$ ch11s2
What are your first, last and middle names?
Kamran Husain Bilal
First Name: Kamran
Last  Name: Husain
Middle Name: Bilal
$ ch11s2
What are your first, last and middle names?
Who wants to know
First Name: who
Last  Name: wants
Middle Name: to know
```

Analysis

Note how the last variable was assigned a value of `to know` (the extra text in input).

See how you can use this new command and the previously learned information to create an application to manage your todo list.

Working with a Sample Application

The specifications for this list manager are kept simple because they are meant as an example only. However, the concepts presented here will be very useful for you when you create other scripts. Naturally, you can add your own specifications to this skeletal specification if you want to customize this example to make this into a utility you use daily.

Begin with what you want this application to do and what problem it's trying to solve for you. If you are like me, you can have several items to do in a month and would like to track the progress of the more important ones. Rather than leave notes all over the place, I have decided to store them in my UNIX account directory, where I can use them as things develop.

Here are some of the requirements for this application:

- ☐ A one-line description of the task. I have limited each to one line for simplicity.
- ☐ The priority (0-9) as a digit, with 0 as the lowest priority and 9 as the most important.

- Status (p for pending, d for done, i for impossible). You can expand this list with your own specifications.
- Date due. This is kept in a *YYYYMMDD* format.

> **Note:** The *YYYY* is for the year, *MM* is for the month, and *DD* is for the day of the month. This format makes it easy to sort by time because years change less frequently than months, which in turn occur less frequently than days. For example, 19940702 will be the second day of July in 1994 and will be earlier than 20040512 (May 12th, 2004). To avoid any problems at the turn of the century, use the four-digit year instead of two digits. (If you used two digits and used 00 to indicate the year 2000, it would be interpreted as preceding 94.)
>
> This problem is not unique. In fact, there is old code today that relies on two-digit years and is expected to break when the year 2000 rolls around. If you are thinking about working on old banking software, this is your chance to make it!

For storing the list of items, I chose a simple text format so that I can edit the file when I want to. The format on each line is

```
<priority> <status> <duedate> <task>
```

Write this as a menu-driven shell script that will let you add items to the list, sort them by due date or priority, and list all the items. To edit my list of items, I like to use my `vi` editor, but you are free to choose the editor of your choice.

Writing a Menu-Driven Shell Script

Write the menu for this application. See the following code lines for an example of this.

Input Output

```
$ nl todo1

#
# todo1: The first pass at creating the menu for the
#     todo list manager
#
while :
do
echo "
     TODO MANAGER
```

Input Output

```
9             ------------
10
11            Change [F]ile
12            [A]dd Item
13            sort items by [D]ate
14            sort items by [P]riority
15            [E]dit the list
16            [L]ist sorted items
17            E[X]it
18            Enter Selection:"
19      read response
20      case $response in
21            f|F) echo "File functions here"
22                 ;;
23            a|A) echo "Add functions here"
24                 ;;
25            d|D) echo "Sort by Date"
26                 ;;
27            p|P) echo "Sort by Priority"
28                 ;;
29            e|E) echo "Edit the list"
30                 ;;
31            l|L) echo "Lising the TODO list as of `date`"
32                 ;;
33            x|X) echo "Bye"
34                 exit 0
35                 ;;
36
37            *)
38                 echo "Please Enter a selection shown in [ ]";
39                 ;;
40            esac
41      done
```

Analysis

This `todo1` script is written in two parts. The first part presents a menu to the user (lines 7 through 18), and the second part reads the user selection back and acts on it (lines 19 through 40).

Both parts reside within a continuous `while` loop. You exit from the shell script when you type an **X** or **x** at the response.

When you run the shell script, it will produce the menu and ask you for a response. Look at the following example.

Input Output

```
$ todo1

                TODO MANAGER
                  ------------

             Change [F]ile
             [A]dd Item
             sort items by [D]ate
             sort items by [P]riority
             [E]dit the list
```

Input
Output

```
                [L]ist sorted items
                E[X]it
                Enter Selection:
A
Add functions here


                     TODO MANAGER
                     ------------

                Change [F]ile
                [A]dd Item
                sort items by [D]ate
                sort items by [P]riority
                [E]dit the list
                [L]ist sorted items
                E[X]it
                Enter Selection:
X
Bye
$
```

Analysis

The shell script worked as you expected. Now add some functionality behind each case statement and work with a file. The first thing you'll do today is work with a file to store all the data in it. Use the default file called `items` in the `HOME` directory, where you know the file will be available. Of course, you should have the liberty to change to another list too, which is why you have the `[F]` option on the menu.

Add the following lines in the `todo` shell script to ensure that the `items` file exists. Place these lines before the `while` statement.

```
if [ ! -f $HOME/items ]
then
     echo "Creating the items file"
     touch $HOME/items
fi

datafile=$HOME/items
```

The condition **datafile** first tests to see if the file `items` does exist in my `HOME` directory. If `items` does not exist, the script will create an empty file for me. The second line sets the `dataflle` variable to this file.

I am now guaranteed that this file will always exist while I am running this script. Now run this script to create the file and confirm that the file is there.

Input Output

```
$ ls $HOME /items
ls: /home/kamran/items: No such file or directory
$ todo

                         TODO MANAGER
                           ------------

                    Change [F]ile
                    [A]dd Item
                    sort items by [D]ate
                    sort items by [P]riority
                    [E]dit the list
                    [L]ist sorted items
                    Enter Selection:
X
Bye
$
$ ls $HOME/items
/home/kamran/items
```

Analysis

Next, add some code in order to add items to this file. Remember that you want to append the items in the file one line at a time. Each line will have the following items, in this order:

```
<priority> <status> <duedate> <task>
```

You will add the following lines to the part of the shell script that adds items to the list of `items` file:

Input Output

```
echo -e "Enter task priority:\c"
read priority
echo -e "Enter status [p d i]:\c"
read tstat
echo -e "Enter due date [YYYYMMDD]:\c"
read duedate
echo -e "Enter Task:"
read tasktodo

echo $priority $tstat $duedate $tasktodo >> $datafile
```

Analysis

These lines ask the user for the required items for the `todo` file entry. The first line asks for the priority of the task and then waits for input from the user.

Note: Note the use of the `-e` option on the `echo` command. This option enables the `\c` to ignore any trailing newlines. You may or may not need it in your shell.

The following is a partial list of special escapable options to the `echo` command.

\a Alert (bell)
\b Backspace
\c Suppress trailing newline
\f Form feed (new page)
\n New line (line feed)
\r Carriage return
\t Tab
\\ Another \
\nnn Explicit ASCII code for a character in octal

Therefore, the command

```
echo "Wake up ! \a"
```

should ring a bell on your terminal. If this does not work, try the command with the -e option.

```
echo -e "Wake up ! \a"
```

Run this script to see whether your additions work.

Input Output

```
$ todo

                TODO MANAGER
                  -----------

           Change [F]ile
           [A]dd Item
           sort items by [D]ate
           sort items by [P]riority
           [E]dit the list
           [L]ist sorted items
           E[X]it
           Enter Selection:

A
Add functions here
Enter task priority:8
Enter status [p d i]:p
Enter due date [YYYYMMDD]:19940808
Enter Task:
I have to finish this book soon.

...
X
Bye
$ cat $HOME/items
8 p 19940808 I have to finish this book soon.
$
```

Analysis The ellipses indicate another menu and a subsequent exit. The task is now recorded in the `items` file. The `cat` command confirmed the file's existence.

Using Default Values

If, in the course of adding new items, you made the mistake of pressing Enter when the script asked for input, then you would write a blank field to that value. The first method is to use the following `if` statement to determine whether each variable is empty:

```
If [ ${priority}X = X ]
```

However, this statement gets cumbersome to type and read in a shell script. To make things easier, you can use the shortcut


```
${var=defaultValue}
```

This tells the shell to use the word `defaultValue` as the value of this statement if `var` is not set. The contents of `var` are not set. If you want to check if the value is not set, or is `NULL`, use the construct

```
${name:=default}
```

The colon option is the one you want, because if you do not type any value, you would like the variable to be assigned a `defaultValue` instead of the `NULL` value.

So, to give the default value of `5` for priority, `p` for pending, and `19940101` as the default, you would use

```
echo -e "Enter task priority: [5] \c"
read priority
echo -e "Enter status [p d i]: [p]\c"
read tstat
echo -e "Enter due date [YYYYMMDD]: [19940101]\c"
read duedate
echo -e "Enter Task:"
read tasktodo

echo ${priority=5}  ${tstat=p} ${duedate=19940101} $tasktodo >> \
$datafile
```

Now when you run this shell script you will get the following output.

Input Output

```
$ todo
...
     Enter task priority: [5] <enter>
     Enter status [p d i]: [p] <enter>
     Enter due date [YYYYMMDD]: [19940101] <enter>
     Enter Task:
Another line with defaults
...
```

```
x
$ cat $HOME/items
8 p 19940808 I have to finish this book soon.
5 p 19940101 Another line with defaults
```

Analysis

The `<enter>` is used to indicate that you have not typed anything at the prompt. The default values were assigned correctly. When you are writing shell scripts, it is very important that you provide default values for the end user to work with. This provides user-friendly shell scripts and enables the user to have fewer typing mistakes.

The Types of Assignments

There are several test and assignment statements for you to work with. The following is a list of these statements:

- `${name}` is replaced with the value of name.
- `${name-word}` is replaced with the value of `name` if it is defined; otherwise, it is replaced with the value of `word`.
- `${name:-word}` is replaced with the value of `name` if it is defined; or set to `NULL`; otherwise, it is replaced with the value of `word`.
- `${name+word}` is replaced with the value of `name` if it is defined; otherwise, it is replaced with nothing.
- `${name:+word}` is replaced with the value of `name` if it is defined or set to `NULL`; otherwise, it is replaced with nothing.
- `${name?error}` is replaced with the value of `name` if it is defined. Otherwise, the shell exits with an error message of the form `name: error`.
- `${name:?error}` is replaced with the value of `name` if it is defined or set to `NULL`. Otherwise, the shell exits with an error message of the form `name: error`.
- `${name=word}` is replaced with the value of `name` if it is defined; otherwise, name is assigned the value `word` and the expression is replaced with the value `word`.
- `${name:=word}` is replaced with the value of `name` if it is defined or set to `NULL`; otherwise, name is assigned the value `word` and the expression is replaced with the value `word`.

Using ${x} is helpful when you want to concatenate one string to another when the second string begins with a letter or digit. The following are some examples of this:

```
$ ds='$'
$ echo "Salary: $cs1000.00"          <---- wrong
$ echo "Salary: ${cs}1000.00"        <---- right
$ echo "Salary: $cs"1000.00          <---- right
```

Also, as Day 3 discussed, when creating new variables from others, you can use ${x}. The following example creates tarnation:

```
$ f1=tar
$ f2=nation
$ echo ${f1}
tar
$ echo ${f1}nation
tarnation
```

As you work with this application, you will work with these variable assignment loops and clarify them as you come across them.

Using UNIX Tools

You still need to add more functionality to this application by incorporating these features:

- Changing the default file you work with
- Invoking the editor
- Listing the items
- Sorting the file

Rather than re-create the functionality in the shell, you will use the UNIX tools already available to you—namely sort, more, and vi. Then use these tools from within the todo application.

Adding a Default File

Add the following lines to the todo script file in order to add the functionality of using a default file:

```
if [ $# -gt 1 ] then
     datafile=$1
else
     datafile=$HOME/items
fi
```

Now the script will work with the filename `todo`'s list file `$HOME/items` as the first name. Using the shortcuts you used earlier, you could just as easily specify

```
datafile=$(1-$HOME/items}
```

in one line and be done with it. The two constructs are equivalent. I prefer to use the one-line version because it's concise and easier to read.

Starting an Editor

Because the data file is a text file, you can use a standard text editor on it. For example, you can add the following lines to the `case` statement.

```
e¦E) echo "Edit the list"
     $EDITOR $datafile
     ;;
```

This means that whatever your `EDITOR` variable is set to will be called to edit the datafile. Because my `EDITOR` variable is set to `vi`, the visual editor, selecting the `E` option will start the `vi` editor on this datafile. It is therefore my responsibility to ensure that the `EDITOR` variable exists before using it in this context. What if it does not exist? In that event

```
$EDITOR $datafile
```

will become just

```
$datafile
```

and your system will attempt to execute the `$datafile` itself. Therefore, add the default `EDITOR` variable as `vi` with the following line:

```
EDITOR=${EDITOR-vi}
```

This will assign the value of the `vi` to `EDITOR` if `EDITOR` does not exist or is not defined when this shell script is run.

The added benefit of this default assignment is that if you add more options to the menu that require the `EDITOR` variable, you have to make the change at one location rather than having to change the variable all over the shell script. For example, the statement `EDITOR=${EDITOR-emacs}` changes the editor from `vi` to `emacs` for all references to `$EDITOR` in the shell script. Changing the word `vi` may also unexpectedly change all references to livid, vivid, provide, and so on. This way, you can make the change once and be done with it.

DO | **DON'T**

DO assign default values to shell variables at the beginning of the script, where the user can see them immediately. Explain why you are overriding any standard shell variable value.

DON'T expect shell variables, such as `EDITOR`, to be assigned values. For example, for the `EDITOR` variable, use a default. It's easier to make any future changes on this one variable than to globally change a word in a script file.

DO use the `${word-value}` whenever possible. It's easier to read than an equivalent `if-then-fi` statement.

Listing a File

To list a file, you will use the sample shortcut, which uses a standard UNIX utility to view `items`. You can use the `more` command to view `items`, but if you have a command called `less` it is better to use that instead. The pun "less is better than more" applies here, because the `less` command offers more functionality than the `more` command. (For example, you can scroll backwards with the `less` command, but you cannot do so with the `more` command.)

As before, you will assign the value `less` to the `MORE` variable if `MORE` is not already defined. Use the statement:

```
MORE=${MORE-less}
```

In the `case` statement you will add the following lines:

```
1|L) echo "Listing the TODO list as of `date`"
     $MORE $datafile
     ;;
```

This will print a header with the present date.

What if you wanted to change the listings to include the line numbers for all subsequent locations? Similar to what you learned with the `EDITOR` variable, you could change the `MORE` command setting to

```
MORE=${MORE-more}
```

if the `less` command does not exist on your machine.

Sorting by Date and Priority

The todo list is currently being printed in the order that it's being appended to, with no regard to the time or priority. At the beginning of the day, you should look at the most important item(s) on the list. Use the following list.

Input/Output

```
$ cat $HOME/items
8 p 19940808 I have to finish this book soon.
5 p 19940415 File taxes
1 p 19940101 Pay your bills
9 p 19940721 Get anniversary present
8 p 19940705 Respond back to irate customers
8 p 19940709 Get parts to manufacturing
0 d 19940621 Remove A/P Items from Stafford Account
3 p 19940912 Return home lobotomy kit
6 p 19950101 Send apology letters after new year party
6 p 19950103 Post bail for Company President
6 p 19941015 Assign project to Smith
2 p 19941031 Send Check to IRS
4 d 19940311 Remove A/P Items from Stafford Account
7 d 19940711 Send FAX to JT Brown about manuals
```

One of the options you have to support is to sort *by priority*. You can do this with the `sort -r` command (because you want to see priority 9 before 0) and this will sort on the first field per line. Try using `sort -r` at the command line first.

Input/Output

```
$ sort -r $HOME/items
9 p 19940721 Get anniversary present
8 p 19940808 I have to finish this book soon.
8 p 19940709 Get parts to manufacturing
8 p 19940705 Respond back to irate customers
7 d 19940711 Send FAX to JT Brown about manuals
6 p 19950103 Post bail for Company President
6 p 19950101 Send apology letters after new year party
6 p 19941015 Assign project to Smith
5 p 19940415 File taxes
4 d 19940311 Remove A/P Items from Stafford Account
3 p 19940912 Return home lobotomy kit
2 p 19941031 Send Check to IRS
1 p 19940101 Pay your bills
0 d 19940621 Remove A/P Items from Stafford Account
```

Analysis

This did sort the file by priority. Now add it to the case statement:

```
p|P) echo "Todo list by priority `date`"
     sort -r $datafile | $MORE
     ;;
```

Note that you should pass this through the `MORE` command in case the number of lines is greater than one screenful.

What about sorting by date? The dates are shown in numerical order, as described earlier, to ensure that 1994 is less than the year 2000 and above, years are sorted before months, and months are sorted before days. To sort by date, you have to know how to get to the date in the line.

Each line to be sorted consists of fields separated by fields. To get to the date in each line you have to go to the third field per line. To rephrase this in an expression for the `sort` command, you have to skip the first two fields, then sort up to the end of the third field. To put this in the syntax that `sort` would understand you have to use the options `POS1` and `POS2` in the command:

```
$ sort +POS1 -POS2 filename
```

Therefore, to get to just the third field, you would use `+2` and `-3`. The `+2` skips two fields and the `-3` stops the `sort` key after the end of the third field.

To illustrate this, try the commands sort `-3 $HOME/items` and `sort +2 $HOME/items`. See the following example.

Input Output

```
$ sort -3 $HOME/items
Try `sort --help' for more information.  (...did not work at all...)
$ sort +2 $HOME/items
1 p 19940101 Pay your bills
4 d 19940311 Remove A/P Items from Stafford Account
5 p 19940415 File taxes
0 d 19940621 Remove A/P Items from Stafford Account
8 p 19940705 Respond back to irate customers
8 p 19940709 Get parts to manufacturing
7 d 19940711 Send FAX to JT Brown about manuals
9 p 19940721 Get anniversary present
8 p 19940808 I have to finish this book soon.
3 p 19940912 Return home lobotomy kit
6 p 19941015 Assign project to Smith
2 p 19941031 Send Check to IRS
6 p 19950101 Send apology letters after new year party
6 p 19950103 Post bail for Company President
$
$ sort +2 -3 $HOME/items
1 p 19940101 Pay your bills
4 d 19940311 Remove A/P Items from Stafford Account
5 p 19940415 File taxes
0 d 19940621 Remove A/P Items from Stafford Account
8 p 19940705 Respond back to irate customers
8 p 19940709 Get parts to manufacturing
7 d 19940711 Send FAX to JT Brown about manuals
9 p 19940721 Get anniversary present
8 p 19940808 I have to finish this book soon.
3 p 19940912 Return home lobotomy kit
6 p 19941015 Assign project to Smith
2 p 19941031 Send Check to IRS
6 p 19950101 Send apology letters after new year party
6 p 19950103 Post bail for Company President
```

Analysis

The first command did not work. Therefore, you cannot try the `-POS2` option without the `+POS1` option.

The second command sorted on lines beginning at field 3 but included the rest of the line. This is not exactly what you wanted.

Ah, the third try got you what you wanted. The dates are in order now. Confirm this by looking at the third column of the output.

Okay, so go ahead and add this to the case statement, which will handle the `sort by date` command. This section will look like the following:

```
d¦D) echo "Sort by Date"
     sort +2 -3 $datafile ¦ $MORE
     ;;
```

Complete Listing of the *todo* List Manager

The application as it stands now is more or less complete as you wanted it in the beginning. Obviously, there are a lot of nice things that you can add to this as you go along, but step back and view the entire shell script in its entirety to get a grasp of what the shell script looks like. I have added comments and line numbers to highlight the important sections.

```
#!/bin/sh
###############################################################
##
#                   Kamran Husain
#
# todo: A task list manager for personal use only.
#
# Use at your own risk, copy and modify freely, just credit the
# author with the idea. No warranty of any sort is implied.
#
#
###############################################################
##

#
###############################################################
##
#    Set your required defaults.
#
###############################################################
##
EDITOR=${EDITOR-vi}
MORE=${MORE-less}

#
###############################################################
##
#    Check if the user specified a filename to work with
```

```
#
####################################################################
##
datafile=${1-$HOME/items}

#
####################################################################
##
# For debug: uncomment these lines
# echo $datafile
# echo $EDITOR
# echo $MORE
#
####################################################################
##

#
####################################################################
##
#
# Create the file if it does not exist.
#
#
####################################################################
##
if [ ! -f $datafile ]
then
     echo "Creating the items file"
     touch $HOME/items
fi

#
####################################################################
##
#    Now process the commands in a while loop.
#         First present the menu
#
####################################################################
##
while :
do
echo "

     TODO MANAGER
     ------------

     Change [F]ile
     [A]dd Item
     sort items by [D]ate
     sort items by [P]riority
     [E]dit the list
     [L]ist sorted items
     E[X]it

     Enter Selection: (F, A, D, P, E, L, X ):"

read response
```

```
#
####################################################################
##
# Parse the response
#
####################################################################
##

case $response in

     f¦F) echo "File functions here"
          ;;
     a¦A) echo "Add functions here"

     #
     #  Ask the user about the item.
     #
          echo -e "Enter task priority: [5] \c"
          read priority
          echo -e "Enter status [p d i]: [p]\c"
          read tstat
          echo -e "Enter due date [YYYYMMDD]: [19940101]\c"
          read duedate
          echo -e "Enter Task:"
          read tasktodo

     # ######################################
     # Now write the data to end of the file
     # ######################################
echo ${priority:=5}  ${tstat:=p} ${duedate:=19940101} $tasktodo
>> $datafile


          ;;
     d¦D) echo "Sort by Date"
          sort +2 -3 $datafile ¦ $MORE
          ;;
     p¦P) echo "Todo list by priority `date`"
          sort -r $datafile ¦ $MORE
          ;;
     e¦E) echo "Edit the list"
          $EDITOR $datafile
          ;;
     l¦L) echo "Lising the TODO list as of `date`"
          $MORE $datafile
          ;;
     x¦X) echo "Bye"
          exit 0
          ;;

     *)
          echo "Please Enter a selection shown in [ ] ";
          ;;
     esac
done
############### end of shell script ################
```

Automating the List

The last item you have to do is to remind yourself what to do today when you log in. This cannot be done with the application, but can be done as part of your `.profile` script. In the `.profile` script, you have to determine whether the date of an item matches that of today's date; then you should print this line out. To do this you would need to do the following:

- Determine today's date in the *YYYYMMDD* format.
- Search for this date in the `$HOME/items` file.
- Print all items, with the highest priority first.

To get today's date in the YYYYMMDD format, you can use the date command's format option:

```
$ date    +'%Y%m%d'
19940711
```

where `%Y` gives the year with century, `%m` gives the month, and `%d` gives the day of the month. The + and single quotes give you the format in the `date` command syntax. (Do a `man date` command for the complete list of options to the `date` command.)

Next, take this output and pass it to the `grep` command for use in searching the `$HOME/items` file for any matches.

```
$ grep `date +'%Y%m%d'` $HOME/items
7 d 19940711 Send FAX to JT Brown about manuals
```

Now you can add this line with the `grep` command to your `.profile` file, and it will tell you automatically what items need to be done today. The catch to using this method is that it will only work with the items in the `$HOME/items` file.

UNIX Commands Learned Today

- `read`
- `sort`
- `less`

Summary

Today's material introduced you to reading shell variables and assigning default values. It also introduced you to some additional features of the `sort` and `read` commands.

- The `read` statement is used to read from the keyboard into variables. Words from the line are assigned one each to the `read` command's arguments. The last variable gets the rest of the line. If there are more variables than words, the extra variables are assigned a `NULL` value.
- You can assign default values to variables when you test them.
- The `-e` option to the `echo` command is sometimes required to enable the parsing of the special options following the backslash.
- The output from the `date` command can be formatted to print various formats.
- The `sort` command can be used to sort on field numbers on a per-line basis using `POS1` and `POS2`.
- The `case` statement makes multiple options easier to handle, especially when you are working with an interactive menu shell script.

What's Next?

Tomorrow you will add to today's application by giving it the sort and search capabilities using other UNIX tools. Also, you will add the capability to remove lines from the file, search for tasks by keyword, and work with signals, traps, and functions.

Q&A

Q Can I read a complete line into a shell variable?

A Yes, just specify the variable by itself at the `read` command.

Q What's wrong with the following script? What happens when you run it, and why?

```
echo "Hello"
read  $a $b $c $d
echo  $a $b $c $d
```

A The `read` command should be of the form:

```
read a b c d
```

The erroneous `$` in front of the variable causes the shell to read into the variable specified by the value of `a b c` and `d` rather than `a b c` or `d` themselves. If these are not defined at this point, you will be assigning a `NULL` variable. Consequently, nothing will be printed out.

Q Currently the `p|P` and other cases force the response to be one character long. Why doesn't the string `priority` work where `p` does?

A The regular expression `p|P` implies either `p` or `P` and nothing else. If you want to use regular expressions to catch the first `p` or `P` on a new line, use `^P"|"^p` or `^p*|P*`.

Workshop

The Workshop provides quiz questions to help you solidify your understanding of the material covered. Some Workshop sections of this book also contain exercises to provide you with experience in using what you've learned. Try to understand the quiz and exercise answers before continuing on to the next chapter. Answers are provided in Appendix D, "Answers."

Quiz

1. What happens if you do not specify any variable at the read prompt?
2. What's the result of the last `echo` command in these commands? (The colon forces the execution of the `${ }` construct.)

```
$ feet=
$ : ${feet:=Two}
$ echo $feet
Two
$ : ${feet:=Two}
$ echo $feet
$-----------
```

3. What does the following command do in a shell script?

```
${datafile:?"FILE NOT FOUND"}
```

4. What is the end result of the following command?

```
echo ${EDITOR:-/usr/bin/vi} ${datafile:-${defaultFile:+todolist}}
```

Exercises

1. Write a shell script that tests and prints out the names of all the files in a directory that are executable. Do not print any other file or directory names. If there are subdirectories, go down recursively.

   How would you change this script to not go down recursively?

   How can you make a shell script accept its argument list to the `ls` command from the command line?

2. Add the capability to work with comments in the `todo` data file. All comments should begin with a `#` and a white space at the start of a line. (To make life easier, do not consider a `#` in the middle of a line as a comment.)

3. Think of other features you would like to add to this application and come up with ways to do so. For instance, create a numbered list of all the output options or change the exit X option to include a Q for quit option.

4. Enable sorting by pending, impossible, or done in the `todo` manager. (Hint: use the `+POS1` and `-POS2` options to the `sort` command.)

5. Think of ways to remove items from the `todo` list. (Hint: use the `grep -v` option to search for and print items that do not match a specification.)

6. Add the option to print the `todo` data file to the printer with the `lp` command. Add today's date to the beginning of the file.

   (Hint: See Days 6 and 7 on subshells and sending print jobs in one blob to the printer.)

11

WEEK 2

UNIX Tools in Shell Scripts

Today, you'll learn about more UNIX tools that you can use in your shell scripts. These tools are powerful enough to build more complicated applications and handle error situations. At the end of the day, you will add a few more features to the `todo` list manager you created yesterday.

Today's lesson offers a grab bag of UNIX utilities for you to work with. The information given here will show you how to do the following:

- Use the `cut` and `paste` commands to extract data from a line at a time
- Use the `sed` command to search and replace specific strings
- Handle interrupts via the use of traps
- Use the desktop calculator within UNIX

The *cut* Command

The `cut` command is used to extract columns of data out of text streams.

For example, the `who` command gives a listing of all the users, their terminals, and login times and dates. If you wanted to get only the user names from this command, you would use the `cut` command to cut the output of the `who` command.

The syntax to the `cut` command is as follows:

```
$ cut -cchars file
```

where `chars` specifies the number and range of characters to cut out.

The `-c5` option cuts the fifth character from the input, `-c1,2,3,4` cuts the first four characters of the input string. A range of characters also can be specified with the -. For example, the range of the first four characters is specified via the `-c1-4` option:

To get the first eight characters of each output from the `who` command, you would do the following:

```
$ who | cut -c1-8
geoff
kamran
carol
```

The rest of the output on each line is not printed.

If you want to get all the characters from the start of a line to the end of the line, do not specify the last part of the `cut` command. To get all but the user name from the `who` command, use the `-c9-` option:

```
$ who | cut -c9-
 tty1     May  7 10:16
 tty1     May  8 12:16
 tty2     May  8 12:23
```

Sometimes your input is not cleanly aligned on column boundaries. Consider the system file /etc/passwd. To look at the contents of this file, use the cat command. This is short for concatenate.

Input Output

```
$ cat /etc/passwd
root:*:0:0:root:/root:/bin/bash
bin:*:1:1:bin:/bin:
daemon:*:2:2:daemon:/sbin:
adm:*:3:4:adm:/var/adm:
lp:*:4:7:lp:/var/spool/lpd:
sync:*:5:0:sync:/sbin:/bin/sync
shutdown:*:6:0:shutdown:/sbin:/sbin/shutdown
halt:*:7:0:halt:/sbin:/sbin/halt
mail:*:8:12:mail:/var/spool/mail:
news:*:9:13:news:/var/spool/news:
uucp:*:10:14:uucp:/var/spool/uucp:
operator:*:11:0:operator:/root:/bin/bash
games:*:12:100:games:/usr/games:
man:*:13:15:man:/usr/man:
postmaster:*:14:12:postmaster:/var/spool/mail:/bin/bash
ftp:*:404:1::/home/ftp:/bin/bash
```

Analysis How do you cut some specific information from this file? In this case, the -c option cannot be used. However, all the fields are separated by colons. Look at the man pages for the cut command, and you'll see that the -d option specifies a delimiter and -f specifies the fields you want to look at.

To get the user name and description of all the users listed in the password file, /etc/passwd, use the following command.

Input Output

```
$ cut -d: -f1,5  /etc/passwd
root:root
bin:bin
daemon:daemon
adm:adm
lp:lp
sync:sync
shutdown:shutdown
halt:halt
mail:mail
news:news
uucp:uucp
operator:operator
games:games
man:man
postmaster:postmaster
ftp:
```

Analysis If you want to keep track of the names and phones numbers of your favorite pizza parlors in a file, for example, start with a sample phone book called pizza. The numbers are listed here:

```
Mr. Gatti      265-3419
Dominoes      256-1000
Pizza Hut     345-2174
Dirty's     980-2314
Gut Wrench     980-3184
Pizza Inn     265-2213
Slimey's    266-9876
Jorges' Pub     265-1987
```

In this file, you separate the pizza name from its phone number with tabs.

```
$ cut -c1-10 pizza
```

will not yield the expected results. Instead, you will get this:

```
Mr. Gatti
Dominoes    2
Pizza Hut
Dirty's     9
Gut Wrench
Pizza Inn
Slimey's    2
Jorges' Pu
```

However, if you were to use

```
$ cut -f1 pizza
```

you would get this result:

```
Mr. Gatti
Dominoes
Pizza Hut
Dirty's
Gut Wrench
Pizza Inn
Slimey's
Jorges' Pub
```

Note that you did not have to specify the `-d` option because the `cut` command assumes the tab field to be the default separator for all fields.

The *paste* Command

The `paste` command is the inverse of the `cut` command. The syntax for `paste` is as follows:

```
paste files
```

In this command, all corresponding lines from data files are pasted together to form one line. For example, if you have two files, `parlor` and `phone`, you would do the following:

Input Output

```
$ cat parlor
Mr. Gatti
Dominoes
Pizza Hut
Dirty's
Gut Wrench
Pizza Inn
Slimey's
Jorges' Pub
$
$ cat phone
265-3419
256-1000
345-2174
980-2314
980-3184
265-2213
266-9876
265-1987
$
$ paste phone parlor
265-3419        Mr. Gatti
256-1000        Dominoes
345-2174        Pizza Hut
980-2314        Dirty's
980-3184        Gut Wrench
265-2213        Pizza Inn
266-9876        Slimey's
265-1987        Jorges' Pub
$
$ paste parlor phone
Mr. Gatti       265-3419
Dominoes        256-1000
Pizza Hut       345-2174
Dirty's         980-3184
Gut Wrench      265-2213
Pizza Inn       266-9876
Slimey's        265-1987
Jorges' Pub     265-1934
$
```

Analysis

The `paste` command takes the first line from each file and pastes the lines into one contiguous line. In the first `paste` command, the phone number is placed in front of the name. In the second command, the name is placed before the phone number.

The output from the `paste` command can either be redirected to a file or piped to another program. See the following code for an example of this:

```
$ paste parlor phone ¦ sort
Mr. Gatti      265-3419
Dominoes       256-1000
Pizza Hut      345-2174
Dirty's        980-3184
Gut Wrench     265-2213
Pizza Inn      266-9876
Slimey's       265-1987
Jorges' Pub    265-1934
Billy Bobs     499-8347
Cici           498-8666
```

DO	DON'T

DO use the same number of lines per file when you are pasting. If the number of lines is not the same, you can mix unrelated items together.

DO sort the input files to a `paste` command to ensure that all lines in the files match.

DON'T use the `-c` option if your data is not aligned on columns; instead, use the `-f` option to get items by fields.

Using *sed*

Now you can create files with the `paste` command. The number of operations that you can do so far are still somewhat limited. To use the advanced text manipulation features, you can use another program called the stream editor, `sed`. This is a noninteractive editor and is most often used within shell scripts.

You will pass the text through `sed` one line at a time. `sed` will then apply one or more commands to these lines and pass the output to the standard output. This operation on the stream of input through itself gives `sed` the name of stream editor. Unlike an interactive editor, which will copy the entire file to a buffer and let you move around and move it, `sed` will not give you any choices once you have invoked it. So why use it?

- `sed` is great for doing simple changes on several files. Rather than invoke an editor on every file, make the change and repeat for the next file; you can make the change in a script file once and use `sed` to make the changes on all the files in one command.
- `sed` has the same powerful regular expression capabilities as `egrep`.

- sed can take its editing commands from the command line or a script (called sed script). By using scripts, you can save the actual editing commands for later use on other files.
- For large text files, it's sometimes easier to save sed changes rather than different files themselves; this also saves disk space. It's faster to send small changes than to send the whole file across a slow communications interface.

The syntax for a sed command is as follows:

```
sed -e commands -f sed_script -n filenames ...
```

where -e causes the commands to be entered from the command line. -f asks sed to read the sed_script file for its commands. A sed_script is simply a text file containing the sed commands. By default, each line of input is echoed after the sed commands are applied to it. The -n option suppresses this echo.

For example, in the parlor file you could rename all Pizza instances with the word Burger by using the command. I've added a couple entries in the file to make it longer. I will use this now-modified file for illustrating the substitution command through the end of the chapter. The four lines that are different are as follows:

```
Pizz Hut - West
Pizza Hut - East
Billy Bobs
Cici
```

Input Output

```
$ cat parlor
Mr. Gatti
Dominoes
Pizza Hut - West
Pizza Hut - East
Dirty's
Gut Wrench
Pizza Inn
Slimey's
Jorges' Pub
Billy Bobs
Cici
$ sed -e "s/Pizza/Burger/" parlor
Mr. Gatti
Dominoes
Burger Hut - West
Burger Hut - East
Dirty's
Gut Wrench
Burger Inn
Slimey's
Jorges' Pub
Billy Bobs
Cici
```

Analysis The construct `s/Pizza/Burger/` replaced the word `Pizza`, on every line, with the word `Burger`. Note how the substitution was interpreted for the `sed` command.

The syntax for the substitution command is as follows:

```
s/original string/new string/
```

sed Commands and Ranges

There is no concept of current line in `sed`. All `sed` commands operate on each line in all the input files. All line numbers in `sed` are absolute.

If you want the `sed` command to operate only on a certain number of lines, you must specify the line numbers in the following syntax:

```
starting,ending command
```

where *`starting`* is the line number to begin when the first line in a file is line 1, and *`ending`* is an absolute line number of the last line on which this command will apply. If you do not specify any line numbers, the *`command`* is applied to all the lines in the file.

If you specify one line number only (that is, without the , and n), the *`command`* works only on the one line number. The first line in the file is 1, and the last line in the file can be specified by a `$`.

To apply this substitution command only on the first four lines of the file, you would do the following.

Input Output

```
$ sed -e "1,4s/Pizza/Burger/" parlor
Mr. Gatti
Dominoes
Burger Hut - West
Burger Hut - East
Dirty's
Gut Wrench
Pizza Inn
Slimey's
Jorges' Pub
Billy Bobs
Cici
```

Analysis Note how the `Pizza` in `Pizza Inn` was not modified since it was not in the range of lines specified for the substitution command.

Similarly, to apply the changes on all but the first four lines in the file, you would do the following:

```
$ sed -e "5,$s/Pizza/Burger/" parlor
```

where the `$` specifies the last line in the file.

`sed` enables you to print text in the input file with the `p` command. You can specify a range of commands on which to operate by using the syntax *m,np*. For example, the command

```
$ sed -e 1,8p chap11
```

will print the first eight lines of the file `chap11`. It will also print out every line in the file too, unless the `-n` option is specified. If it is, the command will look like this:

```
$ sed -n -e 1,8p chap11
```

You do not have to specify the range via the use of numbers only. You also can specify the starting regular expressions to specify the starting and ending line numbers. Here's a sample file:

Input Output

```
$ cat sedtext1

  Towards the end of his life, though living in Paris, Isaac Albiez
  had become the leading spanish composer of his day. His final
  masterpiece, Iberia, was instantly recognized by his generation of
  Spanish composers as showing them a way out of the impasse
  pictoralism.

  After Manuelle de Falla and Joaquin Turinna had their celebrated
  encounter with Albeinz in Oct. 1907 Turinna wrote that "Music is an
  art and not a diversion for the frivolity of women and dissipation of
  men. ..."

  Falla's Night in the Garden of Spain was conceived in Paris before
  his return to Spain and the outbreak of war in 1917.


$
$ sed -e "/Towards/,/picto/" sedtext1

  Towards the end of his life, though living in Paris, Isaac Albiez
  Towards the end of his life, though living in Paris, Isaac Albiez
  had become the leading Spanish composer of his day. His final
  had become the leading Spanish composer of his day. His final
  masterpiece, Iberia, was instantly recognized by his generation of
  masterpiece, Iberia, was instantly recognized by his generation of
  Spanish composers as showing them a way out of the impasse
  Spanish composers as showing them a way out of the impasse
  pictoralism.
  pictoralism.

  After Manuelle de Falla and Joaquin Turinna had their celebrated
  encounter with Albeiz in Oct. 1907 Turinna wrote that "Music is an
  art and not a diversion for the frivolity of women and dissipation of
  men. ..."
```

Input Output

```
  Falla's Night in the Garden of Spain was conceived in Paris before
  his return to Spain and the outbreak of war in 1917.
$
$ sed -n -e "/Towards/,/picto/p" sedtext1
  Towards the end of his life, though living in Paris, Isaac Albiez
  had become the leading Spanish composer of his day. His final
  masterpiece, Iberia, was instantly recognized by his generation of
  Spanish composers as showing them a way out of the impasse
  pictoralism.
$
$
```

Analysis

The first command correctly specified the range of the first paragraph with the starting line containing the word `Toward` and the ending line containing the word `picto`. However, it also printed out all the lines in the file, including the ones requested. The result is not what you wanted, so you used the `-n` option and you got only the lines you requested.

Using Script Files

When you use `sed` with the `-f` option, you can specify a file that contains the editing commands. This is helpful when you have to make several changes to several files and want to keep track of them for later use. It also keeps you from having to type several `sed` commands on one command line.

You can create a `sed` script with a standard text editor, or from the command line, by redirecting the output from the input to a file or by using the `diff` command with the `--ed` option. You learned the first two methods earlier when creating shell scripts. The `diff` command option is a bit new and deserves some attention.

The `diff` option `--ed` (`-e` on some old versions of `diff`) will create a series of `ed` commands that can generally be used with `sed`. This method is not guaranteed, and I have occasionally seen some editing commands that did not work with `sed`. I do not have examples to show you because all the examples in this book work with `sed`. However, you have been warned. Also, sometimes the editing command output will exceed the length of the original file itself, so you have to decide whether to save the new file as is or the changes themselves.

Here's an example from earlier. You know that `sed1` has more lines than `sed2`.

Input Output

```
$ sed -e "/Towards/,/picto/p" sedtext1 > sed1
$ sed -n -e "/Towards/,/picto/p" sedtext1 > sed2
$ diff sed1 sed2
1d0
<
3,4d1
<   Towards the end of his life, though living in Paris, Isaac Albiez
```

Input/Output

```
<   had become the leading spanish composer of his day. His final
7d3
<   masterpiece, Iberia, was instantly recognized by his generation of
9,10d4
<   Spanish composers as showing them a way out of the impasse
<   pictoralism.
12,20d5
<
<   After Manuelle de Falla and Joaquin Turinna had their celebrated
<   encounter with Albeinz in Oct. 1907 Turinna wrote that "Music is an
<   art and not a diversion for the frivolity of women and dissipation of
<   men. ..."
<
<   Falla's Night in the Garden of Spain was conceived in Paris before
<   his return to spain and the outbreak of war in 1917.
<
$ diff --ed  sed1 sed2
12,20d
9,10d
7d
3,4d
1d
$
```


Analysis

The output from the `diff` command produces some deletion commands. If these were applied to the `sed1` file, do you get `sed2`? Let's try it.

Input/Output

```
$ diff --ed  sed1 sed2 > sedmake
$ sed -f sedmake sed1  > sed4
$ diff sed2 sed4
$
```

Analysis

There isn't a difference between the edited versions of `sed2` and `sed4`. This confirms that the changes requested from the `diff` command when applied to `sed1` did create a file identical to `sed2`. If there would have been a difference between `sed2`'s and `sed4`'s contents, you could have seen output from the `$diff sed2 sed4` commands.

DO	DON'T

DO use the `diff -e` or `--ed` option to create a `sed` script for keeping track of changes to large files.

DO track the size and complexity of changes via the `diff` command, because it may sometimes be better to save the new file rather than the changes.

DON'T use `sed` on files that are not text files.

> **Note:** Over the years, I used `sed` for substitution only. I also have found `grep` to be much faster in finding specific strings. When I want to delete specific lines from files, I use the `head` and `tail` commands to get faster responses. Still, the `sed` command has been indispensable when I have had to send configuration changes for C source files on overseas calls. The time required to send the changes were minimal compared to what they would have been if I had sent all the files.

Other *sed* Commands

The `sed` command to delete text into input files streams is `d`. To delete lines use the command:

```
m,nd
```

where lines `m` through `n` from the input stream will be deleted. As before, you can specify `m` and `n` via regular expressions.

Input
Output

```
$ sed -e "4,9d" sedtext1

  Towards the end of his life, though living in Paris, Isaac Albiez
  had become the leading spanish composer of his day. His final
  art and not a diversion for the frivolity of women and dissipation of
  men. ..."

         Falla's Night in the Garden of Spain was conceived in Paris before
  his return to spain and the outbreak of war in 1917.
```

Analysis

Lines 4 through 9 are missing. To add lines to a file, use the `a` (append) command in a script. The `a` command appends lines to every line that it can be applied to. To append a blank line to every line in a file, use the script:

```
$ cat blankline
a\



$
```

The `\` is used to escape a new line. Since no line number was specified before the `a` command, the new line will be applied to all the lines in the input file. To add four lines to the first line of a file, use the command:

```
$
1a\
\
```

```
\
\
$
```

Note how each new line in the line to be appended is escaped with a `\` to keep it all together as one append command.

This introduction to the `sed` command is by no means complete. The command is very powerful when used with shell scripts to track changes to files, modify files interactively, or even create shell scripts. When used with shell scripts and filename expansion, this command is used to apply several changes to several files with one shell script.

For example, if you want to change all occurrences of the word `Widget` to `Gadget` in all the files in your current directory, you would use the following shell script.

Input Output

```
$ cat sample
tempfile=/tmp/$0$$
for i
do
    sed -e "s/Widget/Gadget/g" $i > $tempfile
    mv $tempfile $i
done
rm $tempfile   2>$1  >/dev/null
```

Analysis

The shell script applies the substitution to all filenames specified at the prompt.

The `/tmp` directory is a location in the UNIX system that's reserved for temporary files. In some installations, it's usually located on a disk with the quickest access time because `/tmp` is very heavily used as a temporary placeholder for files in large operations. The `/tmp` directory is writeable by everybody.

The `$$` is the process id of the shell script being executed. The `/tmp/$0$$` creates a file called `cx152` for a shell script `cx` running with a process id of 152. (`tempfile` is assigned this value. `$tempfile` is used to store the output from the `sed` command and input for the `mv` command.)

After the shell script is finished, you have to be sure to remove this file from the `/tmp` directory. Otherwise, on the next invocation of this shell script, you will create a new file because you will have a new process id for your shell script. This could create a whole lot of files in the temp space in a hurry. If the `mv $tempfile $i` command doesn't remove the `$template`, you'll still remove the temporary file with the `rm` command. Any error messages resulting from trying to remove a `$temp` file that does not exist will be sent to `/dev/null`.

Note: On some systems, the access time on the `/tmp` directory may actually be faster than the drive you are on. Ask your system administrator how your system is set up.

Also, you can stop the for loop in mid-execution with a Ctrl+c, at which point the temp file will not be removed. This is where you have to trap the Ctrl+c commands and other assorted errors.

The *trap* Commands

The `trap` command executes a command when it receives a signal from the system. A process can receive a signal (also known as an interrupt) from a hardware source, terminal input, or a kill call from another process. When a process receives such a signal, it takes an action based on the signal. The default action is to take `SIG_DFL`, which causes the process to terminate. The syntax for the `trap` command is as follows:

```
trap ['command'] [n ... ]
```

If `command` is omitted, `trap` resets traps for the given signals to the original default values. If the command is a null string, the shell script will ignore that trap. If *n* is 0, the shell will execute this command on exit. If you want to execute more than one command, you can separate the commands with semicolons.

The most common signals you will have to deal with are signals `1`, `2`, and `9`. These refer to a hang-up, an interrupt from the user, or a kill signal from another process, respectively. If you are interested in knowing the rest of the signals, look at the file `/usr/include/signal.h` for a list of the signals on your system. The statement

```
trap 'rm $tempfile 2>/dev/null; exit' 1 2 9
```

will remove the temporary file, send all spurious error messages to the `/dev/null` file, and then exit for all signals `1`, `2`, and `9`.

All signals can be trapped to perform a default action when received except signal `9` (also known as `SIGKILL`), which is not stoppable. For a demo of this type of trapping, run the following script.

```
$ cat nostop
trap 'echo "OUCH!"' 1 2
read c
while [ c != "END" ]
do
        sleep 1
        read c
done
$ nostop  (now hit a few ctrl-c's)
OUCH!
OUCH!
OUCH!
OUCH!
OUCH!
END
$
```

The `OUCH!` string is printed on every Ctrl+c (when the `trap` command is executed). You do not have an `exit` statement in the `trap` command. The program continues where it left off after the signal is over.

DO | **DON'T**

DO put an `exit` command in the `trap` command sequence. If you do not, the shell script will continue where it was interrupted.

DON'T put the `trap` statement within a loop. The most effective place to place the statement is before the loop.

```
trap ...
...
while :
...
```

This is an absolute statement because you may want to trap only in small portions of a long `for` loop.

DO put single quotes around the command. It's better to be safe than sorry.

DO use `' '` as the null command when you want to ignore interrupts.

DON'T try to ignore signal `9`. UNIX will not let you.

More Functions for Your Desktop

Now that you have some more information to work with, you can add a few more features to the `todo` script (from Day 10). These features are as follows:

- Remove some `todo` items
- Print strings based on a string pattern
- Add a calculator and a calendar

Removing *todo* Items

The first thing to do before removing any items is to identify them. Since this is a text file, it's easier to number the lines in the input file and then delete the lines you want.

To display the lines in the file, you can use the `nl` command piped into the `more` command. Then ask for the line numbers to delete, create a `sed` script, and do the delete.

First, add the option to the menu.

```
>  [R]emove items
```

Then add the commands to list the file with the `nl` command.

Input Output

```
# ########################################################
#    Remove items.
# ########################################################
     r¦R)
         nl $datafile ¦ $MORE
         echo "Enter the line number:"
         read delLine
         echo "$delLine is the line to delete"
         echo "${delLine}d" > temp
         sed -f temp $datafile > temp2
         mv temp2 $datafile
         ;;
```

Analysis

This displays the entire list of items in the datafile and numbers them for you to review. Since you will be in the `$MORE` command, you will have to press the `q` command to get out.

The script will then ask you for the line number to delete. It will accept the line number and create a `sed` script for the line to delete. The `sed` script then removes the offending line from the script file.

Finally, the script moves the newly edited file (`temp2`) back on to the `$datafile`.

Note how the shell script created the sed script and executed it for you. The actions taken in this program are somewhat simplistic because they are used as examples only. However, they can show you the power of shell programming. You can create your own shell or other scripts from within shell scripts, and execute them.

Another application function you might want to add is to search for strings. What if you wanted to search for items that you have to send to someone? With a small list, you would also like to be able to create a report.

To create a shell script that will take the input and print it out, you would find the text in the form of a regular expression and then apply grep -e (or egrep) on it, as follows:

```
#    ##################################################
#     Search for item.
# ####################################################
    s¦S)
        echo "Enter the string to search for:"
        read findStr
        grep -e "$findStr" ¦ $MORE
        ;;
```

The possibilities are endless in this mode. You can see how to add more and more functions to your desktop shell script. As you see more functions that you want, you can add them into your shell scripts. In UNIX, the power comes from being able to put together the tools in a shell script.

Other UNIX Utilities

Another utility you can add to your menu program is a calendar utility. The UNIX cal command is handy when you want to add get some dates out to work with. The format for using the cal command is as follows:

```
cal month year.
```

The month is a digit between 1 and 12. To get the current month, use the options %m and %Y to the date command, and then get the current calendar. If you do not specify a month or year, you will be presented with the current month's calendar. The option to add this would be coded as follows:

```
case C¦c)
    cal
    ;;
```

Because using the cal command requires an integer input to the month command, it's a bit clumsy to use. To make the calendar accept strings as month names, you could write a new shell script called calx, which does accept month names.

Input
Output

```
$ cat calx
#!/bin/sh
if [ $# -lt 1 ]
then
    echo "Usage: $0 month [year]"
    exit 1;
fi
if [ $# -eq 1 ]
then
    year=`date +%Y`
fi

if [ $# -eq 2 ]
then
    year=$2
fi

case $1 in
    [Jj]an*)    month=1 ;;
    [Ff]eb*)    month=2 ;;
    [Mm]ar*)    month=3 ;;
    [Aa]pr*)    month=4 ;;
    [Mm]ay*)    month=5 ;;
    [Jj]un*)    month=6 ;;
    [Jj]ul*)    month=7 ;;
    [Aa]ug*)    month=8 ;;
    [Ss]ep*)    month=9 ;;
    [Oo]ct*)    month=10 ;;
    [Nn]ov*)    month=11 ;;
    [Dd]ec*)    month=12 ;;
    *)
        echo "Enter a correct month please"
        exit 2
        ;;
esac

#
# Do the cal command.
#
cal  $month $year
$
$
$
$ calx Aug 1994
    August 1994
 S  M Tu  W Th  F  S
    1  2  3  4  5  6
 7  8  9 10 11 12 13
14 15 16 17 18 19 20
21 22 23 24 25 26 27
28 29 30 31
```

Analysis

The `cal` command accepts the month input as a string.

Summary

You learned the following items today:

- The shell can create `sed` scripts so that you can create special functions.
- You can create your shell wrappers around standard UNIX commands as you did today with the `calx` command.
- You can intercept signals such as hang-ups and Ctrl+c with the `trap` command. The only signal you cannot stop is signal `9`, which the `SIGKILL` requests.
- Signal `9` cannot be ignored or stopped. This is the last resort method of stopping a process that is ignoring all other signals.
- The UNIX calendar utility is a good tool to have in any desktop.

todo Application Listing

Following is the complete listing for the `todo` application. This includes all the topics covered in yesterday's and today's text.

```
######################################################################
#                 Kamran Husain
#
# todo: A task list manager for personal use only.
#
# Use at your own risk, copy and modify freely, just credit the
# author with the idea. No warranty of any sort is implied.
#
# ####################################################################
# Set up default trap
# ####################################################################
trap "Type X to exit;" 1 2


# ####################################################################
#    Set your required defaults.
# ####################################################################
EDITOR=${EDITOR-vi}
MORE=${MORE-less}
# ####################################################################
#     Check if the user specified a filename to work with
# ####################################################################
datafile=${1-$HOME/items}

# ####################################################################
# For debug: uncomment these lines
# echo $datafile
# echo $EDITOR
```

```
# echo $MORE
# ######################################################################

# ######################################################################
#
# Create the file if it does not exist.
#
# ######################################################################
if [ ! -f $datafile ]
then
     echo "Creating the items file"
     touch $HOME/items
fi

# ######################################################################
#    Now process the commands in a while loop.
#        First present the menu
# ######################################################################
while :
do
echo "

    TODO MANAGER
    ------------

    Change [F]ile              [A]dd Item
    sort items by [D]ate or       by [P]riority
    [R]emove items                   [E]dit the list
    [L]ist sorted items         [S]earch for item
    [C]alender                    [k]alkulator

    E[X]it

    Enter Selection:"

read response

# ######################################################################
# Parse the response
# ######################################################################

case $response in

    f¦F) echo "File functions here"
        ;;

# ########################################################
#    Search for item.
# ########################################################
    s¦S)
        echo "Enter the string to search for:"
        read findStr
        grep -e "$findStr" ¦ $MORE
        ;;
```

```
# ########################################################
#    Remove items.
# ########################################################
    r¦R)
        nl $datafile ¦ $MORE
        echo "Enter the line number:"
        read delLine
        echo "$delLine is the line to delete"
        echo "${delLine}d" > temp
        sed -f temp $datafile > temp2
        # mv temp2 $datafile
        ;;

# ########################################################
#    Display this month's calendar
# ########################################################
    c¦C)
        cal `date +%m` `date +%Y`
        ;;


# ########################################################
#    Fire up the calculator
# ########################################################
    k¦K)
        bc
        ;;

# ########################################################
#    Fire up the calculator
# ########################################################
    a¦A)
        echo -e "Enter task priority: [5] \c"
        read priority
        echo -e "Enter status [p d i]: [p]\c"
        read tstat
        echo -e "Enter due date [YYYYMMDD]: [19940101]\c"
        read duedate
        echo -e "Enter Task:"
        read tasktodo

    # ########################################
    # Now write the data to end of the file
    # ########################################
echo ${priority:=5}  ${tstat:=p} ${duedate:=19940101} $tasktodo >> $datafile
        ;;

# ########################################################
#    Sort by date
# ########################################################
    d¦D)
        sort +2 -3 $datafile ¦ $MORE
        ;;
# ########################################################
#    Sort by priority
# ########################################################
```

```
    p¦P) echo "Todo list by priority `date`"
        sort -r $datafile ¦ $MORE
        ;;
# ########################################################
#    Edit the list
# ########################################################
    e¦E) echo "Edit the list"
        $EDITOR $datafile
        ;;
# ########################################################
#    List the file without sorting
# ########################################################
    l¦L) echo "Lising the TODO list as of `date`"
        $MORE $datafile
        ;;
# ########################################################
#    Exit
# ########################################################
    x¦X) echo "Bye"
        exit 0
        ;;

# ########################################################
#    Error handler
# ########################################################
    *)
        echo "Please Enter a selection shown in [ ] ";
        ;;
    esac
done
############### end of shell script ################
```

What's Next

Tomorrow's lesson is devoted to the most powerful of UNIX tools, called `awk`. This is a language in itself and when used with shell programs can prove to be a very effective programming tool. Tomorrow's lesson will cover this in detail by showing how to handle a phone book manager with multiline records using the `awk` command.

UNIX Tools Learned Today

- ☐ `sed` Streaming editor
- ☐ `trap` Interrupt handler
- ☐ `cal` Calendar

Q&A

Q How can I ensure that my shell script will clean up after it executes?

A The `trap` command `0` executes the command when the shell script executes. You can place other shell scripts in place of the command.

Q When is it a good time to use the `sed` editor?

A You should consider using the `sed` editor when you're working with editable files and when the changes you make are minor compared to the file you are creating. It's then more economical to save the changes than the file itself. You also would work with the `sed` editor when you want to send changes across a slow or expensive transmission medium.

Q Can the output from the `diff` command be used to re-create a new file?

A Yes. In most cases, the output from the `diff --ed` command can be used to create a new file.

Workshop

The Workshop provides quiz questions to help you solidify your understanding of the material covered. Some Workshop sections of this book also contain exercises to provide you with experience in using what you've learned. Try to understand the quiz and exercise answers before continuing on to the next chapter. Answers are provided in Appendix D, "Answers."

Quiz

1. Why is signal `9` not stoppable?
2. How do I perform multiple `sed` operations on a file when it's not clear whether the operations are mutually exclusive? (Mutually exclusive means that you cannot be trying to substitute lines you are just creating.)

Exercises

1. Write a `sed` script to add blank lines to every line in a file.
2. Write a shell script to extract the year, month, and day from the date shown in the `todo` list: `YYYYmmDD ?` year from an item in the `todo` list?

3. Add more options to the `todo` list generator to incorporate the `bc` or `dc` calculator.
4. Make the calendar option in the `todo` application accept a month and year as input, and then default to the current month.

   Hint: Use `calx` as a starting point.

WEEK 2

12

awk

Today's text deals with a powerful, flexible, and easy-to-use programming tool in the UNIX environment—awk. In UNIX, awk is perhaps one of the most important tools you will use, and so it deserves a day to itself.

The programs here illustrate only some of the power available to you in awk. Today's lesson is not meant to be a complete tutorial in awk, nor can it encompass all the features in awk. I cover only the basics of awk and how they would apply to shell programming in today's text.

A word of caution before you start—today's text may actually be a little confusing at first. What you will learn today, however, will be programming knowledge that will serve you well in your UNIX exploits.

After reading today's text, you should be able to decide whether to write a shell script for what you want done, or whether the task at hand requires a special awk program. These decisions will become easier with practice, so don't worry if this information seems overwhelming at first. There will be plenty of examples for you to work with and to extend for your own use.

The topics you will cover on awk are the following:

- ☐ Why learn awk?
- ☐ Syntax of awk programs
- ☐ Mathematical operations in awk
- ☐ Pattern matching
- ☐ Loop constructs
- ☐ Writing and debugging awk programs
- ☐ Writing to multiple files
- ☐ Writing an awk program to work with data
- ☐ Writing stand-alone programs that do not require an input file
- ☐ How to tie awk programs to shell scripts

Why Learn *awk*?

As you work with computers, you might work with data. To do any specialized operation with data, you will find yourself having to do a task by writing code in a specialized programming language such as C or Pascal.

Keep in mind that awk is not the cure-all for all your UNIX programming needs. For searching and printing strings, you would be better off using grep. For searching and replacing strings, you might consider sed. For simple math operations, expr will suffice, and you can always rely on bc or dc calculators. So where does awk fit in?

awk is a special programming language that enables you to create small, efficient programs that can handle complex tasks such as tracking a database, calculating mortgage annuities, and so on. To one degree or another, it combines all the features of grep, bc, dc, and expr because it is capable of handling regular expressions and doing mathematical operations. In addition, it has most of the specialized printing capabilities of the C programming language's printf statement. The awk program adds more features to these UNIX tools by handling arrays, field splitting, and data storage mechanisms. When combined with the powerful file handling capabilities of the shell, awk is sure to become a very valuable tool in your set of UNIX tools. awk is named after its inventors, Ano, Weinberger, and Kernighan.

Note: If you do not know the C language, do not despair. I will cover its relevant features today. As you learn about the awk language, you will learn a little about the C syntax for statements.

If you would like to know more about the C programming language, consider getting Sams Publishing's *Teach Yourself C in 21 Days*, by Peter Aitken and Bradley Jones.

Also, awk programs are usually very short and generally easily modifiable. When awk programs are one or two lines long, it's easy to try different combinations very quickly, just as it is with shell scripts. You can think of awk as an entity between a script and compiled binary program.

How Does *awk* Work?

An awk program scans input files and splits the input file into fields automatically. It then checks a set of patterns and determines whether a pattern is matched with these fields. If the combination of fields match, awk performs the action on it. The patterns and actions are placed together either at the command line or in a file (referred to as an awk script).

Every input line is tested against all of the patterns in an awk program. The patterns could be string comparisons, mathematical operations, or a combination of both. For each pattern that matches (that is, for each where the result of the comparison is true), the corresponding action between the braces { } is executed. Actions can span several lines of code or can be as short as one line.

If no action is specified for a pattern, each line that matches a pattern is printed. If no pattern is specified for an action, that action is taken for all lines in the file.

Running *awk* Programs

The awk program is run from the command line and is typed between the single quotes. The syntax for the entire command is this:

```
awk "program" inputfiles...
```

The program is generally between single quotes to prevent any regular expressions from being mangled by the shell.

If the program is in a text file to save you a lot of typing, then

```
awk -f progfile inputfiles...
```

will tell awk to take all its commands from the file *progfile*. When dealing with programs of two or more lines, you should consider using a program file to keep your awk script. Even though this adds to the clutter of files on your disk, the most frequently used awk programs would always be at your disposal.

For multiline programs, it's best to work with an awk program file. This prevents errors by preventing a lot of typing at the command line. You *can*, however, type multiline programs at the command line. The following example is of a program that shows a header printed at the top of a file and the number of lines read at the end. Be aware that on some systems, awk is called gawk (GNN awk) or nawk (new awk).

```
$ awk 'BEGIN { print "This is a new file"; }
>      END   { print "Lines read ", NR; }'
```

I will cover the details of this program later. This example simply shows how a multiline program can be entered at the prompt.

The best place to start learning awk is with an example. Let's say that you have a file of the stock prices (at the close of a day) in a text file. The three columns are your stock's ticker symbol, its closing price, and the number of shares you own. You would like to know what each stock in your portfolio is worth. I show the data and the program first and then explain the program.

Input/Output

```
$ cat q1
KTWC      9.875     4000
NING      11.25     1200
ITNC      60.125     104
WAOL      22.50      224
MPSI      87.00     1900
NIPP      92.00     1222
$ awk ' { print $1 "" $2 * $3 } '  q1
KTWC 39500
NING 13500
ITNC 6253
WAOL 5040
MPSI 165300
NIPP 112424
```

Analysis

The awk program is between the curly braces:

```
{ print $1 " "  $2 * $3 }
```

Notice how the program is enclosed between single quotes to prevent the dollar sign (`$`) from being interpreted by the shell.

Each input line from the file `q1` is split (by default at the whitespaces) into fields. The first field is referred to by `$1`, the second by `$2`, and so on. The entire line can be referred to by `$0`. The number of fields in the entire line is kept in a special variable `NF`.

The program uses its `print` command to print two fields—`$1` and the result from the multiplication of `$2` and `$3`. The printed fields are shown in the output of the example.

The comma (,)in the print statement causes a whitespace to be printed in the output between each field in the input to the print command. If you left out the comma, the fields would be placed immediately next to each other without any spaces between them.

Now you want to print out the values of just those stocks whose price is 60 or greater. For this output, you would have to test a pattern where `$2` (stock price) is greater than 60.

The program would be as follows:

Input/Output

```
$ awk ' $2 > 60  { print $1, "at "$2 , " is $" $2 * $3 } '  q1
ITNC at 60.125  is $6253
MPSI at 87.00  is $165300
NIPP at 92.00  is $112424
```

Analysis

This time, the program consists of two components—the match condition and the action to take. The match condition is outside the curly braces. The `$2 > 60` condition, which tests whether the price of the stock is greater than 60, is applied to each line.

12

The action component

```
{ print $1, "at "$2 , " is $" $2 * $3 }
```

prints a descriptive statement for you. This `print` statement is executed only when the stock-price check condition is true.

The action is first to print the first field, followed by the `"at "` string, followed by field `$2`, then another string `" $"`, followed by the product of `$2 * $3`.

awk Variables

By now, you have learned that variables are assigned from input lines as `$1`, `$2`, and so on, with the entire line as `$0`. The `awk` program also provides special variables for line processing. Some of these special variables are the following:

- `NR` This is the number of lines read up to now. Each line is treated like a "record" by default; hence, `NR` stands for *Number of Records.*
- `NF` This is the number of fields in the current record (or line).
- `FS` This is the field separator, by default a blank.
- `RS` This is the record separator, by default a newline.
- `ARGC` This is the count of the number of arguments to the `awk` program.
- `ARGV` This is the array (the *V* is for *vector*) of the arguments to this file. `ARGV[0]` is the program name; `ARGV[1]` is the first argument, `ARGV[2]` is the second argument, and so on. This is comparable to the arguments to a shell script.
- `FILENAME` This is the name of the current input file.

Let's look at some small `awk` programs so that you can see how to use these variables. The `nl` program is excellent for printing a line number before every line in the file. On some systems, it may not exist, however. No problem—you can write an `awk` program to do just that.

Input/Output

```
$ cat nl.awk

.....{
.....print  NR, " ", $0;
.....}
```

Input Output

```
$
$ awk -f nl.awk awk.1
1
2   Question: What is a BogoMip ?
3
4   `BogoMips' is a contraction of `Bogus MIPS'.  MIPS stands for (depending
5   who you listen to) Millions of Instructions per Second, or Meaningless
6   Indication of Processor Speed.
7
8   The number printed at boot-time is the result of a kernel timing
9   calibration, used for very short delay loops by some device drivers.
10
11   As a very approximate guide the BogoMips will be approximately:
12            386SX                  clock * 0.125 + 0.2
13            386DX                  clock * 0.20 - 0.6
14            486SX/DX               clock * 0.49 + 0.25
15            486DX2                 clock * 0.50 + 0.37
16            Pentium                24.0
17
18   If the number you're seeing is wildly lower than this you may have the
19   Turbo button or CPU speed set incorrectly, or have some kind of caching
20   problem [as described in Q6.8 `When I add more memory it slows to a
21   crawl.'.]
22
23
```

Analysis

This time, I ran the awk command with the f option to read the program from a disk file. I ran nl.awk on itself to get a line-numbered output. Notice how no qualifying search pattern was specified, so every line in the file was executed.

Now I can convert this awk program into a shell script called nl.

```
$ cat nl
-#!/bin/sh
#
# Read the input from a file for the nl.awk program
#
if [ $# -lt 1 ]
then
     echo "Usage: $0 filename ..."
     exit 1
fi

for i
do
     awk -f nl.awk $i
done
```

This shell script will be the nl script with a twist. Instead of reading from the standard input, it will always expect to read from a file.

Formatted Output

As it stands, the `nl.awk` program has a bug. It prints line numbers correctly for the first 10 lines. Then it "bumps" every line over as it prints the tens, and it bumps the lines again when it gets to hundreds, and so on. This output is definitely not as good as I would like.

I'll modify the program to print the line numbers in five columns and print a form feed after every 60 lines. A form feed is a Ctrl+l, and it shows up as `^L` on a display.

The output I am talking about is a *formatted output.* This requires the use of a powerful `awk` statement called `printf`. It has the form:

```
printf format arg1, arg2, arg3, ....
```

where *`format`* is a string containing text that will be printed verbatim, interspersed with specifications regarding how each of the values should be printed. A specification is a `%`, followed by a few characters that control the format of value. The first specification designates how `arg1` is printed, the second specification designates how `arg2` is printed, and so on.

The specifications for the `printf` statements include at least the following:

`%c`	ASCII character
`%d`	Decimal number
`%o`	Octal number
`%s`	String
`%x`	Unsigned hexadecimal number
`%f`	Signed floating-point number *`[xxx.yyyyyy]`*
`%g`	Signed exponential number *`[x.yyyyyyE{+-}zz]`*

You can specify the length of the output-formatted field with a number between the `%` and its specification. For example, a `%4d` will print the decimal number in four characters.

The precision for floating-point numbers can be specified as `%x.y`, where `x` is the total number of fields (including the decimal point) and `y` is the number of decimal places to the right of the decimal point. For example, `%7.2f` will print the floating-point number in seven characters: four digits to the left of the decimal point, one decimal point, and then two digits to the right of the decimal point.

Let's revisit the example of the new `nl` program and apply this knowledge of the `printf` function. To print each line with a five-digit number in front of it, I can use the following statement:

```
printf "%5d %s\n", NR, $0;
```

The `\n` is the specification for a new line. The `printf` statement does not print a new line for you automatically. The `%5d` will print the value of `NR` as a five-digit decimal number, and the `%s` will print the entire string `$0`.

Let's test this script.

Input Output

```
$ awk -f nl.awk awk.1
    1
    2 Question: What is a BogoMip ?
    3
    4 `BogoMips' is a contraction of `Bogus MIPS'.  MIPS stands for
      ➥(depending
    5 who you listen to) Millions of Instructions per Second, or Meaningless
    6 Indication of Processor Speed.
    7
    8 The number printed at boot-time is the result of a kernel timing
    9 calibration, used for very short delay loops by some device drivers.
   10
   11 As a very approximate guide the BogoMips will be approximately:
   12           386SX                 clock * 0.125 + 0.2
   13           386DX                 clock * 0.20 - 0.6
   14           486SX/DX              clock * 0.49 + 0.25
   15           486DX2                clock * 0.50 + 0.37
   16           Pentium               24.0
   17
   18 If the number you're seeing is wildly lower than this you may have the
   19 Turbo button or CPU speed set incorrectly, or have some kind of caching
   20 problem [as described in Q6.8 `When I add more memory it slows to a
   21 crawl.'.]
   22
   23
```

Analysis This is much better. Now, as you can see, the line numbers are formatted correctly and are not indenting the text.

BEGIN and *END*

There are times when you must do some special initialization before you start processing each statement through the `awk` pattern-matching statements. The statements in the `BEGIN` section of an `awk` program are executed before the first line of the input is processed. The statements in the `END` section are processed after the last line in the input is processed. These statements are optional.

The syntax for each command is as follows:

```
BEGIN {
     statement;
     statement;
     ...
}
```

and

```
END {
     statement;
     statement;
     ...
}
```

So, in the listing program, I can have the following awk script to print a banner page for me before I start printing.

Input Output

```
$ cat npr.awk
    1
    2 BEGIN     {
    3       printf "\n\n\n Filename: %s", FILENAME;
    4       "date " | getline thisDay;
    5       printf "\n\n\n Date: %s" , thisDay;
    6       printf "\f";
    7 }
    8
    9 {
   10       printf "%5d %s\n", NR, $0
   11 }
```

Analysis First, in the printf section, the \n prints a new line and \f prints a form feed (or new page). So the line \n\n\n will print three lines, and a \f will start a new page.

The preceding example shows several new features of awk in addition to the BEGIN and END statements. I will discuss these in detail shortly. The BEGIN section, in this case, prints out the input filename by using the %s format for the special awk variable called FILENAME.

> **Note:** This awk program is good for sending output to the printer. If you send the output to your terminal, you may have to pipe it through the more filter. Keep in mind that on some terminals a new page will clear the screen (or on some as ^L, Ctrl+l).
>
> Also, you can pipe the output from the awk command to lp. So you can use the following line:
>
> ```
> $ awk -f prog.awk datfile | lp
> ```
>
> It sends the awk-processed output to the printer command lp.

The first item in the "date" part in the example's line 4 is the shorthand for executing a shell command in a subshell. The results from the date command are then piped into a routine called getline, which reads its standard input into the variable thisDay.

The " " in the awk program is actually run as a script in a subshell and replaces the standard input with the results of the UNIX command between the quotes. Notice that this behavior of quotes in awk differs from the behavior of quotes in shells.

So, in line 4, the output from the date command is piped into the variable `thisDay` by the `getline` function, which reads its standard input into one or more variables listed as its arguments.

DO DON'T

DO initialize any variables you use in awk to zero or a null string for half-page or longer awk programs. Even though awk enables you to create and initialize variables when they are first used, it's still a good idea to explicitly declare and set the variables in the BEGIN block. This makes the code much more readable.

DO pipe the output from the "*command*" to a getline function. This is the only way you can capture the output from the command.

DON'T expect to use more than 1,023 characters per string variable. This is the most common default length.

DON'T use `getline` for output that is more than one line from "*command*". The pipe is efficient only for small programs with short, one-line outputs. For larger programs, you might want to use a shell script instead to break the output to smaller lines.

The `END` statement is very helpful when you want to do something after calculating the processing of all the input. An example would be to print the number of lines and number of pages in the input file. So, you would set two counters, `pages` and `lines`, to `0` before the first line is processed (in a `BEGIN` statement). Then, in the `END` segment, print the sum of the number of lines and pages.

Input Output

```
$ cat np2.awk

BEGIN     {

#
#     Initialize the page count to zero
#
    lines = 0;
    pages = 1;
}

```

Input Output

```
11 #
12 #     Print out the number of pages and line numbers
13 #
14 END   {
15      printf "\n *** %5d lines in %5d pages *** ", lines, pages;
16 }
17
18 {
19
20      printf "%5d %s\n", NR, $0
21      lines = lines + 1;
22 #
23 #     Print out the number of pages and line numbers
24 #
25      if ((lines % 60) == 0)
26           {
27           pages = pages + 1;
28           printf "\n [Page %5d ]\f", pages;
29           }
30 }
```

Analysis

The page banner is commented out in this example. You can "uncomment" it by removing the `#` in front of the line. The `awk` program comments work the same way as shell comments: all text from the `#` to the end of the line is ignored.

The `BEGIN` statement does the initialization of the variables `pages` and `lines` to 0. So, lines 7 and 8 are quite unnecessary, but they do provide better readability of the code. Also, because they are done at the start of the program and are done once only, they do not compromise the speed of execution in any appreciable degree.

Line 21 adds 1 to the `lines` variable as a record is read.

Then, in line 25, I check whether the remainder of `lines` divided by 60 is `0`. The `%` operator returns the remainder of the division between two integer values. So 8/2 will have a remainder of 0, but 8/5 will have a remainder of 3. This `%` operator is known as the modulu operator. If you are getting confused, don't worry; I will talk about operators in a moment.

The comparison operator is `==`, not a single `=` sign. The `==` returns a Boolean value. Unlike the `TRUE` and `FALSE` values for the shell, `TRUE` in `awk` is a non-zero value, and `FALSE` is a zero value. So, in this case, the value of `lines` divided by 60 is `TRUE` when the remainder is 0.

If this condition is true—that is, I have printed 60 lines of text—then in lines 27 and 28, I increment the `page` counter by 1 and print the page number out with a form feed and reset the line counter.

> **Note:** When you are programming in awk, it's easy to forget that comparisons in awk are exactly the opposite of how they work in shell scripts. A returned value of 0 in awk is FALSE, whereas in a shell test, 0 indicates a successful operation, generally interpreted as TRUE.
>
> Similarly, a non-zero return value in a shell test indicates that something was amiss and that the response is "not true." However, in awk, a non-zero return value is interpreted as meaning that the test returned a true value.

You can use multiple BEGIN and END statements; if you do so, they are executed in the order they are found in the program.

awk Operators

In awk, you have seen performed several comparisons that use the same operators as you saw in shell programming. A list of some of these is provided in Table 12.1.

Table 12.1. awk operators.

Operator	Meaning
a = b	Assigns *b* to *a*
a += b	Adds *b* to a, and assign the result to *a*
a -= b	Subtracts *b* from a, and assign the result to *a*
a *= b	Multiplies *b* to a, and assign the result to *a*
a /= b	Divides *b* by a, and assign the result to *a*
a %= b	Gets the remainder of *b* divided by a, then assign the result to *a*
||	Boolean OR
&&	Boolean AND
==	Equal to
!=	Not equal to
<	Less than

continues

Table 12.1. continued

Operator	Meaning
<=	Less than or equal to
>	Greater than
>=	Greater than or equal to
+ - * /	Math operators for add, subtract, multiply, divide
a ^ *b*	Exponentiates *a* to the power of *b*
++*a*	Increments *a* by one before using it
--*a*	Decrements *a* by one before using it
a++	Increments *a* by one after using it
a--	Decrements *a* by one after using it

Try some of these operators in a sample program.

Input Output

```
$ awk -f nl.awk sample.awk
     1
     2 BEGIN {
     3      i  = 10; j  = 2;
     4      printf " \n set values, i = %d, j = %d \n", i, j;
     5      printf " i++ = %d \n", i++;
     6      printf " i-- = %d \n", i--;
     7
     8      printf " \n set values, i = %d, j = %d \n", i, j;
     9      printf " --i = %d \n", --i;
    10      printf " ++i = %d \n", ++i;
    11
    12      i  = 10; j  = 2;
    13      printf " \n Reset values, i = %d, j = %d \n", i, j;
    14
    15      i += j;
    16      printf" i += j gives %d \n", i;
    17
    18      i -= j;
    19      printf" i -= j gives %d \n", i;
    20
    21      i *= j;
    22      printf" i *= j gives %d \n", i;
    23
    24      i /= j;
    25      printf" i /= j gives %d \n", i;
    26
    27      i %= j;
    28      printf" i %= j gives %d \n", i;
```

```
29
30       i  = 10; j  = 2;
31       printf " \n reset values, i = %d, j = %d \n", i, j;
32
33       i  = i ^ j;
34       printf" i ^= j gives %d \n", i;
35
36 }
$ awk -f sample.awk

 set values, i = 10, j = 2
 i++ = 10
 i-- = 11

 set values, i = 10, j = 2
 --i = 9
 ++i = 10

 Reset values, i = 10, j = 2
 i += j gives 12
 i -= j gives 10
 i *= j gives 20
 i /= j gives 10
 i %= j gives 0

 reset values, i = 10, j = 2
 i ^= j gives 100
```

Analysis Post-increment and post-decrement examples are shown in lines 5 and 6. In line 5, `i` is incremented after being used by the `printf` statement, so that a 10 is printed. In line 6, `i` is decremented after it is used in the `printf` statement.

Pre-decrement and pre-increment examples are shown in lines 9 and 10. The value of `i` is decremented and incremented before it is used in the `printf` statement.

The rest of the lines show how the operators can be used on the same variables and the result stored in the same variable.

Boolean Operators

The Boolean operators are very useful in creating combinations of patterns. The program

```
$1 >= 5 && $3 <= 10
```

will print those lines in which the first field is greater than or equal to 5 *and* the third field is less than or equal to 10. Similarly, the program

```
$1 >= 5 || $3 <= 10
```

will print those lines in which either the first field is greater than or equal to 5 *or* the third field is less than or equal to 10.

The NOT operator is the ! symbol. So,

```
!( $1 >= 5 || $3 <= 10 )
```

will print all lines *except* those lines in which either the first field is greater than or equal to 5 *or* the third field is less than or equal to 10.

More on Printing with *awk*

print is an awk action. You can use the following program to swap the first two fields of an input file:

```
{ print $2, $1  }
```

If fields are separated by commas on the print statement, they are separated by spaces on the output. If the comma is omitted, the values are concatenated together. For example, if $1 = can and $2 = not, then

```
print $1, $2 ;
```

will print can not, but

```
print $1 $2 ;
```

will print cannot.

The output fields are printed with a special awk variable OFS between each field. If you modify OFS to be something else, say a comma, you can then print a comma-delimited output that's great for spread sheets. So

```
{ OFS = ","; print NF, $1, $2, $3 }
```

will print the number of fields per line along with the first three parameters.

Assignment of Variables

In awk, depending on the value, variables can be numbers or strings. The following statements will assign to x a number and string, respectively:

```
x = 1
x = "now"
```

Strings are interpreted as numbers when an arithmetic operator exists between them. So, given the statement

```
x = "1" + "2"
```

x will be assigned a value of 3. However, an operator between double quotes will be assigned as part of a string. The statement

```
x = "1 + 2"
```

will assign a string to x.

You can concatenate strings by omitting commas in the print statements.

Pattern Matching

Another awk strength is its pattern matching. The patterns for matching can be specified as strings or as regular expressions. For example, the program

```
/atom/ { print $0; }
```

will print every line containing the word *atom.* The regular expression

```
/[aA]tom/ { print $0 }
```

will match *Atom* and *atom.*

The -y option will specify a case-insensitive search. In other words, you specify your search statement in lowercase letters only, and awk does the work of capitalizing the characters to do the search for you. This works in a manner similar to egrep.

In fact, you are allowed to use all of egrep's expressions in a search pattern. Some examples of the programs employ egrep are as follows:

Input Output

```
$ cat a1.awk
# All lines consisting only of digits
/^[0-9]+$/       { print }

$ cat a2.awk
# All lines with numbers with exactly 3 digits.
/^[0-9][0-9][0-9]$/

$ cat a2.awk
# All lines with numbers with 3 digits in a row anywhere on a line.
/[0-9][0-9][0-9]/

$ cat a3.awk
# Find all lines with a (a), (b), or (c) in the beginning
/^\([abc]\)/ { print }
```

Analysis

There are four programs shown in the preceding listing.

The first program searches for lines that have digits only. The second program searches for lines that have exactly three digits. The third program shows lines that have three-digit numbers anywhere on the line. The fourth program picks out patterns `(a)`, `(b)`, or `(c)`. Notice how the `()` are escaped in the same way as they would be in a shell program.

Loops

The `awk` program provides loop constructs similar to, but more powerful than, those of the shell. Those types of loop constructs are listed here:

- `while` loops
- `for` loops
- `break`
- `continue`

while Loops

The `while` loop continues while a condition is true. The following code example uses a `while` loop to print all the fields in a line in reverse order.

```
{
     i = 1;
     while (i <= NF) {
          printf "%s ", $(NF - i);
           i++;
     }
     printf "\n";
}
```

Notice the use of the `$(NF - i)` to print the items in reverse order.

for Loops

The `for` statement enables you to execute a statement a specified number of times. The syntax is

```
for (initialization; condition; increment)
```

The initialization statement sets up a variable, say `i = 0`. The condition tests to see whether the condition is met. If the condition is false, the loop will stop. The last increment is done at the end of every iteration and before each condition testing. The following example shows a `for` statement to reverse an entire line:

```
{

for (i = NF; i >= 1; i--)
     printf "%s ", $i;

printf "\n";
}
```

As with shell programming, you can use the `break` statement to break out of a loop and the `continue` statement to move to the top of the loop. The `exit` statement stops the `awk` program.

The *next* Command

The `next` command skips to the next record in the input file without going back to the top of the file. For example, the following code will print every odd record:

```
NR % 2 == 1 { print $0; }
```

Working with Files

In addition to writing to standard output, you also can write to another file of your choice. For example, the program

```
{ print $2 > "field2" }
```

will create a file called `field2` with all the second fields from the current file. You can even separate the input from one file into separate files, with one field for each file. For example, the program

```
{ print $1 > "field1"; print $2 > "field2" }
```

will create two files: one with the first field of the current input file and the other with the second field.

Also, for an input field separator, you can specify something other than a whitespace by changing the `IFS` variable. `IFS` stands for the input field separator.

Let's run the previous `awk` program, `{ print $1 >= "field1"; print $2 > "field2" }`, on the `/etc/passwd` file to get all the user IDs in one file and get the user names in another file. The problem is that some users in the passwd file do not have a password, so the two fields are jammed together, as on this line. For example:

```
dbarry::503:100:Dave B. Arry:/home/dbarry:/bin/bash
hira::505:100:Hira H. :/home/hira:/bin/bash
    ^^
```

This will cause me some grief with awk. So I'll separate these out with a sed script and then pipe the results through awk.

```
$ sed -e 's/:/ : /g' /etc/passwd
```

Input Output

```
$ head +6 /etc/passwd ¦ sed -e 's/:/ : /g'
root :  : 0 : 0 : root : /root : /bin/bash
bin : * : 1 : 1 : bin : /bin :
daemon : * : 2 : 2 : daemon : /sbin :
adm : * : 3 : 4 : adm : /var/adm :
lp : * : 4 : 7 : lp : /var/spool/lpd :
sync : * : 5 : 0 : sync : /sbin : /bin/sync
$
```

Analysis This code will separate the colons out into separate fields.

Next, I want to get the output from this script into two files, uid and unm. So I use the following statements:

Input Output

```
$  sed -e 's/:/ : /g' /etc/passwd ¦
>     awk '{ print $1 > "uid"; print $5 > "unm" }
$
```

Analysis The output will be sent to the respective files, uid and unm.

Handling Errors with *print* Statements

If you make an error in an awk program, the program will probably stop immediately and print an error message at the line where the error occurred.

Input Output

```
$ awk -f bad.awk datafile
awk: bad.awk:1: /$3 == 0
awk: bad.awk:1:   ^ unterminated regexp
$ cat bad.awk
/$3 == 0
     {
     printf "%5d %s\n", NR, $0;
     }
$ cat > bad.awk
/$3 == 0/
     {
     printf "%5d %s\n", NR, $0;
     }
^D
$ awk -f bad.awk datafile
... output here
```

Analysis Notice that the missing / caused awk to print an error message at about line 1. The messages of awk are somewhat hard to understand at times, but in this case awk pointed to the problem immediately.

DO DON'T

DO check that your conditions are readable without ambiguity. Use parentheses `()` to group together logical statements.

DO end each `awk` statement with a semicolon. This is not necessary if the next statement is a `}`.

DON'T forget to check that you have the same number of opening braces, parentheses, and brackets as you have closing braces, parentheses, and brackets.

You do not have to end a statement with a semicolon if the next line happens to be a closing brace `}`. I recommend that you include it anyway, however, because it makes the code readable and if you later add extra lines, you won't inadvertently forget to put the semicolon. For example, given the following code,

```
{
i = i + $3 * $3
}
```

if you add a line,

```
{
i = i + $3 * $3    ## THIS IS BAD!
j = i / 32
}
```

you must have a semicolon after the `$3`. Otherwise, you will get an error message.

Programmers call this type of error a *syntax error*. Such errors causes the program to stop without ever executing through to the end. Some errors occur only while executing—for example, dividing something by `0` or writing blank lines because of a typographical error. These are called *runtime* errors and are more difficult to catch. In my experience, the best way to catch runtime bugs in `awk` is to pepper the program with two types of statements:

- *Error-checking statements:* These include checks for `0` before a number is used as a divisor.
- *Debug `printf` statements:* These print the value of suspect variables at important stages of the program. You pipe the output to a file and then examine the file to see how things were at the time of the "crash."

Some Sample *awk* Applications

The best way to learn about awk is through practice. I have been using awk for about a decade, and to this day I am surprised by its features. After you are hooked on awk, it's hard to find other languages as useful. So for practice, let's start with some sample awk files that are small but powerful.

```
#
# Print the 10th line. Note that the default action { print }
# is not even typed here.
#
NR == 10


#
# Print the last two fields of every line.
#
{ print $(NF -1), $NF }


#
# Swap and print the first two fields in a file
#
{ print $2, $1; }

#
# Swap the first two fields then print the whole line
#
{ print t = $2; $2 = $1; $1 = t; print }


#
# Print the last line in the file
#
     { sline = $0; }
END { print sline }


#
# Print all the lines in which the input is between 80 and 100
#
($NF >= 80) && ($NF <= 100)
#
# Print the number of lines with the word shell in it.
#
/[sS]hell/      { nl = nl + 1; }
END     { print nl }


#
# Print the number of fields in the entire file.
#
```

```
     { count = count + NF ; }
END      { print count; }

#
# Print all the lines that are less than 80 characters long
#
length($0) < 80
```

Some Mathematical Operations

The program covered in this section does some statistics for you. Let's say you have the test scores for some students and you want to get the values for the following:

- The highest score
- The lowest score
- The average score

Input Output

```
$ cat scores
Billie Lord       56
Dale Carrington    68
Carl Carlock       12
Candy Walker       89
H E Konx         88
Aurora Garcia     44
Sherri Hodges      20
Gwen Foster        96
Timothy K Jackson       85
Robert Goble       22
```

Analysis

Note how the data is not in aligned columns. Some names have two fields (`Candy Walker`) and some have three (`H E Knox`). This means that I have to be able to access the data backwards; that is, the `NF` field will be the score.

DO	DON'T

DO use a `\n` to print a new line in a printf statement.

DON'T use an `\n` at the end of a print statement, because a new line is automatically printed for you by print.

DO initialize variables whenever possible. It's easier to track them that way.

Input Output

```
$ awk -f nl.awk score.awk
     1 BEGIN {
     2       maxscore = 0;
     3       minscore = 100;
     4 }
     5       {
     6       sum += $NF;
     7       if ( $NF < minscore) minscore = $NF;
     8       if ( $NF > maxscore) maxscore = $NF;
     9
    10 }
    11
    12 END  {
    13
    14       printf "\n Maximum Score = %d", maxscore;
    15       printf "\n Minimum Score = %d", minscore;
    16       printf "\n Average Score = %d", sum / NR;
    17       print;
    18 }
$ awk -f score.awk scores

 Maximum Score = 96
 Minimum Score = 12
 Average Score = 58
```

Analysis Lines 2 and 3 initialize the `maxscore` and `minscore` to absurd values. Notice that `sum` does not have to be initialized to `0`.

Line 6 sums up all the scores. Lines 7 and 8 perform a comparison to see whether the limits are reached.

Lines 14 through 17 print the results. The results are shown when the program is executed.

Sample Mortgage Amortization

The `awk` programming language can be a valuable tool for you to do some serious programming. Consider the following example, which deals with calculating how much you can save if you make accelerated payments on a loan. This example is designed for homeowners who are trying to accelerate the payoff of a loan by repaying an extra 1/12 of their monthly payment per month. You can, however, easily turn this into an analysis of another loan type.

As you examine the listing, consider these points:

- All the variables are declared and initialized at the beginning of the program. This makes it easier for you to modify the parameters you are working with.

- To output the results from an awk program, use print and printf format statements.
- Notice the use of comments, marked by the # sign, in the source file. Use comments with reason. Too many comments will clutter the code, but too few comments may not provide enough information for you to look at later.

Input Output

```
$ awk -f nl.awk amort.awk
    1 #
    2 #      This is an example of a stand-alone awk program
    3 #      that does not require an input file because it
    4 #      does everything between the BEGIN and END
    5 #      statements.
    6 #
    7 #
    8
    9
   10 BEGIN {
   11      # --------------------------------------------------
   12      # This awk program calculates the estimated savings from
   13      # making extra principal payments on a conventional loan.
   14      # --------------------------------------------------
   15      # Modify these parameters for your loan then run
   16      #     awk -f amort.awk
   17      # --------------------------------------------------
   18      rt =   6.625;         # Annual Interest Rate
   19      points = 1.00;        # including LOP
   20      loanAmt = 110000.00;  # Loan balance
   21      rolledCost = 2500.00; # Roll in any closing costs
   22      yr = 30.0;            # Years to finance for
   23      # --------------------------------------------------
   24      #      End of modifiable parameters
   25      # --------------------------------------------------
   26
   27      if (cmdRoll != 0) loanAmt += cmdRoll;
   28      if (cmdRate != 0) rt = cmdRate;
   29      if (cmdPts  >= 0) points = cmdPts;
   30
   31
   32      #
   33      #
   34      regac = 0;     # accumulated principal - regular
   35      mcsac = 0;     # accumulated principal - accelerated
   36      loanAmt += rolledCost;     # roll in amount
   37      pointAmt = loanAmt * points * 0.01;  # Add the points
   38      regpr =  loanAmt + pointAmt;     # start with principal
   39      mcspr = regpr;     # same for accelerated principal
   40      npaymts = yr * 12; # total payments over loan
   41
   42      #
   43      # Calculate the monthly payment based on canned formula
   44      # store result in regmo.
   45      #
   46      exp1 = (1 + rt/1200.00)^(yr * 12.0);
   47      regmo = (rt/1200.00)
```

```
regmo *= exp1;
regmo *= regpr
regmo /= (exp1 - 1);

#
# Make 1/12 payment extra per month. So mcsmo is
# the accelerated payments.
#
mcsmo = regmo * 13 / 12.0;
mcsmo = regmo + 100.00;

#
#
printf "\n                         Mortgage Acceleration Analysis";
printf "\n  Period of loan   = 30 years";
printf "\n  Interest         = %5.3f APR **** with %5.3f points",
➥ rt, points ;
printf "\n  Loan Amount      = $%9.2f (rolled cost $%8.2f)",
➥ loanAmt, rolledCost;
printf "\n  Money for points= $%9.2f", pointAmt;
printf "\n  AMOUNT FINANCED = $%9.2f", regpr;
printf "\n";
printf "\n  Mo. Payment(PI) = $%6.2f", regmo;
printf "    With Extra Principal (PI) = $%6.2f", mcsmo;
printf "\n  Difference in Mo. Payment(PI) = $%6.2f", mcsmo -
➥ regmo;
# printf "\n  Savings over current Mo. pmt  = $%6.2f",
➥ 1052.00 - regmo;
printf "\n";
printf "\n         Regular   %2d years    vs.    Prepayment",yr;
printf "\n Yr  Principal    Interest       Principal     Inter
➥ est";

rt = rt/1200;
yr = 0;
# -----------------------------------------------------------
# For all payments.
# -----------------------------------------------------------
for (i = 1; i <= npaymts ; i++)
{
intr = rt * regpr;
regac += intr ;
regpr += intr ;
regpr -= regmo;

#
# -----------------------------------------------------------
# If principal still exists, print its value out
# -----------------------------------------------------------
#
if (mcspr > 0)
  {
  intr = rt * mcspr;
  mcsac += intr ;
```

```
97        mcspr += intr ;
98        mcspr -= mcsmo;
99        }
100       if (i %12 == 0)
101       {
102       yr++;
103       if ((mcspr < 0) && (done == 0))
104          {
105          done = 1;
106          early = yr;
107          }
108     # -----------------------------------------------------------
109     # Uncomment the next four lines for a more detailed output
110     # -----------------------------------------------------------
111       #   printf "\n %4d   $%9.2f   $%8.2f     $%9.2f   $%8.2f",
112       #          yr, regpr, regac, mcspr,mcsac;
113       #   else
114       # printf "\n %4d   $%9.2f   $%8.2f", yr, regpr, regac;
115       }
116
117     if (((yr % 5) == 0)  && ((i %12 ) == 0))
118         printf  "\n %2d $%9.2f   $%9.2f     $%9.2f   $%9.2f",
119          yr, regpr, regac, mcspr,mcsac;
120     }
121     # -----------------------------------------------------------
122     # Print out the savings
123     # -----------------------------------------------------------
124     printf "\n                                          =============";
125     printf "\n Total Interest Paid Regular Payments  = $%9.2f",
        ➥      regac ;
126     printf "\n Total Interest Paid Extra Payments    = $%9.2f",
        ➥      mcsac ;
127     printf "\n Total Savings via Extra Principal     = $%9.2f",
        ➥      regac - mcsac ;
128     print "\n Early Pay off in ",early, " years";
129
130 }
```

Analysis

Lines 18 through 22 define the variables for this program. You can set these values and run the program with your set of numbers.

Lines 27 through 29 are variables that are set from the command line (see the section on command-line arguments in awk). You will learn how to set these variables from the command line. They are used in this example to override the coded awk values. This is why the value is checked before it is used in the addition.

Lines 34 to 40 initialize the loan parameters for the balance.

Lines 46 to 50 calculate the monthly payment, given the loan amount, time, and interest rate. This is from a finance textbook and could perhaps be coded in a faster manner. Do you think you can make this part more readable or faster?

Line 57 calculates the accelerated monthly payment. Lines 61 through 74 print the header for the output. Line 76 gets the interest rate per payment period (12 months).

Line 81 starts a `for` loop for all the payments to be made for this loan. The `npaymts` was set in line 40.

The program checks to see whether the curtailed principal is greater than 0 before printing it. If the amount is less than `0`, the program will not print out the principal.

Lines 117 to 119 print out, in column, the balance after every five years. Notice how the spaces are set in the `printf` statements to match the printed headings before the loop. The `%9.2f` corresponds to the nine spaces each for the floating-point numbers.

Finally, in lines 124 to 129, the results of the analysis are printed.

Let's run this program and see the results.

Input Output

```
$ awk -f amort.awk
                     Mortgage Acceleration Analysis
  Period of loan  = 30 years
  Interest        = 6.625 APR **** with 0.000 points
  Loan Amount     = $112500.00 (rolled cost $ 2500.00)
  Money for points= $     0.00
  AMOUNT FINANCED = $112500.00

  Mo. Payment(PI) = $720.35    With Extra Principal (PI) = $820.35
  Difference in Mo. Payment(PI) = $100.00

        Regular   30 years    vs.     Prepayment
 Yr  Principal    Interest        Principal     Interest
  5 $105462.52   $ 36183.51      $ 98372.29   $ 35093.28
 10 $ 95670.28   $ 69612.26      $ 78714.43   $ 64656.41
 15 $ 82044.98   $ 99207.95      $ 51361.71   $ 86524.68
 20 $ 63086.20   $123470.16      $ 13302.04   $ 97686.00
 25 $ 36706.19   $140311.14      $   -792.24  $ 98358.01
 30 $      0.00  $146825.94      $   -792.24  $ 98358.01
                                               =============
 Total Interest Paid Regular Payments    = $146825.94
 Total Interest Paid Extra Payments      = $ 98358.01
 Total Savings via Extra Principal       = $ 48467.92
 Early Pay off in  22  years
```

Analysis

Notice how, with the help of the format fields of the `printf` statements, the output is aligned to fit in a column. (The results of this example were an eye-opener to me.) This output shows that the loan can be paid off about seven or eight years early, with substantial savings in interest over the life of the loan.

Passing Values at the Command Line

What if you want to be able to change the APR to a different number, given the same loan amount. Faced with a refinance decision, you have to play with a number of interest rates and rolled costs. Editing the file will be a little tiresome after a while. So, let's add to the program the capability to specify these values at the command line.

The syntax for setting values at the command line to an awk program is

```
awk ... -v var=val -v var1=val1 ...
```

where *var* is the variable that is set to a value before even the BEGIN statements are executed. Let's use a shell script to set these values.

Input/Output

```
$ cat amort.sh
#!/bin/sh
#
# cmdRate = APR  (e.g. 6.875)
# cmdPts  = LOR + Buydown pts
# cmdRoll = amount of closing costs rolled back in
#
if [ $1 = "-?" -0 $# -eq 0]
then
     echo "USAGE: $0 awk -f amort.awk APR PTS ROLLEDCOST"
     exit 1
fi
awk -v "cmdRate=$1" -v "cmdPts=$2" -v "cmdRoll=$3 " -f amort.awk
```

Analysis This program takes three arguments: the APR, points, and any additional rolled costs. Notice the double quotes around the set variables:

```
-v "cmdRate=$1"
```

These variables correspond to those tested for in lines 27 through 29 in amort.awk.

Summary

The awk program is a powerful pattern-scanning language. It uses one type of statement with two components, a pattern and an action. Patterns select the data to be processed, and actions specify the action to be taken when data matches the pattern.

- The entire line can be referred to by $0. Each field in the line is referred to by $1 for the first, $2 for the second, and so on. The number of fields in the line is represented by the awk special variable NF.

- The `print` command will print all its arguments on one line. Arguments must be separated by commas. Otherwise, they will be connected together; no blank spaces will separate them.
- The `awk` program has special variables for the number of lines read, the number of fields in the current line (`NF`), and the input field separator (`IFS`).
- The `printf` statement is a special-purpose statement that performs a formatted print. You specify a format string as the first argument, followed by zero or more variables to which the format is applied. The `printf` statement does not automatically print a new line.
- As with other UNIX tools, if you omit the input filenames with the `awk` command, `awk` will accept input from the keyboard instead.
- With the `-v` option, the `awk` program will accept variables at the command line.
- The simplest program is the `{ print }` program, which prints every line in the file. You do not have to specify the `$0`, which is the default in this case. Nor do you need the semicolon as the delimiter for the line.
- The default action of `{ print $0; }` is taken when the action portion is left out.
- `{print $0 }` is equivalent to `{ print }`.
- The `length(var)` function returns the length of a string.
- Consider using `awk` for most tasks, especially when the task seems overly complicated if performed with other UNIX tools.

Today's text only scratched the surface of this program. The `awk` program is a powerful tool for UNIX tasks and offers many more features than can be described here.

Despite its appeal, however, `awk` may not be suitable for tasks for which other UNIX tools are specifically designed. Use `grep` for searching, `sed` for searching and replacing, `cut` for columnar output removal, and so on. Rather than think "How can I use this tool to do the job?" you should learn to think "What tool should I use for this job?"

What's Next

Tomorrow, I will discuss a newer shell, the Korn shell. The Korn shell has been widely distributed in recent versions of UNIX. You will come across it sooner or later. The Korn shell follows the syntax of the Bourne shell and adds many more features that greatly use the flexibility in UNIX.

Q&A

Q Must all `awk` statements end in a semicolon?

A As a general rule, yes. The exception is when the next statement is a `}`. In this case, a semicolon is not necessary.

Q Can I put more than one statement on one line?

A Yes. As in shell commands, statements are terminated with a semicolon. You therefore can put multiple statements on one line, for example:

```
i++; j++; k--; printf "hello %d", k;
```

Q Can I skip records when a pattern is matched?

A Yes. Use the `next` command.

Q I want to learn more about `awk`. Where do I go?

A Start by trying the man pages. For more examples, check out any reference book on using UNIX. Other Sams books include *Teach Yourself UNIX in a Week*, by Dave Taylor, and *UNIX Unleashed*, by the Sams Development Team.

Q If you have to locate a short string in several files, which of the following UNIX tools would you use? Why?

`awk`

`grep`

`sed`

A For small strings, use `grep` to find and print the string. For complicated string expressions, use `egrep`. For combinations of strings, use `awk`. Leave `sed` for search-and-substitute tasks, because the other tools are better designed for search-only operations.

For example, to search for `cat`, use `grep`. For `cat` by itself on a line with a two-digit number after it, use `egrep`. To count the number of such occurrences, pipe the output to `wc`.

To add the numbers following the word `cat` and to print the output after the numbers are added, use `awk`.

Q Do I have to use parentheses to group together multiple statements?

A No. Doing so is not necessary all the time, but using parentheses does remove any ambiguities. Commands in `awk` are processed in order of precedence.

Command precedence means that commands with higher precedence will be executed before those of lower precedence. For example, in the line

```
c * b + a
```

`b` will be multiplied to `c` before being added to `a` because the multiplier is of higher precedence that the addition operation. To add `b` to `a` before multiplying, use

```
c * (b + a)
```

Table 12.1 listed the operators in the order of precedence.

Workshop

The Workshop provides quiz questions to help you solidify your understanding of the material covered. Some Workshop sections of this book also contain exercises to provide you with experience in using what you've learned. Try to understand the quiz and exercise answers before continuing on to the next chapter. Answers are provided in Appendix D, "Answers."

Quiz

1. Given the `awk`, `sed`, `egrep`, and `grep` commands, which tool would you use if you wanted to do some substitution? Why?
2. Your printout is printing `%d` and `%f` in your print statements. What could be wrong?
3. Can you use multiple patterns to qualify a search? How would you print only those lines in which field 1 is greater than 10 and field 3 is a string "dog"?
4. What's the default action in `awk`? That is, what action is taken when the action part of a statement is omitted?

Exercises

1. Modify the following shell script to accept input from the keyboard if no input files are specified:

```
if [ $# -lt 1 ]
        then
```

```
        echo "Usage: $0 filename ..."
        exit 1
fi
for i
do
        awk -f nl.awk $i
done
```

2. In the `amort.awk` program, the monthly payment calculation is done in several statements. Can you rewrite the program so that it has fewer statements?
3. Write an `awk` script to find out if any passwords are missing in the `/etc/passwd` file. (Hint: Check whether the field in a colon-delimited file is blank.)
4. Write an `awk` program to simulate the `cut` program, with fields as "`:`" instead of spaces. (Hint: Use `IFS`.)

12

13

WEEK 2

Korn Shell Programming

Today, you will work on another popular shell in the UNIX environment. Although the Bourne shell is still the "standard" shell for UNIX, the Korn shell is becoming a popular replacement on later UNIX releases. Its popularity probably can be best attributed to its compatibility with the Bourne shell and its incorporation of some of the features of the C shell.

You will learn about the following topics:

- Why use the Korn shell?
- Am I running the Korn shell?
- `ksh` command-line options
- The environment of the Korn shell
- The command history
- Functions, reserved words, and parameter substitution
- The tilde operator
- Arithmetic substitution
- Tests
- Creating menus
- Command substitution
- Aliases and arrays
- Built-in commands
- Special files in the Korn shell

Today's lesson serves only as an introduction to the Korn shell; I cannot hope to encompass all the features of the Korn shell in one day. After reading today's text, you should have enough knowledge to be comfortable with the Korn shell.

Why Use the Korn Shell?

The first thing you should do now is relax. Except for minor differences, all the Bourne shell commands that you have learned will work under the Korn shell. You already have a running start.

You may be asking yourself, "So what is this Korn shell anyway, and why is it so important after all?"

The Korn shell was developed at AT&T Bell Labs by David Korn. He designed this shell to be upwards-compatible with the Bourne shell so that programs written in the Bourne shell and then run under the Korn shell would continue to work as before.

Some of the features in the Korn shell that make it so popular are the following:

- A command history mechanism that enables you to edit any commands previously entered during this shell. A built-in command editor will run like `vi` or `emacs`.
- Built-in integer arithmetic that is better than using the `expr` command.
- Jobs and process control. Under the Korn shell, you can manage jobs in the background.
- Arrays. These enable you to group together several items.
- Command aliasing.

I will cover these popular features today. All the knowledge you have of the Bourne shell will help you grasp these topics.

Am I Running the Korn Shell?

The binary program for the Korn shell is called `ksh` and is usually found in the `/bin` directory. Look for it there first.

Input
Output

```
$ ls /bin/ksh
/bin/ksh
```

Analysis

The default prompt in the Bourne and Korn shells is a `$`, so looking at the prompt will not tell you which shell you are running. For a quick test of which shell you are running, you could type the following command at the prompt:

```
$ echo $RANDOM $RANDOM
```

In the Bourne shell, you should get a blank line. In the Korn shell, you will see two different numbers:

```
$ echo $RANDOM $RANDOM
2668 8551
```

If you do see a blank line, type `ksh` at the prompt. This will start the Korn shell for you. If you do not see an error message, try the `RANDOM` command test again. If it works, you are in the Korn shell.

Note: You can talk to your system administrators about having this as your default shell. If it's not on your system, ask them to get it for you.

Note: On some systems, you may have the public domain version of the Korn shell (`pdksh`). This is another version of the Korn shell, one whose source is available on the Internet, along with instructions on how to build it.

The `pdksh` shell is not the full-featured version of the Korn shell because it lacks support for arrays, has limited regular-expression parsing, and does not support the `[[ ]]` conditional testing. In addition, you may need some programming knowledge to be able to compile and link the sources for your system. Lastly, the `pdksh` documentation is incomplete.

Despite its lack of such features, it still has the advantage of the source-on-hand for you to review. Being free, its price is good for the pocketbook.

ksh Command-Line Options

If `ksh` finds the `ENV` environment variable set when it begins execution (after profile processing), `ksh` executes the file named by the expansion of the value of this variable.

The shell accepts the following options on the command line:

- `-c` *`cmdstring`* executes *`cmdstring`* as if it were an input line to the shell and then exits. The `ksh` assigns arguments after the *`cmdstring`* positional parameters.
- `-i` invokes an interactive shell as opposed to running a script. With `-i`, the shell catches and ignores interrupts. Without `-i`, an interrupt terminates the shell. For shells that read from the terminal, `-i` is the default.

- `-rm` invokes a "restricted" shell. (As noted earlier, you also can invoke a restricted shell by using the name `rsh`). In a restricted shell, you cannot do the following: use the `cd` command; change the values of the variables `ENV`, `PATH`, or `SHELL`; use > or >> to redirect output; or specify command names containing `/`. These restrictions do not apply during execution of your profile file.

As with the Bourne shell, if you want to use any of these characters inside an actual argument, you must quote the argument so that the shell doesn't use the special meanings of the characters. See Day 4 for more information about quoting.

Environment

The Korn shell works with the `.profile` file just as the Bourne shell does. It looks for this file by using the `ENV` environment variable, which contains information about the file's location. The Korn shell also needs the `SHELL` variable set and exported for all the programs that need to start an interactive subshell, such as the `:!` in `vi`.

See Appendix A for a detailed list of the environment variables used in the Korn shell.

The Command History

The command history is a history of all the commands in the shell session. Every time you press the Enter key, the command you typed will be entered in this list. The list is in a file called `.sh_history` in your login directory and can be referred to by the `HISTFILE` environment variable.

The size of this list is set by the `HISTSIZE` environment variable; typically the size is set to 128. You can increase the history by resetting the variable to a different value.

With a feature called command-line editing, you can edit the commands in your history. You can choose these popular editors: `vi`, `gmacs`, or `emacs`. I will discuss the `vi` editor here.

> **Note:** If you are an `emacs` fan, you will find that the Korn shell editor faithfully emulates most `emacs` line-edit commands. Don't worry if you do not know how to use `vi`. I will cover the editing commands here.

13

Here are several environment variables that determine which mode you are in. You can use any one of these methods turn on the `vi` editor support, but it's safer to put these lines in your `.profile` script so that you do not have to type them in every time you log in. The values are the following:

- `VISUAL` can be set to `vi`, `emacs`, or `gmacs`.
- If `VISUAL` is not set, the Korn shell checks the `EDITOR` variable for the same values.
- The `set -o` mode command sets one of the preceding modes, for example:

```
$ EDITOR=vi
$ VISUAL=vi
$ set -o vi
```

All of these methods will turn on the `vi` editor support.

To work with `vi`, you have to remember that you are working in two modes of operation—*input* and *command.* In input mode, whatever you are typing will be entered verbatim. In the command mode, your keyboard strokes mean special commands to `vi`.

You go from the input mode to the command mode by pressing the Esc key on your keyboard. To get from the command mode to the input `mode`, you can press the lowercase I key (i).

After entering the `set -o vi` command, you are automatically in the input mode. When you are in the input mode of the `vi` editor, whatever you type will be sent to the shell.

Enter a few commands at the prompt:

```
$ date
Mon Aug  1 21:37:10 CDT 1994
$ echo Howdy
Howdy
$ pwd
/home/kamran/sams
$
```

To get to the command mode, press the Esc key. When you enter the command mode, the cursor will move one space to the left of the last character typed. (The shape of the cursor may change on certain terminals.) In the command mode, you can move the cursor without disturbing the command line.

To move the cursor to the left one character, press the lowercase H key. To move the cursor right one character, press the lowercase L key. Do not press the Enter key after these commands! The Enter key is reserved for executing the command on the current line.

If you try to move the cursor beyond the left or right limits of the line, the shell beeps at you. To move to the previous command, press the lowercase K key; to move forward in the history, press the lowercase J key.

As shown in the preceding example, you press Esc at the prompt and then press the lowercase K key. You should see the `pwd` command. Press the Enter key to execute this command. If you want to back further instead of executing the command, press the lowercase K key as many times as you want to go back. If you get to the top of the list, you will hear a beep for every K key you press. On some terminals, the screen might flash. To move forward in the command history, you can press the lowercase J key. Try it.

DO | **DON'T**

DO press the Esc key several times if you are not sure which mode you are in. If you are already in the command mode when you press the Esc key, you will hear a beep for every Esc key pressed.

DON'T press the Enter key after every `vi` command in the command mode! The Enter key is reserved for executing the command on the current line.

What commands do you have available for you to edit these history commands? They are presented in Table 13.1.

Table 13.1. Some `vi` edit commands at the prompt.

Letter	Action
`x`	Deletes the current character under the prompt
`dw`	Deletes the word from the current character to the first white space
`D`	Deletes the entire line from the present cursor position
`p`	Restores the last deletion (character or word) at the cursor location
`i`	Puts `vi` into insert mode at the current character location
`a`	Puts `vi` into insert mode after the current character location
`A`	Puts `vi` into insert mode at the end of the line
`I`	Puts `vi` into insert mode at the start of the line

continues

Table 13.1. continued

Letter	Action
`h`	Moves the cursor left
`l`	Moves the cursor right
`j`	Moves the cursor down the history file (beeps if the cursor is at the end)
`k`	Moves the cursor up the history file (beeps if the cursor is at the top)

To see your command history, use the `history` command:

Input/Output

```
$ history
  484  cd
  485  cd sams
  486  vi *.faq
  487  cd /cdrom/usr/doc
  488  cd faq/faq
  489  ls
  490  ls
  491  ls -l
  492  zless linux-faq.ascii.gz
  493  exit
  494  cd sams
  495  vi *.awk
  496  vi nl.awk
  497  vi nl.awk
  498  awk -f nl.awk nl.awk
  499  vi nl.awk
  500  exit
  501  history
```

Analysis: The numbers to the left of the command are simply command reference numbers in ascending order.

To view one or more commands from your history file, type the `fc` command. For example, `fc -l 492 498` enables you to view all the file. Commands 492 through 498 in your history file will be selected for the editor in a temporary file. The `-r` option to the `fc` command reverses the order; and the `-n` option puts you into the editor set by the variable called `EDITOR` for the list of commands not preceded by line numbers. After you are finished editing this temporary file and you exit the editor, the file is run as temporary shell script.

This feature is indispensable for re-executing a complex sequence of commands because you can edit all the command at once and execute them as a shell script.

To re-execute any previously entered commands, you can use the `r` command.

Input Output

```
$ who
kamran    tty1      Aug  5 14:52
kamran    tty2      Aug  5 15:21
$ r
who
kamran    tty1      Aug  5 14:52
kamran    tty2      Aug  5 15:21
```

Analysis

The `who` command was re-executed by the `r` command. This is helpful when you do not want to re-edit the command history.

Foreground and Background

Terminals that support multiple windows are replacing the single-window terminal, especially with X Windows on UNIX systems. If you have multiple terminals available to run multiple shells simultaneously, you do not need to learn background and foreground processing. However, if you are stuck in the Dark Ages and have only a single-window terminal, you will appreciate the use of background processing.

Let's say you want to run some script that takes a long time to execute or that periodically tests some condition. If this script takes over your terminal while it executes or waits, you would be out of luck and would have to find another terminal. This is where the Korn shell features of job control can help.

If you try the following command in the Korn shell, you will get the output shown here:

Input Output

```
$ who ¦ wc &
[1] 489
```

Analysis

The `[1]` is the job number, and `489` is the process ID of this job. The ampersand (`&`) at the end of the command puts the job in the background.

When the job terminates, you will see

```
[1] + Done  who ¦ wc &
```

to indicate that the job is done.

To see what jobs you have currently running in the background, use the jobs command.

Input Output

```
$ jobs
[1]  + Runnning      vi ch1 &
[2]  + Runnning      vi ch2 &
[3]  + Runnning      vi ch3 &
```

Analysis

This output indicates that I have three `vi` sessions in three different jobs. Notice that the process ID is not given in this output.

13

To kill any of these jobs, I would use the following command:

```
kill %jobnumber
```

`kill %1` would kill the first job.

```
$
$ jobs
[1]   + Runnning       vi ch1 &
[2]   + Runnning       vi ch2 &
[3]   + Runnning       vi ch3 &
$ kill %1
[1] + Terminated      vi ch1 &
```

Suspending a Job

To suspend a job in the foreground, press Ctrl+z. You will then be presented with a prompt of the form

```
[n]   + Stopped command
```

where *n* is the job number for the stopped command. You will then be in a new shell. The process is not running, however. To keep it running in the background, enter the `bg` command. You will see a message of the form

```
[n]   command
```

which indicates that the command is now running in the background.

The `bg` command is helpful if you accidently send a print job in the foreground and you simply want to move it to the background.

To bring a job to the foreground, use the `fg` command. For example, the command

```
fg %1
```

brings job number 1 to the foreground.

Functions

Functions are available in the Korn shell just as in the Bourne shell. You invoke a function like any other command; when you actually call the function, `ksh` saves the current positional parameters. The function's command-line arguments then replace those parameters until the function finishes.

Either of the following forms defines a function named *`variable`* as a body that consists of the sequence of commands:

```
function variable {
        command
     [...]
}
```

or,

```
variable() {
        command
     [...]
}
```

The second case is available only in the ksh and not in the Bourne shell.

The function ends either by falling off the end of the code of the function body or by reaching a `return` statement. If the function uses `typeset` to declare any variables in the function body, the variables are local to the function. The `ksh` also saves the current `ERR` and `EXIT` traps and any flags manipulated with the `set` command; these are restored when the function finishes.

The `ksh` functions can have local variables defined by the `typeset` command, making recursion possible. For example:

```
typeset i j
```

This way, if a variable of the same name (`i` or `j`) exists in the function, it is saved when the function is called and is restored when the function returns. Look at the following example.

Input Output

```
$ ddd=100
$ function doit
> {
> echo $ddd
> ddd=10
> echo $ddd
> }
$ doit
100
10
$ echo $ddd
10
$ ddd=100
$ function doit
> {
> typeset ddd
> echo $ddd
> ddd=10
> echo $ddd
> }
$ doit
100
10
$ echo $ddd
100
$
```

13

Analysis

When the local variable was typeset, the value of a variable in the same shell was not changed.

The values returned from the function are in `$?`, and I assign this value with the `return $var` statement.

Input/Output

```
$ function sqr
>{
>(( s = $1 * $1 ))
> return $s
>}
$ typeset -f
function sqr()
      {
      (( s= $1 * $1))
      return $s
      }

$ sqr 5
$ ret_val=$?
$ print $ret_val
25
```

Analysis

Sometimes the output of the `typeset -f` command lists only the name of the function on not the defunction. The `typeset -f` command displays all the functions listed in my environment. Notice that I used the `$?` immediately. If I had not done that—that is, if I had put a `print` statement between the `sqr` call and the `ret_val` assignment—the value of `$?` would be changed to the value of the return from the `print` statement.

To load these functions at login time every time you use the Korn shell, you can set `FPATH` to point to the directory (or directories) with these function names. The format is similar to that of the `PATH` variable.

The Korn shell will search this `FPATH` and load all the files you specify with the `typeset -f` command, or the shell will try to execute a function that is not defined.

To use `FPATH`, put the following items in your `.profile` file:

- `typeset -f` *`name`*, for all the functions you want defined this way
- The command `set -o autoload`, for turning on this option

To remove a function definition, use the `unset` command as shown here:

Input/Output

```
$ type sqr
ksh: sqr is a function
$ unset sqr
$ type sqr
ksh: sqr: command not found
```

Analysis In this example, I used the `unset` command to remove the function definition for `sqr`.

DO	DON'T

DO assign the `$?` returned value of a function immediately. This value is changed on every function or program execution.

DO use the `typeset -f` command to get the list of all functions in your environment.

DON'T forget to use the `print` command instead of the `echo` command. The `print` command is the standard for the Korn shell.

The `typeset -Rn` command right-justifies and fixes the length of a string variable. For example:

```
typeset -R12 dosname
```

sets the length of `$dosname` contents to 12 characters. The `print` statement will now always print 12 characters when it prints `$dosname`.

This would be useful for an application like the `nl.awk` program you saw developed on Day 12.

Similarly, the command

```
typeset -L12 dosname
```

defines a left-justified string that is 12 characters long. If `dosname` is less than 12 characters, it will be padded with spaces and extra characters will be truncated.

Reserved Words

The `ksh` shell recognizes reserved words only when they are the unquoted first token of a command. This enables you to pass these reserved words as arguments to commands executed from the shell. Here is the full list of reserved words:

```
!        {        }
case     do       done
elif     else     esac
fi       for      function
if       select   then
time     until    while
```

When parsing commands, before performing filename generation, `ksh` examines the command name against currently defined aliases and functions, and then against the set of built-in commands.

Built-in commands are those commands that the `ksh` can execute directly, without searching for program files. See Appendix A.

If the command name is not a function or a built-in command, the shell looks for a program file or script file that contains an executable version of that command. The ksh uses the same procedure to search for commands that is used with the Bourne shell.

Parameter Substitution

The shell uses three types of parameters: positional parameters, special parameters, and variables. A *positional parameter* is represented either by a single digit (except 0) or by one or more digits in curly braces. For example, `7` and `{15}` are both valid representations of positional parameters. Positional parameters are assigned values from the command line when you invoke `ksh`.

A *special parameter* is represented with one of the following characters:

```
*   @   #   ?   !   -   $   0
```

The values to which special parameters expand are listed later today.

In the Korn shell, you have some additional parameter substitution options (compared with parameter substitution in the Bourne shell). The following list summarizes these options, including for completeness those found in the Bourne shell:

- ☐ `$1, .. $9 .. $`*n* provides each positional parameter, where `n` could be greater than 9 if used with the `${}`—that is, `${12}` for the twelfth parameter. In the Bourne shell, you have to shift to get to the tenth parameter or higher. In the Korn shell, you can use numbers greater than 10, as long as they are between curly braces. For parameters indexed lower than 10, you can use either `$`*n* or `${`*n*`}`.
- ☐ `$#, ${#*}`, and `${#@}` each expand to the number of positional parameters.
- ☐ `$@` expands to the complete list of positional parameters, each as a separate argument in the command line being processed. This means that `$@` is equivalent to `"$1" "$2" "$3" ....`

- $* expands to the complete list of positional parameters, all put together as a single argument, with parameters separated by the first character of the value of IFS. So, if the first character of IFS is a blank, then "$*" is equivalent to "$1 $2 ...".
- $- expands to all options that are in effect from previous calls to the set command and from options on the ksh command line.
- $? expands to the exit status of the last command executed.
- $$ expands to the current process number of this shell. For example, print "I am $$" will tell you what your shell's process ID is.
- $! expands to the process number of the last command.
- ${myarrary[*arithmetic expression*]} expands to the value of an element in an array named myarray. The arithmetic expression gives the subscript of the array. For example:

```
i = 2
t=${cards[((i * 13))]}
```

  will give the 27th item in the card array. Notice that the array is indexed from 0 and up.

- ${*variable*[*]} expands to all the elements in the array *variable*, separated by the first character of the value of $IFS. So the value of t in this example will be set to "1 2 3 4" given the array num.

```
$ num[0] = 1
$ num[1] = 2
$ num[2] = 3
$ num[3] = 4
$ t=${num[*]}
$ echo $t
1 2 3 4
```

- ${*variable*[@]} expands the items of the array. When unquoted, it is the same as ${*variable*[*]}. When quoted as "${*variable*[@]}", it expands to all the elements in the array *variable*, with each element quoted individually. This is helpful if you want to put these elements into a for loop or pass them as parameters.

- `${#parameter}` expands to the number of characters in the value of the given parameter. To test the length of characters in the string, you would use the following:

```
$ t="Kamran"
$ echo ${#t}
6
```

- `${#variable[*]}` expands to the number of elements in the array named *variable*. Elements that do not have assigned values do not count. For example, if you assign values only to elements 0 and 4, the number of elements is two. Elements 1 through 3 do not count and are set to `NULL`, for example:

```
$ num[0]=1
$ num[1]=2
$ num[4]=3
$ num[5]=4
$ t=${#num[*]}
$ echo The number of elements =
The number of elements = 4
```

Note: In some versions of the Korn shell, the `${#array[*]}` returns the highest index used, plus `1`, instead of counting only the assigned values. In other words, the value of `t` in the preceding example would be 6, not 4.

Use the preceding example to test your `ksh` and to find out the behavior of your `ksh`.

- `${parameter:-word}` expands to the value of `parameter` if it is defined and has a non-empty value; otherwise, it expands `word`. This means that you can use `word` as a default value if the `parameter` isn't defined.
- `${parameter-word}` is similar to the preceding construct, except that the *parameter* is expanded if defined, even if the value is empty. This is the same as in the Bourne shell.
- `${variable:=word}` expands *word* with parameter expansion and assigns the result to *variable*, provided that *variable* is not defined or has an empty value. The result is the expansion of *variable*, whether or not *word* was expanded. This is the same as in the Bourne shell.

- `${variable=word}` is similar to the preceding construct except that the `variable` must be undefined (it can't be null) for `word` to be expanded.
- `${parameter:?message}` expands to the value of `parameter` provided that it is defined and non-empty. If `parameter` isn't defined or is null, `ksh` expands and displays the `message`. If `message` is empty, `ksh` displays a default message. In a non-interactive shell (for example, a script file), the shell will terminate after displaying this `message`.
- `${parameter?word}` is similar to the previous construct, except that `ksh` displays the *word* only if `parameter` is undefined.
- `${parameter:+word}` expands to `word`, if `parameter` is defined and is non-empty.
- `${parameter+word}` expands to `word`, if `parameter` is defined.
- `${parameter#pattern}` attempts to match `pattern` against the value of the specified `parameter`. The `pattern` is the same as a case pattern. `ksh` searches for the shortest prefix of the value of `parameter` that matches `pattern`. If `ksh` finds no match, the construct expands to the value of `parameter`; otherwise, the portion of the value that matched `pattern` is deleted from the expansion. This is not available in the Bourne shell.
- `${parameter##pattern}` is similar to the preceding construct, except that `ksh` deletes the longest part that matches `pattern` if it finds such a match. This is not available in the Bourne shell.
- `${parameter%pattern}` searches for the shortest suffix of the value of `parameter` matching `pattern` and deletes the matching string from the expansion. This tests whether the `parameter` ends in the pattern; if so, it removes the shortest part that pattern. This is not available in the Bourne shell.
- `${parameter%%pattern}` is similar to the preceding construct, except that `ksh` deletes the longest part that matches `pattern` if it finds such a match. This is not available in the Bourne shell.

To clear up any confusion about what I've explained in the preceding list, let me illustrate these substitutions with examples.

Input/Output

```
$ var=uttexas
$ echo $var
$ echo ${var%%xas}
utte
$ echo ${var%e*s} # remove the smallest match from right
utt
```

```
$ echo ${var%%xas}  # remove longest from right
utte
$ echo ${var#?t}    # remove 2 character item ?t from the left.
texas
$ echo ${var##*t}   # remove longest match from left.
exas
$ echo ${var##ut)   # remove ut from texas (not a good idea)
texas
$ echo ${var##atm)  # no match (to uttexas) uttexas
```

Analysis These lines give some examples of how to slice up strings in variables.

Now think about how you can create new filenames from these. For example, given files in your directory that begin with `memo.txt`, you may want to create output files from these called `memo.dat` and `followup.txt`.

To get the new filename, you would create the filename from the variable itself, as shown in the following example.

Input/Output

```
$ f=memo.txt
$ g=${f%%txt}dat
$ h=followup${f#memo}
$ echo $g $h
memo.dat followup.txt
```

Analysis The `g` variable is created from removing the `txt` string and tacking on a `dat` at the end. The `h` variable is created by replacing the word `memo` with the word `followup`.

This is usually used in shell scripts to create filenames that are similar to each other.

Special Quoting with Tildes

You can define shell scripts in `ksh` with a tilde (~). For example, if you specify a filename as

```
~dekker/file
```

`ksh` would look up `dekker`'s home directory and put that directory name in place of the `~dekker` construct. If you just specify a ~ without a name, `ksh` replaces the ~ with the current value of your `HOME` variable. That is, `echo ~` displays the name of your home directory. Similarly, `ksh` replaces the construct `~+` with the value of the `PWD` variable (the name of the your current directory) and replaces `~-` (tilde hyphen) with the value of `OLDPWD` (the name of your previous working directory).

This tilde feature is not available in the Bourne shell.

Arithmetic Substitution

The Korn shell provides much better arithmetic facilities than the `expr` command of the Bourne shell. The syntax for arithmetic is

```
$((arithmetic expression))
```

DO	DON'T

DO use the Korn shell arithmetic functions instead of the `expr` command. The Korn shell functions are faster than the `expr` command.

DON'T use double parentheses in the `ksh` to enclose a statement. The single `()` pair is interpreted in a completely different manner than the `(())` pair. The single pair of parentheses executes a command in a subshell, whereas the double pair executes an arithmetic statement.

This sequence is replaced with the value of arithmetic expression that consists of expanded variables, numeric constants, and operators. Numeric constants have the form

```
[base#]number
```

where the optional *`base`* is a decimal integer between 2 and 36 inclusive, and *`number`* is any positive number in the given base. Thankfully, the default base is 10. Undefined variables evaluate to zero. For example, `2#1010` is the binary representation of decimal 10; `5#20` will also show the decimal number 10.

The `let` command is a command built in to the Korn shell that does work equivalent to the `((..))` sequence. The format for the `let` command is

```
let expression
```

where *`expression`* is a mathematical expression. So, in the Bourne shell you would use ``i=`expr $i + 1` ``, whereas in the Korn shell you would use `let i=i+1`.

With the use of quotes, you can evaluate multiple expressions:

```
let "i=i+1" "k=7*19"
```

You can compare the values of numbers by using the `(( ))` and `let` operators. For example, to test whether `x` is between 100 and 232 inclusive, you would use the test `(( x >= 100  && x <= 232))`.

13

You also can use binary numbers with the *base#digits* format. For example:

```
y = 2#1001 << 2
```

will give the value of `2#100100` to `y`. The `2` before the `#` is the base `2`, followed by the digits of the number.

Notice that you do not need the `$` between the `((..))` operators. So

```
(( y = y  - 1 ))
```

is the same as

```
(( y = $y  - 1 ))
```

In `ksh`, when you omit the `$`, you are asking the variable `y` to be interpreted as an integer instead of a string. With the `$`, the `y` is first converted to a string, and then back to an integer.

Arithmetic expressions may be used without the enclosing `$(( and ))` in assignment to an integer variable (see the man page for the `typeset` command); as an argument to the following built-in commands:

```
break
continue
exit
let
return
shift
```

Aritmetic expressions also can be used without the `((..))` when used as arguments to test numeric comparisons (`-eq`, `-ge`, `-gt`, `-le`, `-lt`, and `-ne`). See the following example to test the `((..))` operator.

Input Output

```
#
# Test Ksh math
#
print -n "Enter you age in years:"
read older

(( months = older * 12 ))
print "You are $months months old"
```

Analysis

Notice how the `older` variable did not need the `$` in the arithmetic statement.

I will cover these tests in detail in the next section, titled "Tests."

Tests

The Korn shell provides several ways to do tests of strings and integers. If you are now comfortable with the Bourne shell's `test` command, you will have no problem appreciating the power of testing in the Korn shell.

Math Tests

Let's look at an example of some of the tests for mathematical operations.

Input Output

```
$ cat testKsh
print "Enter two numbers: "
read x y

if (( x == y))
then
     print "the same     "
fi

if  test $x -eq $y
then
     print "the same     "
fi

if let "$x == $y"
then
     print "the same     "
fi

if  [ $x -eq $y ]
then
     print "the same     "
fi

if  [[ $x -eq $y ]]
then
     print "the same     "
fi

if  [[ $x -eq $y ]]
then
     :    # non-commital
fi
```

Analysis Notice that there are five different ways of testing whether two numbers are equal. In the last test, because the shell would give an error if nothing was between the `then` and `fi`, I used the colon operator that does nothing except act as a placeholder.

String Comparison

You also can compare strings in the ((..)) or [[ ]] operators. With the use of regular expressions, you can create very flexible testing statements. Let's look at some examples.

Input
Output

```
for i in $*
do
     if [[ $s = *c ]]
     then
          print "$s ends in a letter c "
     fi

     if [[ $s != *c ]]
     then
          print "$s does not end in a letter c "
     fi
done
```

Analysis

This test prints two messages based on the comparison of strings to simple regular expressions.

The Korn shell provides for more types of patterns than does the Bourne shell. The Korn shell's list of pattern-match operations is the following:

`?(pat1¦pat2¦ ... ¦patN)`	Matches zero or more patterns
`+(pat1¦pat2¦ ... ¦patN)`	Matches one or more patterns
`@(pat1¦pat2¦ ... ¦patN)`	Matches exactly one pattern
`*(pat1¦pat2¦ ... ¦patN)`	Matches zero, one, or more patterns
`!(pat1¦pat2¦ ... ¦patN)`	Matches any pattern except in the list

For example, `car?` matches `cart` and `carp` but not `carpet`; `car?(?¦??)` matches any three-letter word whose first three characters match `car` exactly.

Likewise, `car@(td)` matches `cart` and `card` but not `car`, because either `t` or `d` must be in the pattern. `care*(ful¦less¦ly)` matches zero, one, or more in the list; so it would catch `careful`, `careless`, `carefully`, and `care`.

`care+(ful¦less¦ly)` matches one or more in the list. So it would catch `careful`, `careless`, `carefully`, but not `care`.

The expression `@(bus¦car¦van¦bike)` matches only `bus`, `car`, `van`, or `bike`, and nothing else. This is useful for enumerating a specified response.

You could use the following example for a yes/no response shell script.

```
print "enter yes or no in lower case"
while :
do
     read response

     if (( response != @(yes¦no) ))
     then
          print "Okay I will do something "
          break
     else
     print "enter yes or no in lower case"
     fi
done
```

This script reads a response from you and compares the response with the answer it expected to get. This may not work on some old Korn shells.

Creating Menus

Use the `select` statement to create simple menus. Select menus enable you to create menus with responses of the form of `1`, `2`, `3` and so on. It's an antiquated method, but it works on all terminals (from old VT52 terminals to X terminal windows with a prompt). Let's look at a sample script.

```
# Demonstrate a menu driven item.

PS3="hello: Please enter you order"

select feedme in Burger Fries Combo1 Combo2 Nothing "Thank You"
do
     case $feedme in

          Burger) echo "One Burger "  ;;
          Fries) echo "Greasy Fries " ;;
          Combo1) echo "Combo1 ";;
          Combo2) echo "Combo2 ";;
          Nothing) echo "Nothing... ???? ";;
          "Thank You") break;;
          *) print " Are you going to order or what?"
     esac

done
$ sel
1) Burger
2) Fries
3) Combo1
4) Combo2
5) Nothing
6) Thank You
hello: Please enter your order
```

Analysis

This program demonstrates several features:

- The `select` statement specified the items for the menu.
- The items in the select list could be grouped by means of double quotes.
- The `*)` is the catch-all for bad user input.
- The `PS3` variable is used to set the prompt for the `select` statement.

Of course, you can opt to use the method we used in the Bourne shell to rewrite the `todo list` manager. The method of using the `select` call can be better if you want to present a consistent set of menus and submenus. Also, it handles blank lines automatically, whereas you would have to do it yourself in the `while` loop. You can choose whichever one you like in the Korn shell. This `select` call is not available in the Bourne shell.

Command Substitution

In `ksh`, you have the same features as the Bourne shell for command substitution. You can put together several complicated shell scripts.

Input Output

```
$     vi $(grep -l download $(find . -name '*.c' -print ))
```

Analysis

This command uses `find` to search the current directory and its subdirectories to find all files having names that end in `.c`. The command then uses `grep` to search each such file for those that contain the string `download`. Finally, it calls `vi` to edit each such file.

Note: There is an historical inconsistency in the backquoting syntax. A backslash `(\)` within a backquoted command is interpreted differently depending on its context. Backslashes are interpreted literally unless they precede a dollar sign `$`, grave accent `` ` ``, or another backslash `\`; in these cases, the leading backslash becomes an escape character to force the literal interpretation of the `$`, `` ` ``, or `\`.

So, the command `echo '\$x'` issued at system level produces the output `\$x`, whereas the same command nested in a backquoted syntax `` `echo 'echo '\$x'` `` produces the output `$x`.

I recommend the `$(command)` syntax for command substitutions. The `ksh` performs command substitutions as if a new copy of the shell is invoked to execute the command. This affects the behavior of `$-` (standing for the list of options passed to the shell). If a command substitution contains `$-`, the expansion of `$-` does not include the `-im` option in the interactive mode, because the command is being executed by a non-interactive shell.

Aliases

An *alias* is a synonym provided by the Korn shell to allow customization of your environment. The Korn shell keeps a list of all the aliases on every session. You can set the items in this list in your `.profile` or `$ENV` file by means of the `alias` command. The Korn shell searches this list and compares the first word of the command with this list. If it finds a match, it substitutes the first word with its `alias`.

For example, `alias lm='ls -Cl'` sets up the string `lm` as `ls -Cl`. Now when `lm` is typed in, it will be interpreted as `ls -Cl`.

To list all your aliases, type the `alias` command by itself. To list a specific alias for a specific command, type `alias` *`command`* by itself on a line. Aliases export only to the Korn shell.

As a rule, aliases are not exported to subshells. Use the `-x` flag when setting an alias to allow the alias to be exported.

To remove an alias, use the `unalias` command. The syntax is

```
unalias name
```

where *`name`* is the name of an alias.

DO | **DON'T**

DO define the alias with single quotes if you want the alias to be set at the time it's executed. If you define the alias with double quotes, it will be set at the time it is set and not when it is executed.

DON'T specify aliases for every command you use. It may be easy to alias some options for commands now, but if you go to another UNIX machine, you may not remember all the options you had aliased. Use aliases with discretion and care.

13

Arrays

Arrays are one-dimensional containers of strings or integers. You can implicitly declare a variable as an array by using a subscript expression when you assign a value, as in

```
variable[index]=value
```

The index can be an arithmetic expression as well. The array is never declared as such and is created by subscripting a variable. The maximum size of an array is 512 or 1024 (depending on your system), and the array indexed is from 0 up.

You can use a subscripted array variable anywhere that the shell allows an ordinary variable. Here is an example.

Input
Output

```
$ chap[0]="done"
$ chap[1]="done"
$ chap[2]="done"
$ chap[3]="done"
$ chap[4]="done"
$ chap[9]="done"
$ chap[10]="doing"
$ i=11
$ chap[$i]="halfway"
$
$ print "Chapter 10 = ${chap[10]}"
Chapter 10 = doing
$ print $chap[5]
$ print $chap[4]
done
$
$ print "Enter chapter 13 status:"
$ read chap[13]      # reads the answer in element 13
```

Analysis

The array variables that are not assigned a value are left null. See the output from printing the fifth item `[5]` of the array. Also, the `read` statement shows how you can read into an element of an array.

DO | **DON'T**

DO use the `${ }` when the expression you are working with is on the right side of the equal sign. For example:

```
array[2]="hi"          #okay

${array[2]}="hi"       # not good
```

DON'T use the `${ }` when the expression you are working with is on the left side of the equal sign, for example:

```
achh=array[2]           # not good

achh=${array[2]}        # good
```

DO remember how to assign values between two arrays with the $ on the right side of the equal sign. For example:

```
array[2]=${array[4]}
```

is correct. However,

```
${array[4]}=array[2]
```

is not correct.

More on the *ksh* Environment

A ksh execution environment is the set of conditions affecting most commands executed within the shell. It consists of

- Open files
- The current working directory
- The traps currently set
- The shell parameters and exported variables
- The shell functions currently defined
- The file creation mask
- Options (see the man pages for the set command)

A subshell environment starts as a duplicate of the shell environment, except that traps caught by the shell are set to default values in the subshell. Changes made to a subshell environment do not affect the parent shell environment as they do in the Bourne shell.

Built-In Commands

The following list shows the commands that are built into the Korn shell. Such commands are built into the shell to increase performance of shell scripts or to access the shell's internal data structures and variables. These internal commands are designed to have semantics indistinguishable from external commands.

```
:         .          [       aliasbg break
cd        continue   echo    eval    exec
exit      export     false   fc      getopts jobs
let       newgrp     print   read    readonly
return    set        shift           times
trap      type       typeset ulimit  umask
unalias   unset      wait    whence
```

The POSIX.2 standard recognizes a subset of these commands as special built-ins. Syntax errors in special built-in commands cause a noninteractive shell to exit with the exit status set by the command. The special built-in utilities are these:

```
:         .          break     continue eval     exec
exit      export     readonly  return   set      shift
trap      typeset    unset
```

As well as built-in commands, the shell has a set of predefined aliases:

```
autoload false     functions            history
         integer   nohup         pwd    suspend...true type
```

The Search for Commands

With functions, aliases, built-in commands, and so on, it's often confusing to remember how the Korn shell executes a command. To make this a bit more clear, here's an explanation of the sequence of events that the Korn shell takes to execute a command:

- Check whether the command is a reserved word and then execute it.
- Check the alias list. If command is found on the list, perform substitution. After substitution, check whether the alias definition ends in a space. If it does, check the reserved words again. If not found, proceed to next step.
- Check and execute if this command is built in.
- Check and execute its function list.
- Check and execute if found on the `PATH`
- This is the default action of the shell; it displays "command not found" when all the previous avenues have been exhausted, and the user has to be told that the command has not been found.

After the command has been "found," the Korn shell performs the following steps:

- Tilde expansion
- Parameter or variable substitution

- Command substitution in `$(string)`
- Expand arithmetic operations on `$((..))`
- Takes `IFS` and splits the words apart

In the case of `((..))` as the first command, the Korn shell skips all the first steps and starts taking steps from the variable substitution action.

Special Files Under the Korn Shell

Like the Bourne shell, the Korn shell has some special files it works with. They are listed in Table 13.2.

Table 13.2. Special files for the Korn shell.

File	Description
`.sh_history`	Default history storage file
`.profile`	Profile for login shell, used by the login
`/etc/profile`	System-wide profile for login shells, used by the login
`/etc/suid_profile`	Profile used under the privileged option and when effective and real UIDs are different, used by the login
`/tmp/sh*`	Temporary files for command substitution, history files re-execution, loops, and so on

13

Summary

Here are some points to remember:

- The Korn shell runs almost all Bourne shell scripts. The Korn shell is designed to be upward-compatible. (The only significant difference is that the Bourne shell can use the `^` character as a synonym for the `|` character as a pipe. This use is now archaic.)
- The command history file can be referred to by the `HISTFILE` environment variable.
- The command editor mode can be set by the `EDITOR` or `VISUAL` environment variables, or by the `set -o` mode command.

- The Korn shell provides many types of conditional tests with the `((..))` and `[[ ]]` operators.
- Korn shell arrays are either 512 or 1,024 elements long and are indexed from 0 and up. They are automatically created by subscripting a variable.
- It's easy to create simple menus in the Korn shell with the `select` command.
- The tilde (~) is a special character for creating a synonym for the user name. It's also used in `+~` for the current directory and `~-` for the previous directory.
- Built-in commands act like their similar-named, on-disk programs but run faster because they are built in to the shell; thus, the `PATH` does not have to be searched.
- The `RANDOM` variable is set to a random number in the Korn shell every time it is used.
- The `print` statement is more useful than the `echo` statement.
- A Ctrl+z puts the foreground process into a stopped state. The `bg` command runs the stopped process in the background. The `jobs` command lists all the jobs.
- Commands are searched for in a predefined order in the Korn shell: reserved words, aliases, built-in commands, functions, and `PATH`.
- Aliases provide a shorthand for complicated commands.

Today's text gave you only a snapshot of what the Korn shell can do for you. However, you do have enough knowledge about the Korn shell to proceed in learning on your own. Read the man pages and try out different commands.

If a command does not work the way you think it should, try to break it into smaller pieces. Then check to see whether the pieces work by themselves. Check for whitespaces in the proper places. Did you remember to use `${ }` on the right and not the left? Did you use one pair of parentheses `()` or two `((..))`? Before you berate your shell scripts, make sure you are running the Korn shell. (Remember the `RANDOM` test?)

The best way to learn the Korn shell is to use it.

What's Next

Tomorrow, I will discuss all the odds and ends of shell programming, material that did not fit in the earlier days' texts. You will then have some fun with Bourne and Korn shell scripts and create some helpful utilities, which are based on the commands you have learned so far.

Q&A

Q Should I learn the Korn shell and why?

A The Korn shell is quickly becoming the UNIX industry's standard shell. Soon you will see it in the latest UNIX distributions. It is also upward-compatible with the Bourne shell, so you will not be relearning a new syntax.

Q What are the uses for random numbers in the Korn shell?

A You can use random numbers to create temporary files for your shell scripts. Generating filenames with a combination of your current process ID (`$$`), user name (~), and the `RANDOM` variable almost guarantees that you will not overwrite any other files in your session.

Q When is the `select` statement useful?

A It's useful when you want to keep the types of responses to commands to a known list and create a simple and effective menu-driven interface. You can even nest menus within submenus.

Q Why do we need to use the `$?` immediately?

A If you had do not use it immediately, the value of `$?` would be changed to the value of the return from the next statement.

Workshop

13

The Workshop provides quiz questions to help you solidify your understanding of the material covered. Some Workshop sections of this book also contain exercises to provide you with experience in using what you've learned. Try to understand the quiz and exercise answers before continuing on to the next chapter. Answers are provided in Appendix D, "Answers."

Quiz

1. What's the difference between the `[[ ]]` test and the `(( ))` test?
2. What do these patterns match?

```
/???/?.?m

*/*.[chyl]m

~linux/*.c
```

3. How is a value returned from a function?
4. What's the difference between `$@` and `$*`?

Exercises

1. Write a shell script to reverse the order of an array with 10 elements in it.
2. What does the following shell script do?

```
typeset -i x=${1:-1} y=${2:-1} z
  while     [ x -gt 0 ]     # until overflow
  do
       echo $x
       let z=y+x x=y y=z
  done
```

3. What is the output from the following Korn shell script?

```
typeset x y
x=10
y=3
((z=x + y))
print "$x plus $y = $z"
((z=x - y))
print "x minus y = $z"
((z = x / y))
print "$x divided by y = $z"
((z = x * y))
print "x times $y = $z"
```

14

WEEK 2

The Odds and Ends

Today's discussion is dedicated to those items that did not fall into earlier days' text. Today, you will learn about these topics:

- Mail merge
- Locking the terminal
- Waiting for users
- Users without passwords
- Backup and restore
- Restricted shells
- File compression
- Sending messages to other users
- Using `mail`
- Stupid shell tricks
- Scheduling jobs

Using Mail Merge

With some knowledge of shell programming, you can duplicate in a shell script the mail merge feature available on most word processors today. This involves merging multiline records into one master file and printing it.

The steps you would take to create a merge file are the following:

1. Create a list of all the recipients (in an organized fashion) of your letter. Make standard records for this information. This will be your data file for recipient-specific information.
2. Create a master letter that you have to send to everyone on your list. Insert merge codes in it. The merge codes will be substituted with the recipient-specific information.
3. Create the program that first takes a record and substitutes the value of each merge code with its substitution and then prints out the final version.
4. Repeat step 3 for all records in the data file.

You can use your favorite editor for steps 1 and 2. I will use sed for step 3 and awk for step 4, as I walk you through the steps in the following example.

Beginning with step 1, suppose you had a list of customers in a file that is of the following format:

```
SREC
     name
     address
     city, state zip
     title (Ms. so and so)
     type of order
```

Let's look at the data file for this sample run:

```
$ head tmp.lst
SREC
Ms Horner
123 Corner St.
Anytown ST      12345
Ms Horner
Whey

SREC
Jack B. Nimble
92 W. Any St.
Thistown ST     12345
Mr. Nimble
Bandaids

SREC
Three Little Pigs
Large Brick House
Notown ST       12345
Mr. Pigs
Wolfguard
```

Moving on to step 2, suppose you wanted to send a standard letter along with every purchase, thanking the customer for his or her order. Rather than edit the master letter for each customer, you take the quicker—albeit impersonal—approach of inserting the customer-specific information in obvious places. Look at the following master document:

```
$ cat tmp.master

          Fly By Nite
          Wholesalers
          PO BOX 1234
          HERE, ST 01234


NAME
ADDR1
ADDR2
```

```
Hello TITLE :

This is to confirm your order of ORDER. It will be shipped today
and you should have it within 3 business days.

Thanks for your order.

Sincerely

Haywood Jay Blomey
Fly By Nite Widget Makers
```

The substitutions you would like to make are for the keywords `NAME`, `ADDR1`, `ADDR2`, `TITLE`, and `ORDER`. This is a canned example; you can add more fields as you desire.

Step 3 involves merging the list file with the master template. For this, I will use the following `awk` program.

Input/Output

```
$ cat merge.awk
/^SREC/ {
     getline name
     getline addr
     getline city
     getline title
     getline items
     printf "s/NAME/%s/", name >"tmp.sed"
     printf "\ns/ADDR1/%s/", addr >>"tmp.sed"
     printf "\ns/ADDR2/%s/", city >>"tmp.sed"
     printf "\ns/TITLE/%s/", title >>"tmp.sed"
     printf "\ns/ORDER/%s/\n", items >>"tmp.sed"
     close("tmp.sed")
     "sed -f tmp.sed tmp.mst > letter" | getline
     "lp letter" | getline
     "rm tmp.sed" | getline
     }
```

Analysis

The first line matches a `SREC` string at the top of the line. This marks the beginning of a record.

The next five `getline` commands read the `name`, `addr`, `city`, `title`, and `items`. The `print` commands send the `sed` commands to the `tmp.sed` file. I explicitly close the file with the `close()` statement.

After this `sed` script file is created, I run `sed` on this file and collect the return value from the command by means of the `getline` command. This letter is then sent to the printer with the `lp` command. You can combine these two statements into one:

```
"sed -f tmp.sed tmp.mst | lp" | getline
```

For the moment, it's beneficial to see the output in a file for debugging.

After this letter has been sent to the printer, I remove the file `tmp.sed` for the next record. This step is not really necessary because the first `printf` statement with the > operator will overwrite any existing `tmp.sed` file. All subsequent `printf` statements for the next record will then be appended to `tmp.sed` through the >> operator.

In step 4, the merge is done with the `awk` command:

```
$ awk -f merge.awk template.master
```

Look at the run for the last record in this file. If you remove the `rm ...` statement, the `tmp.sed` file will be left over after the `awk` file is run. The commands generated from the `sed` script will create the file for the last record:

```
s/NAME/Three Little Pigs/
s/ADDR1/Large Brick House/
s/ADDR2/Notown ST   12345/
s/TITLE/Mr. Pigs /
s/ORDER/Wolfguard/
```

`sed` will substitute the fields in the master template for this record to produce the letter for the `Three Little Pigs`.

Input
Output

```
$ cat letter

          Fly By Nite
          Wholesalers
          PO BOX 1234
          HERE, ST 01234


Ms Horner
123 Corner St.
Anytown ST      12345

Hello Ms Horner :

This is to confirm your order of Whey . It will be shipped today
and you should have it within 3 business days.

Thanks for your order.

Sincerely

Haywood Jay Blomey
Fly By Nite Widget Makers
```

Analysis

This merge application demonstrates how to use the `awk` and `sed` utilities to create a powerful application. You can customize this, adding features as you see fit.

Locking the Terminal

Sometimes you have to walk away from your terminal after setting up a lot of environment variables and other things. You really do not want to log out and log back in, nor do you want anyone else to use your terminal while you are away, so what do you do? You can write a shell script to lock out anyone who does not know your password.

For this, you will use the `stty` program to change the line settings. The `stty` program is a very powerful program to set the line settings for all sorts of things—for example, echoing characters, setting parity on the line, and indicating the size of the characters to use. Try the command `$ stty --help` for a long list of options.

DO	DON'T

DON'T practice with the `stty` options unless you have some way to reset the terminal or turn off and back on. The `stty` command is powerful and dangerous; if you are not careful, you could lock up the line.

DO use the `stty sane` command if your terminal starts acting crazy after you've been `cat`ing an executable to the terminal or playing with the `stty` options. The `sane` command is not a guaranteed fix, but it may restore the terminal's setting to a workable state. When all else fails (Ctrl+d, `exit`, and so on), press the power button.

For this example, the option of interest is the one to turn the echo on or off. The echo is the terminal's echoing of the characters you type on the screen. When you type your password, you do not want it echoed on the screen because someone could be looking over your shoulder as you type. Typing the command `stty-echo` turns off the local echo of characters, and `stty echo` turns it back on.

Given this information, let's see how you can lock a terminal until a password is typed.

Input Output

```
#!/bin/sh

trap "echo Sorry; /bin/stty echo; kill $$;" 2 15

PATH=/usr/bin

backupword="sesame"      # Default password

stty -echo    # Do not echo typed characters
##
```

```
## Read a password then clear the screen
##
echo "Enter passkey"
read keyword
clear
while :
do
    read userinput
    if [ "$keyword" = "$userinput" ]
    then
         break
    elif [ "$backupword" = "$userinput" ]
    then
         break
    fi
done

/bin/stty echo     # turn echo back on
```

Analysis This program sets up a trap handler for signals 2 and 15. This prevents an intruder from stopping the script by pressing the Ctrl+c keys while the script is running.

Then you set up a backup password. What if you typed in a keyword, and later when you return to your terminal, discover you have forgotten that keyword? Just to get the terminal started, it would be quite an annoyance to figure out what was on your mind when you locked it. The backup keyword will work just as well.

The program then calls the `stty -echo` command to remove the echo feature, clears the screen, and then waits for you to type in a keyword. It compares the entered word with its two keywords. If they match, the program breaks out of the loop. Otherwise, the loop just goes on forever.

Waiting for Users

This shell script watches for the login of another user and notifies you when that user logs in. Then you can send mail to that person, call up that person, or write to his or her terminal.

Input Output

```
#!/bin/sh

interval=10
if [ $# -ne 1 ]
then
    echo "Usage: $0 username"
fi

username=$1
```

```
until who | grep "$username"
do
     sleep $interval
done

echo "User $username has logged in. Notify security"
```

This program takes the user name as the first argument and waits until the user logs in. It checks the user name with the `who` command until the user logs in. At that point, the program will break out of the `until` loop and take some action.

This program sets the interval between checks to 10 seconds. You can set the interval to a higher value if time is not critical.

Users Without Passwords

Users without passwords is a sore subject for any system administrator. User accounts without passwords represent a security leak for a system because anyone can log into such accounts without being asked for a password. Here's a script to determine whether or not there is a user account without a password.

```
$ cat ckuser
#!/bin/sh
# Check for missing passwds
sed -e 's/:/ : /g' /etc/passwd  | awk -f ckpass.awk
$
$
$ cat ckpass.awk
 {
     if ( $3 == ":")
     printf "\n User %s has no password",  $1;
 }
$ ckuser
 User shutdown has no password
 User dbarry has no password
$
```

This program tells you that the user `dbarry` is not using a password on this account.

Backup and Restore

This is a tricky topic for all users. How do you back up files under UNIX, and how often? For the purpose of making backups, there are several application programs available for you, but I will concentrate on presenting two common UNIX utilities: `tar` and `cpio`.

The original backup command was `tar`, which stands for the *tape archive* utility. The advantages of `tar` are these:

- Its archives can be used on virtually any UNIX system.
- It is reliable and stable.
- It is easy to use.

The `tar` utility stores everything on 1024-byte (or sometimes 512-byte) boundaries. So a 10-byte file will take up 1024 bytes, and a 1025-byte file will take up 2048 bytes. Also, `tar` writes output in one long stream, so if you break off in the middle, you have to start over. The original `tar` program recovered all the files at once. You could not select which filename to get. Now you can get a file at a time.

To create a `tar` archive of all your files on another file on the disk, you would use the command:

```
$ tar -cvf tar_file_name list_of_files_in_directory
```

The `tar` command traverses directories trees down to subdirectories and does not need to be fed complete filenames like the `cpio` command. `cpio` does not pack on 1024-byte boundaries but packs them as contiguously as possible.

tar

Look at an example of using the `tar` command to create an archive.

Input
Output

```
$ tar -cvf chapters.tar ch*
a ch01
a ch02
a ch03
a ch04
a ch05
a ch06
a ch07
a ch08
a ch09
a ch10
a ch11
a ch12
a ch12a
a ch13
a ch13a
a ch14
$ ls *.tar
chapters.tar
$ file chapters.tar
chapters.tar: tar archive
```

Analysis The `tar` command creates a tar archive for you. The `c` option tells the command to create the tar archive; `v` is for a verbose listing. The `chapters.tar` is for the `tar` filename specified by the `-f` option.

Note: On some UNIX machines, you may see the size of each file in 512-byte blocks as an output from the `tar -tvf` command.

To list the files in this archive, use the command:

```
$ tar -tvf chapters.tar
ch01
ch02
ch03
ch04
ch05
ch06
ch07
ch08
ch09
ch10
ch11
ch12
ch12a
ch13
ch13a
ch14
```

The `t` is the option to display the contents. Notice how the `v` and `f` options remain.

To extract files from this archive, use the command

```
tar -xvf chapters.tar
```

where `x` is the extraction request.

cpio

The `cpio` command has three operating modes.

- In *copy-out* mode, `cpio` copies files into an archive. It reads a list of filenames, one per line, on the standard input, and it writes the archive onto the standard output. A typical way to generate the list of filenames is with the `find` command; you should give `find` the `-depth` option to minimize problems with permissions on directories that are unwritable or not searchable.

- In *copy-in* mode, `cpio` copies files out of an archive or lists the archive contents. It reads the archive from the standard input. Any non-option command-line arguments are shell globbing patterns; in the archive, only files whose names match one or more of those patterns are copied from the archive. Unlike in the shell, an initial dot (.) in a filename does match a wildcard at the start of a pattern, and a / in a filename can match wildcards. If no patterns are given, all files are extracted.
- In *copy-pass* mode, `cpio` copies files from one directory tree to another, combining the copy-out and copy-in steps without actually using an archive. It reads the list of files to copy from the standard input; the directory into which it will copy them is given as a non-option argument.

The following options are available for you to use with `cpio`:

`-a`	Append to an existing archive. This works only in copy-out mode. The archive must be a disk file specified with the `-O` option.
`-b`	In copy in mode, swap both halfwords of words and bytes of halfwords in the data. Use this to convert integers between big-endian and little-endian machines.
`-d`	Create directories where needed.
`-f`	Copy only files that do not match any of the given patterns.
`-F`	Archive. Use an archive filename instead of standard input or output.
`-i`	Run in copy-in mode.
`-I`	Archive file to use instead of standard input.
`-l`	Link files instead of copying them, when possible.
`-L`	De-reference symbolic links. (Copy the files that they point to, instead of copying the links.)
`-o`	Run in copy-out mode.
`-O` *`archive`*	Archive filename to use instead of standard output.
`-p`	Run in copy-pass mode.
`-r`	Interactively rename files.
`-s`	In copy-in mode, swap the bytes of each halfword (pair of bytes) in the files.
`-S`	In copy-in mode, swap the halfwords of each word (4 bytes) in the files.
`-t`	Print a table of contents of the input.
`-u`	Replace all files, without asking whether to replace existing newer files with older files.

`-v`	List the files processed.
`-t`	Give an `ls -l` style table of contents listing.
`-V`	Print a dot (.) for each file processed.

You create a `cpio` archive with the `find` command:

```
$ find . -name 'ch*' -print ¦ cpio -v -o > chapters.cpio
```

To restore from this archive, use this command:

```
$ cpio -v -i < chapters.cpio
```

To interactively rename all the files as they are extracted, use the following command:

```
$ cpio -ir < chapters.cpio
```

Restricted Shells

The restricted shell is the same as the original Bourne shell, but it is designed to restrict a user to a particular set of directories and systems. The restricted shell is found as `/bin/rsh` and as the login shell for users who do not need all the capabilities of the system. When in the restricted shell, users cannot do the following:

- Modify the `PATH` or `SHELL`
- Specify an explicit path to an executable file
- Redirect output (no use of >> or >)
- `exec` another program
- Change directories (no use of `cd`)

The restrictions are enforced after the user has logged in and before the `.profile` is executed. The user cannot interrupt the `.profile` while it's executing. If the user presses the Ctrl+c keys while the `.profile` is executing, he or she is logged off.

These restrictions may not look like a daunting list, but they can restrict the user from many of the UNIX directory movement commands. You also can create the `.profile` to set the `PATH` variable and limit the user to only a certain set of directories.

The trick in writing the `.profile` for the `rsh` is to create the `.profile` file in the `HOME` but to keep the user in another directory. The `login` command will execute all the required `set` commands in the user's `HOME` directory and then `cd` over to another data directory after it's done. After the user gains control over the terminal, he or she will not be able to change directories from this directory.

Another thing that you could do with a restricted shell is to place copies of known commands in another directory, for example `/rbin`, and set the `PATH` to this directory in the `.profile`. This will limit the user to this directory; the user will not have access to the complete `/bin` directory. Most UNIX commands are safe, because they recognize `r` as the first character in the `SHELL` variable when they are asked to escape out into a shell. The `rsh` is not fool-proof. Experienced users will find ways to "break out" of the restricted shell into a regular shell if they are given access to the `/bin` or other directories.

File Compression

If you are fortunate enough to have your own workstation, you will most likely not have to worry a lot about disk space. However, as you work more with files, you may find it necessary to compress files to conserve space or to transmit the files over expensive long-distance phone lines. This is where the `compress` and `uncompress` programs are useful.

The `compress` program is a UNIX utility that compresses a file or standard input and replaces it with a file with a `.Z` extension only if the new file is smaller. The syntax is

```
compress [-f] [-v] filename
```

The output is sent to the standard output if no filename is specified. The `-f` option flag will forcefully overwrite an existing file. If the flag is not specified, the program will prompt the user before overwriting a file. The `-v` option will tell you how much a file has been compressed.

Its sister utility, `uncompress`, will uncompress the file for you. The syntax for this command is

```
uncompress [-c] [-f] filename.Z
```

The `uncompress -c` option sends the output from the uncompression to the standard output. This is also called `zcat` on some systems. The uncompressed file is written without the `.Z` extension. The `-f` option will forcefully overwrite an existing file. If the flag is not specified, the program will prompt the user before overwriting any existing file.

You can automate this procedure with a shell script.

```
#!/bin/sh
#
# Provide a listing file.
#
trap "Type X to exit;" 1 2
More = ${More:=/bin/less}
while :
do
```

```
echo "

    DISK MANAGER
    ------------

    [L]ist all files in current directory
    [C]ompress a file
    [U]ompress a file
    [V]erbose mode
    [S]ee the contents of the compressed file

    E[X]it

    Enter Selection:"

read response
#
# Parse the response
#
case $response in

    l¦L)
         echo "Type the filenames:"
         read filename
         ls $filename ¦ nl ¦ $MORE
         ;;

    c¦C)
         echo "Type the filenames:"
         read filename
         if [ -f "$filename" ]
         then
              compress $VERBOSE $filename
              echo "Created ${filename}.Z"
         fi
         ;;

    u¦U)
         echo "Type the filename:"
         read filename
         file $filename ¦ grep "compress"
         if [ $? -eq 0 ]
         then
              uncompress $filename
              echo "Uncompressed ${filename}"
         fi
         ;;
    v¦V)
         if [ -z "$VERBOSE" ]
         then
         VERBOSE="-v"
         echo "Verbose on"
         else
         VERBOSE=
         echo "Verbose off"
         fi
```

```
65          ;;
66
67      s¦S)
68          echo "Type the filename:"
69          read filename
70          file $filename ¦ grep "compress"
71          if [ $? -eq 0 ]
72          then
73               zless $filename
74          fi
75          ;;
76
77      x¦X) echo "Bye"
78          exit 0
79          ;;
80
81 #
82 #    Error handler
83 #
84      *)
85          echo "Please Enter a selection shown in [ ] ";
86          ;;
87      esac
88 done
89
90
```

Analysis This format should be familiar to you. I will discuss in more detail the lines of interest.

> **Note:** If you don't have `zless` (line 73 in the previous listing), use `zcat`, which is a more common—though less powerful—substitute for `zless`.

Lines 56–65 demonstrate how to toggle a shell variable, `VERBOSE`. The value is set to `-v` or `null` and is used as the option flag to the `compress` and `uncompress` commands. Without the `-v` option, no output messages are printed. With the `-v` option, the following messages are printed:

```
$ compress -v ch11
ch11: Compression: 53.21% -- replaced with ch11.Z
$ uncompress -v ch11.Z
ch11.Z:  -- replaced with ch11
```


Line 73 introduces you to yet another UNIX utility, one that enables you to read compressed files: `zless`. Before I invoke `zless` on the input file, I first determine what type of file it is with the `file` command (see line 70). The `file` command tells you what kind of file it is whose name you have typed; the `file` command does so by checking the first few bytes of the input file against a known set of patterns. This set of patterns is stored in file /etc/magic. For a compressed file, the output of the file command will contain the string compress. This is what I search for with the grep command to test whether the filename specified is that of a compressed file.

Stupid Shell Tricks

These are tricks you can learn to demonstrate your UNIX knowledge to your friends. They are also useful to get yourself out of some sticky UNIX situations. By dealing with these quirks in the UNIX shell programming language, you will get an insight into how to be a better shell programmer and debugger.

A Space in Filenames

Having spaces in filenames is perfectly legal, but you may find that is impractical and that you are prone to run into all sorts of errors when trying to access the file whose name has a space. The way to get a filename with spaces is to use quotes.

Input Output

```
$ cat > "ss dd"
Hello
ctrl-d
$ ls ss*
ss dd
$ ls ss dd
ls: ss: No such file or directory
ls: dd: No such file or directory
$ ls "ss dd"
ss dd
```

Analysis

The first line cats the input from the console into the file called ss dd. The quotes are essential because they force the ss and dd to be one argument to the indirection directive. (See Day 3.)

The next line tried to list the file without the quotes, and it failed. The double quotes, however, worked well.

The Unremoveable File

Do *not* try the following command:

```
$ cat > "-r \*"
```

Why? This command creates a file called #-r*# that when you enter at the prompt will turn into

```
$ rm -r *
```

It is not a good command to enter on your files. The reason I've included this section is to remind you that UNIX shells can create some strange situations, some of which can lead to disastrous results if not handled properly.

This file (`-r *`) will be such a pain to remove that you will have to delete the directory in order to delete this file. I got this file in my directory while I was trying out a shell script one command at a time and mistyped a command. After trying various options on the file—moving it, copying it, using all forms of escapes on it—and failing in all attempts, I finally gave up and removed the directory. (Hint: Use

```
$ find .-name '-*' -exec mv {} ff;
$rm ff
```

Send Messages to Other Users

There are several means of sending messages to another user. Two related commands are `wall` and `write`.

The `write` command is used to write to a specific user. The syntax for the command is

```
$ write user [tty]
```

The *user* name is the same name as is shown in the `who` command. If you want to write to a user who is logged in on more than one terminal, the *tty* option can be used to specify which terminal for that user.

The `wall` command is generally only available to the superuser. This command enables the writer to write to all the terminals. Here's an example.

Input Output

```
$ wall "The building is on fire .... Get out now!!!"
Broadcast message from author@nodemama
     (/dev/tty1) at 12:58 ...

The building is on fire .... Get out now!!!
```

Analysis

As you can see, this is reserved for emergencies. It's not a good idea to send unsolicited messages to users.

Users can block such messages with the command `mesg`. To block unsolicited messages, use

```
$ mesg n
```

On the other hand, to allow the unsolicited messages through, use

```
$ mesg y
```

The default is to let the messages through.

mail

The `mail` utility is one of the most important utilities in UNIX. This book would not be complete without a description of its features. `mail` gives you the ability to send electronic messages to other users on your system or to users on other systems connected to your system via a network. There are other uses for `mail`, as you will see when you are doing shell programming. For example, you can send yourself mail messages after a long shell job is done, or you can see your mail periodically using the `at` command.

The major advantage of the `mail` command over the `write` command is that with `mail`, the recipient of the message does not have to be logged in when you send the message. Also, the `write` command is not very polite, and it can be stopped by the `mesg` command.

Using the *mail* Command

Type `mailuserName` at the prompt to send mail to a user `userName` on your system. The command will prompt you for a subject, thus:

```
Subject:
```

Type in your text and terminate it with a single period (`.`) at the end. This will send your mail system to the other user. For example, if you were sending a message to `george`, you would see this.

Input
Output

```
$ mail george
Subject: Ready to eat?
.
(Null body of message, hope it's okay)
```

Analysis

The `Null body` message is `mail`'s way of telling you that you did not type any text in the body of the message.

On the other end, when `george` logs in, he will see the message:

```
you have mail
```

This message will be displayed on his console because the shell periodically checks to see whether there is mail for the user. It is then up to `george` to read his or her mail at a convenient time; `george` would do so by typing the `mail` command with no options. In doing so, the user `george` is put in the interactive mail handler program.

Type a `?` at the mail handler prompt for your list of options. The options that you are most likely to use are these:

- `ENTER` Displays the next message.
- `p` Prints this message again.
- `d` Deletes this message.
- `s` *`file`* Saves this *`file`*. The next mail message is displayed.
- `q` Quits. Any unread messages will remain for the next time. All deleted messages will be lost forever.
- `x` Exits and restores any deleted messages.

If you want to send mail to someone on another system, you have to use `mail` *`username@systemName`* to send that person a free-text message. The mail handler is a very complex and powerful feature of UNIX. You can communicate with anyone connected to the Internet or to various other networks. See your system administrator for more details on how your site's UNIX system is configured. You can use the `man mail` command at the prompt for more information.

You can use the `mail` command with a shell script so that you are notified when the script is done. Consider the following example.

Input
Output

```
$ cat longfile
#
# Do a backup and notify me when you are done
#
# -f /dev/rfd0  use removeable floppy drive 0
# -c for create
#

tar -cf /dev/rfd0 *.[ch]
mail "Done with backup" ¦ kamran

$ longfile &
[1304]
$ vi letter
$ (on exit......)
$
you have mail
$ mail
From kamran Mon Aug 12 15:47
Done with backup

?d
?q
$
```

Analysis

This shell script does a backup of all the `.c` and `.h` files onto the floppy drive. I run this script in the background so that I can do other work. After the backup is complete, the script sends a mail message to me. When I'm done with my work in the `vi` editor, I will be notified that the script is done.

Note: Do not assume that `/dev/rfd0` will be the floppy drive on your machine. The name could be as arcane as `/dev/fd0H1440` or `/dev/rfd1`. Check your UNIX documentation for how to address your system's floppy drive.

The *at* Command

The `at` command is used to execute a command at a specified time. You can specify a.m. or p.m. commands or commands at noon, midnight, or tea-time (4 p.m.). You can even specify the day, month, or year in the form *`MMDDYY`* or *`MM/DD/YY`*. You can mail yourself a message when this is done. This command is useful for periodic backups or other related commands.

For example, to run a job called `backmeup` at 4 p.m. on Monday, type the following command:

```
$ at 4 pm Monday<backmeup
```

If you want to receive a notice of this execution when it happens via a mail message, use the `-m` option.

```
$ at -m 4 pm Monday<backmeup
```

This example assumes that `backmeup` is a shell script. If `backmeup` is a shell script, by default it will be run under the Bourne shell. The `-k` flag will force the execution of the Korn shell instead of the default Bourne shell.

You also can specify time offsets, in terms of now or tomorrow. To run a job three days from now at 4 p.m., you can use

```
$ at 4 pm + 3 days<backmeup
```

To list all the scheduled commands, use the `at -l` command. To remove a command, use the `at -r` command with the index number returned for the job listed in the `at -l` command. This gives the job numbers you need for the `-r` option.

DO	DON'T

DO be frugal with the `at` command. Managing inputs from several `at` commands may actually be more of a hassle than a help.

DON'T use the `at now` command. No matter how fast you press the Enter key, you will be too late for the system. Instead, use the command `at now +1` min to give yourself enough time.

crontab

The `crontab` command is used to do periodic commands. This uses the `cron` daemon (*cron* is short for *chronograph*) to manage a file called `crontab`. Each user has his or her own `crontab` file that lists all the scheduled jobs for him or her.

You will find `crontab` especially useful if you want to run periodic backups or if you want to remind yourself with a mail message to go home at 5 p.m.

The syntax for this command is

```
crontab cfile
```

Use the `-e` option to invoke your editor on your current `crontab` file. The syntax is

```
crontab -e
```

If you do not specify the `-e` option, your previous `crontab` file will be destroyed and you will be given a new file. Be careful. If you want to erase your crontab file, use the command `crontab` without the `-e` option and do not add any entries to the temporary file you are presented with.

The `crontab cfile` command invokes your editor on your crontab file, `cfile`, which will contain all your `crontab` statements. The contents of this file will be copied into a system directory as another filename derived from your user id. Your original `cfile` will not be destroyed.

Note: The instructions for using `crontab` are not consistent across many UNIX systems. Consult your UNIX man pages for details on how to use this command on your machine.

Also, you may have to get your system administrator to set your user name in the `allow` file for `crontab`. If this is not set or if your user name is in the `deny` file, you will be able to use `crontab`. The `allow` file contains a list of users that are allowed to use this utility; likewise, the `deny` file contains a list of users not allowed to use `crontab`. If neither is set, you are allowed to use it. (Use the `find` command to determine the exact location of these two files in your directory structure.)

The usual locations for this file are the `/var/spool` or the `/usr/spool` directories.

The `crontab` file contains one line for each scheduled entry. Each line contains six items:

```
min hour day month dayofweek shellCommand
```

The values each can be assigned are the following:

`min`	0-59
`hour`	0-23
`day`	1-31
`month`	1-12
`dayofweek`	0-6 (0 is Sunday)
`shellCommand`	A shell command, usually with an explicit pathname

An asterisk in any of the first five fields implies a wildcard that matches any value. More than one value can be specified by a range or by separating the values with commas.

Let's say you want to be informed about your timesheets on the 1st and 15th of every month. For this schedule, you would create this entry:

```
0   7   1,15  * *  mailx -s"TIMESHEET DUE" kamran
```

This message will be sent at 7 a.m. on the 1st and 15th day of every month.

To display the time every hour between 8 a.m. and 5 p.m. on the console, use

```
0 8,9,10,11,12,13,14,15,16,17 * * * date  > /dev/console
```

DO	DON'T

DO use absolute pathnames to any shell scripts you use in the `crontab` or `at` commands. This will ensure that you are able to execute the files you want.

DO use the Bourne shell for all your shell scripts. Most `cron` commands use this shell and do not handle `ksh` extensions, such as the tilde (~), very well.

DON'T replace the `crontab` file you find under `/usr/spool`. Use the `crontab` command instead.

DON'T put very many entries in the `crontab` file, even though you can have as many entries as you want. A large number of entries per `crontab` file per user may slow down the system.

To remove the `crontab` file, use

```
crontab -r
```

To list the entries in your file, use

```
crontab -l
```

Summary

Today, you learned about a grab bag of UNIX utilities and programming techniques. You read about the following topics:

- It's possible to create a mail merge using the standard UNIX tools `awk` and `sed`. You have to use two files: a master file with the template and a data file with the individual fields. The example creates a `sed` script and runs `sed` on the data file to create the output files to the printer.
- You learned how to lock the terminal with the `trap` and `stty` commands to prevent unauthorized access.
- Waiting for users is possible with background processing.
- Users without passwords are a threat to any UNIX system. A shell script shown today will find all such accounts in the `/etc/passwd` file.

- Two techniques were presented: `tar` and `cpio`. Both offer powerful backup features. The `tar` is useful for portable backups across different platforms, but it generates large files because it creates files on fixed byte boundaries; `cpio` is easier to use and produces backup files that are more compact.
- Restricted shells are useful when you have to prevent certain users from roaming around your system. Check the `/bin/rsh` man pages for more information.
- File compression is useful when archiving.
- You can send messages to other users with the `write` or `wall` commands. These commands are also reserved for short, quick messages.
- The `mail` utility is the preferred choice for sending messages to users who are not logged in at the time you send the message. The system will save the message for those users until they log in.
- Filenames created with reserved characters may be a nice trick, but using reserved characters can place you in the awkward position of not being able to remove the results easily.
- You can schedule jobs for execution at a specified time with the `at` command or for execution periodically with the `cron` command.

UNIX Commands Learned Today

You learned about the following UNIX commands today:

- `tar`
- `cpio`
- `who`
- `mail`
- `write`
- `at`
- `crontab`

Q&A

Q What's the difference between the `at` and `cron` commands?

A The `at` command runs a command once at a specified time. If you want to reschedule it, you have to do so yourself in the command. The `crontab` command schedules commands for a periodic execution. You do not have to set the commands yourself.

Q The last `write` message from my fellow user wrote over the text on my screen. What should I do?

A First enter Ctrl+l to refresh your screen. If you want to stop any more messages, use `mesg n`. You will not, however, be able to stop messages from the superuser.

Q How do I execute UNIX commands or shell scripts from within an `awk` script file?

A Use the `"UNIX command" | getline` command. This will execute the *`UNIX command`* for you in a subshell and return the result in `$0`.

Workshop

The Workshop provides quiz questions to help you solidify your understanding of the material covered. Some Workshop sections of this book also contain exercises to provide you with experience in using what you've learned. Try to understand the quiz and exercise answers before continuing on to the next chapter. Answers are provided in Appendix D, "Answers."

Quiz

1. How can you stop annoying `write` messages from appearing on your terminal? How do you turn `write` messages back on?
2. How do you get the return value from UNIX commands from within `awk` files?
3. How do you remove entries from the `crontab` file?

14

Exercises

1. Schedule two shell scripts for execution. Execute `gohome` at 5 p.m., Monday through Friday, and execute `backmeup` at 2 a.m. on Saturdays.
2. Schedule a command to remind you of something that will mail a message four days from today at 1p.m. Use the `at` command.
3. Modify the merge program to insert the date of printing on the letterhead. Hint: Use `"date %D %M %Y" ¦ getline today` to read the date into a variable called `today` in the `awk` program.

WEEK 2 IN REVIEW

8 9 10 11 12 13 14

In the second week, you dealt with examples and built on the knowledge you gained from the first week.

On Day 8, you read about the following:

- What shell scripts are and how to write them
- How to use the `colon` command
- The significance of the `$#` and `$*` variables in a script file
- How to use the `shift` command to get all the arguments to a script file
- How to do integer math with the `expr` command
- How to debug your shell script with the `-v` and `-x` options
- How to use the `sh -n` option to work with suspect scripts

On Day 9, you were introduced to the testing and looping commands in the shell. Day 9 covered the following topics:

- How to use the `getopts` commands to parse command-line options in a standard, consistent format to a shell script.
- How to use the `if` conditional test to check for strings and numeric comparison, and for the existence and type of a file.
- How to use the `[]` shortcut, and the `else` and `elif` clauses.
- How to handle multilevel comparison, including regular expressions, with the `case` statement.
- That a shortcut for processing all the arguments in a `for` loop is to leave out the `in` keyword and its list of arguments.
- How quoting mechanisms in the `test` command, for example, and escaping the `()` parentheses works in test conditions with a `\`.
- How to use the looping mechanisms in the shell. The `for` command processes a known number of arguments in a loop. The `while` and `until` commands run until a condition is false or true, respectively.
- How to use the `break` command to break you out of one level of the loop; `break` *n* will break you out of *n* levels of a loop.
- The ampersand (`&`) at the end of the `done` statement will put the entire `for` loop in the background. You can use the indirection command to send the output from the background to another location.
- To wait *n* seconds, you can use the `sleep` *n* command.
- How to use the `getopts` command, which is for processing the incoming options and arguments within a `while` loop and a `case` statement. This command provides a standard mechanism for processing shell arguments.

Day 10 covered shell variables and how to work with assigning default values to them. In addition to this, you discovered how to read the user input via the `read` statement. Day 10 covered the following subjects:

- How to use the `read` statement to read from the keyboard into variables. Words from the line are assigned one each to the `read` command's arguments. The last variable gets the rest of the line. If there are more variables than words, the extra variables are assigned a `NULL` value.

- ☐ How to assign default values to variables when you are testing them.
- ☐ That the -e option to the echo command may sometimes be required to enable the parsing of the special options following the backslash.
- ☐ How the output from the date command can be formatted to print.
- ☐ How the sort command can be used to sort on field numbers on a per-line basis, POS1 and POS2.
- ☐ How the case statement makes handling multiple options easier to handle, especially when working with an interactive menu shell script.

On Day 11, you learned how to handle special situations such as interrupts, and how to put together UNIX tools to create your own shell scripts. You learned about the following:

- ☐ How to create and use sed scripts.
- ☐ How to create your shell wrappers around standard UNIX commands.
- ☐ How to intercept signals (such as hang-ups and Ctrl+c) with the trap command.
- ☐ Why Signal 9 cannot be ignored or stopped. (This is the last-resort method of stopping a process that is ignoring all other signals.)

On Day 12, you learned about awk, a pattern-scanning language. It reads in data from the input file one line at a time and compares it to a list of patterns in an awk program. An awk program is a set of patterns and actions and can be in a text file or specified at the command line. awk takes actions for each pattern that matches in the input line. In Day 12, you learned about the following:

- ☐ About the simplest awk program, `{ print }`, which prints every line of the input file. If the default action of `{ print $0; }` is taken, no action is specified. You do not have to specify the $0, which is the default in this case, and you don't need the ; as the delimiter for the line.
- ☐ How the -f filename option specifies an input file for awk. An awk program also can be specified by placing it in single quotes on the command line.
- ☐ How the entire input line can be referred to by $0. Each field in the line is referred to by $1 for the first, $2 for the second, and so on. The number of fields in the line is the awk special variable NF.

- That awk has special variables for the number of lines read, the number of fields in the current line (NF), and for the input field separator (IFS).
- How the print command will print all arguments to it on one line. Arguments must be separated by commas or they will be connected together with no blank spaces.
- How the printf statement is a special purpose statement that does a formatted print. You specify a format string as the first argument, followed by zero or more variables to which to apply the format. The printf statement does not automatically print a newline.
- That, as with other UNIX tools, if you omit the input filenames with the awk command, awk will accept input from the keyboard instead.
- That awk will accept variables at the command line with the -v option.
- That you should consider using awk for most tasks, especially when the task seems overly complicated when using other UNIX tools.

  awk should be considered for tasks in which a specific UNIX tool will not do the job. For example, grep is faster to use for all but the most complicated text searches. If you want to take an action based on the search, you should consider awk.

On Day 13, you got a short introduction to the Korn shell. The Korn shell will run almost all Bourne shell scripts. It's designed to be upward-compatible. (The only significant difference is that the Bourne shell can use the ^ character as a synonym for the ¦ character as a pipe. Such use is now dated.) On Day 13, you learned about the following:

- That the Korn shell keeps a history of all the commands used in your session. The command-history file can be referred to by the HISTFILE environment variable. You can edit these commands for re-execution with the vi or emacs editors. The command-line editor mode can be set by the EDITOR and/or VISUAL environment variables, or the set -o mode command.
- That the Korn shell provides many types of conditional tests with the ((..)) and [[ ]] operators.
- That the Korn shell enables you to create arrays that are either 512 or 1,024 elements long and are indexed 0 and up. They are automatically created by subscripting a variable.
- How to create simple menus in the Korn shell with the select command. This is another method in addition to the one you discovered in the Bourne shell using case statements on Day 10.

- About special characters, such as the tilde (~) for creating a synonym for the user name, +~ for the current directory, and ~- for the previous directory.
- That the Korn shell has built-in commands that act like its on-disk programs but run faster (since they are built in to the shell and since `PATH` does not have to be searched).
- That the Korn shell has a built-in random number generator. The `RANDOM` variable is set to a random variable in the Korn shell every time it's used.
- That the Korn shell offers a `print` statement that is more useful than the `echo` statement.
- About how the Korn shell supports multiprocessing. A Ctrl+z puts the foreground process into a stopped state. The `bg` command runs the stopped process in the background. The jobs command lists all the jobs.
- How the commands are searched for in a predefined order in the Korn shell: reserved words, aliases, built-in commands, functions, and then the `PATH`.
- That aliases provide a shorthand method for using complicated commands.

Finally, Day 14 showed a hodgepodge of UNIX utilities and programming techniques. You learned the following in Day 14:

- How to create a simple mail merge utility using the standard UNIX tools `awk` and `sed`. You used two files: a master file with the template and a data file with the individual fields. The example in Day 14 created a `sed` script and runs `sed` on the data file to create the output files to the printer.
- How to lock the terminal with the `trap` and `stty` commands to prevent unauthorized access.
- How to wait for specific users to log in via a background process.
- How to find users without passwords, with a shell script and `awk`.
- How to do simple backups and restoration of files. Two techniques were presented here for you to use: `tar` and `cpio`.
- About the use of restricted shells to prevent certain users from roaming around your system.
- How to use file compression for archiving.
- How to use the `write`, `wall`, or `mail` utilities for sending messages to other users.

- How to schedule jobs for execution at a specified time with the at command, or periodically with the cron command.

This week, you completed your mastering of the Bourne shell and its related shells and utilities. You learned how to use shell scripts and tools, and now have examples to see which tool fits the problem you are trying to solve.

A

Bourne Shell Command Summary

This is a summary of all the commands in the Bourne shell and how to use the shell.

Starting the Bourne Shell

If the shell is started by `exec` and the first character of the command is a `-`, the shell will run the system's `.profile` and `$HOME/.profile` files. The following options are supported:

`-c` *`command`*	Executes the command
`-i`	Interactive
`-r`	Restricted shell
`-s`	Commands from standard input

Commands

The syntax for a command is as follows:

`command arguments`

where `command` is the command to be executed given the `arguments`. The command and its arguments are separated by whitespaces (tabs or blanks). Multiple commands have semicolons between them.

The exit status of a command is zero on success and non-zero otherwise.

The pipe symbol (`¦`) can be used to connect the output from one command to the input of another. If a command is terminated with an ampersand (`&`), the command is executed in the background.

Commands can occur on many lines if the last return is escaped with a `\` or between quotes. The shell prompt changes to a `>` symbol to reflect this.

Commands following an unquoted (`#`) are ignored by the shell and are used as comments.

Shell Variables

There are three types of shell variables:

- Normal variables assigned via the `var=value` command.
- Positional parameters `$1`, `$2`, `$3`, and so on.
- Special parameters. (See Table A.1.)

Table A.1. Special variables in the Bourne shell.

Variable	Expands to
$#	The number of command-line arguments
$*	All the arguments to the command in one big quote
$@	All the arguments individually quoted
$0	The name of the program being executed
$$	The process id of the program being executed
$!	The last program executed
$-	List the current options

Environment Variables

As in the Bourne shell, `ksh` maintains a set of variables for its environment. Table A.2 lists these variables, which exist in the Korn and Bourne shells. The text shows those variables that do not exist in the Bourne shell.

Table A.2. Environment variables.

Variable	Function
_ (underscore)	This variable expands to the last argument from the previously executed command. For every command that is executed as a child of the shell, `ksh` sets this variable to the full pathname of the executable file and passes this value through the environment to that child's process. When processing the `MAILPATH` variable, this variable holds the value of the corresponding mail file.
`CDPATH`	This contains a list of directories for the `cd` command to search files for. Directory names are separated with colons on POSIX and UNIX systems. `CDPATH` works similar to the `PATH` variable.

continues

Table A.2. continued

Variable	Function
`COLUMNS`	This contains the maximum width of the edit window in the `ksh`'s `vi` or `emacs` editing mode. It is also used by several other commands to define the width of the terminal output device. This is for the Korn shell only.
`EDITOR`	This variable is set to the name of the default editor for command history editing. It can be set to `vi`, `emacs`, or `gmacs` to enable the corresponding editing mode. This is for the Korn shell only.
`ERRNO`	This contains the system error number of the most recently failed system call. The shell sets only this variable for errors that occur in the current environment. Assigning a value of `0` to this variable clears it. This is for the Korn shell only.
`ENV`	This contains a value on which `ksh` performs parameter substitution to get the name of an initialization file. This file is executed with the `` `.' `` command. This for the Korn shell only.
`FCEDIT`	This contains the name of the default editor for the `fcm` command. If this variable is not set, the default value is `/bin/ed`. This is for the Korn shell only.
`HISTFILE`	This contains the pathname of a file to be used as the history file. When the Korn shell starts, the value of this variable overrides the default history file. This is for the Korn shell only.
`HISTSIZE`	This contains the maximum number of commands that the shell keeps in the history file. If this variable contains a valid number when the shell starts, it overrides the default of 127. This is for the Korn shell only.
`HOME`	This contains your home directory. This is also the default directory for the `cd` command.
`IFS`	This contains a series of characters to be used as internal field separator characters. Any of these characters may separate arguments in unquoted command substitutions or parameter substitutions. In addition, the shell uses these characters to separate values put into variables with the `read` command.

Variable	Function
	The first character in the value of IFS separates the positional parameters in $* expansion.
`LINENO`	This contains the number of the line currently being executed by a shell script.
`LINES`	This contains a numeric value that limits the number of output lines used by the Korn shell's `select` statement in printing its menu.
`MAIL`	This contains the pathname of a mailbox. If `MAILPATH` is not set, the Korn shell tells you when new mail arrives in this file. The shell assumes that new mail has arrived if the file modify time changes.
`MAILCHECK`	This contains the number of seconds of elapsed time that must pass before checking for mail; if not set, the default value is 600 seconds. When using the `MAIL` or `MAILPATH` variables, `ksh` checks for mail before issuing the prompt: `you have mail.`
`MAILPATH`	This contains a list of mailbox files. This overrides the `MAIL` variable.
`OLDPWD`	This contains the name of the previous directory. The `cd` command sets this variable. This is for the Korn shell only.
`PATH`	This contains a list of directories that constitute the search path for executable commands. Directories in this list are separated with colons. This shell searches each directory in the order specified in the list until it finds a matching executable. If you want the shell to search the current directory, put a null string in the list of directories. Starting the list with a colon or semicolon tells the shell to search the current directory first.
`PID`	This contains the decimal value of the process id of the shells parent.
`PS1`	This contains the primary prompt string used when the shell is interactive. The default value is `$`. The shell expands parameters before the prompt is printed. A single `!` in the prompt string is replaced by the command number from the history list; for a

continues

Table A.2. continued

Variable	Function
	real exclamation mark in the prompt, use `!!`. See the man pages for `fc`.
`PS2`	This contains the secondary prompt and is used when completing the input of such things as multiline input, reserved word commands, quoted strings, and documents. The default value of this variable is `>`.
`PS3`	This contains the prompt string used in connection with the `select` reserved word. The default value is `#?`. This is for the Korn shell only.
`PS4`	This contains the prefix for traced commands with set `-x`. The default value is `+`. This is for the Korn shell only.
`PWD`	This contains the name of the current working directory. When the shell starts, the current directory name is assigned to `PWD` unless the variable already has a value.
`RANDOM`	This expands to a random integer. Assigning a value to `RANDOM` sets a new seed for the random number generator.
`REPLY`	This contains the user input from the `select` statement (see Command Syntax). The `read` command also sets this variable if no variable is specified. This is available in the Korn shell only.
`SECONDS`	This contains elapsed time. The value of this variable grows by 1 for each elapsed second of real time. Any value assigned to this variable sets the `SECONDS` counter to that value; initially, the shell sets the value to 0. This is available in the Korn shell only.
`SHELL`	This contains the full pathname of the current shell. It is not set by the shell but is used by various other commands to invoke the shell.
`TMOUT`	This contains the number of seconds before the user input times out. If user input has not been received within this length of time, the shell terminates. This is available in the Korn shell only.
`VISUAL`	This overrides the `EDITOR` variable in setting `vi`, `emacs`, or `gmacs` editing modes for the Korn shell.

Quoting

Table A.3 lists quotes and their actions.

Table A.3. Action of quotes.

Quote	Action
`'..'`	Removes special meaning of all quoted characters
`".."`	Removes special meaning of all quoted characters except `'`, `$` and `\`
`\c`	Removes special meaning of the character `c`. Inside double quotes, it removes the meaning of `'`,`$` and `\` only
`` `cmd` ``	Executes `cmd` and inserts standard output in its place

Filename Substitution

Table A.4 lists the filename substitution characters for the shell.

Table A.4. Filename substitution.

Metacharacter	Expands to
`?`	One character
`*`	Zero or more characters
`[chars]`	Matches a single characters in `[chars]`
`[!chars]`	Matches all except the characters in `[chars]`

I/O Redirection

Table A.5 summarizes the special characters for command-line substitution.

Table A.5. I/O redirection.

Redirection	Action
`< file`	Takes standard input from the file.
`> file`	Sends standard output to the file.

continues

Table A.5. continued

Redirection	Action
`>>file`	Appends standard output to the file.
`<<word`	Reads from standard input until an exact match is found (a line containing only `word`). Parameter substitution occurs on all unquoted characters.
`<<-word`	Same as the preceding, except that leading tabs are removed.
`<&digit`	Standard input is redirected from the digit file descriptor.
`>&digit`	Standard output is redirected to the digit file descriptor.
`<&-`	Standard input is closed.
`>&-`	Standard output is closed.

No filename substitution is performed on the file in the previous table. File descriptor `0` is standard input, `1` is standard output, and `2` is standard error.

Subshells

The (...;) construct executes commands in the parentheses as a subshell. The {...} construct executes commands in the current shell.

Exported variables from the parent shell cannot be modified in the subshell. Input or output from several commands can be redirected via the use of these constructs.

```
(p1; p2; p3) 2>logfile &
```

will execute all three programs in the background and redirect all error output from the three programs to the logfile.

Functions

Functions are of the form

```
name()
{
command
[...]
```

```
command
}
```

where *name* is the name of the function that executes these commands. A return statement will terminate the shell without terminating the shell.

Command Summary

Table A.6 gives a summary of all the commands in the Bourne shell.

Table A.6. Command summary.

: (colon)	The null command.
`. file`	Executes the file as a series of commands in the current shell and not as a subshell.
`break`	Breaks out of the innermost `for`, `while`, or `until` loop.

	`case value`
	`p1)command`
	`[...]`
	`command;;`
	`p2)command`
	`[...]`
	`command;;`
	`[...]`
	`*)command`
	`[...]`
	`command;;`

`continue [n]`	Resumes next iteration in a `for` or `while` loop. If *n* is specified, continue after the *n*th iteration.
`case`	
`esac`	The word's value is compared against all the patterns until a match is found. All commands to the right of the pattern are executed until the `;;` is found. The `*` matches any unmatched pattern up to that point and is the last item in the list since it is the default response for the `case` statement. Patterns can be combined with the ¦ operator as an `OR` operator. The `*)` is optional.

continues

Table A.6. continued

`cd [dir]`	Changes directory to *dir*. If *dir* is not specified, the command goes to the `HOME` directory.
`echo [-n] args`	Writes the `args` to the standard output after filename expansion. The `-n` option suppresses the output of a newline. Escape characters for the echo statement are listed in Table A.7.
`eval args`	Evaluates the arguments and rescans the results.
`exec command [args]`	Executes the command as a subshell with the `args`.
`exit [code]`	Terminates the shell with the exit code.
`export [variables]`	Exports the listed variables to all subsequent subshells. If no variables are specified, the command returns a list of the exported variables.

`for i [in list]`
`do`
`command`
`[ellipse]`
`done`
	Executes the commands in between `do` and `done` by substituting the `$i` with each item in the list. All such commands are executed in a subshell. If the `[in list]` is not specified, the `for` loop is executed on the command-line arguments.

`getopts options var`	Processes command-line arguments, where `options` is the list of options. Each time `getopts` is called, it scans the options list for the command-line arguments. If an argument matches an option, `getopts` stores the value (and parameter, if a colon follows the option) in the variable `var`. The parameter is stored in a special variable called `OPTARG`. If a parameter is expected and none is found, `getopts` prints an error message and exits. `OPTIND` is an index of the next command-line argument to process.

`if condition1`
`then`
`command1`
`[...]`
`[ellipses]`
`elif condition2`
`then`
`command2`
`[...]`
`else`
`command3`
`[...]`
`fi`
	If the condition is tested true, the `command1` set is executed; otherwise the `command2` set is executed if `condition2` is true. If neither is true, `command3` is executed. The `elif` and `else` statements can be nested several levels deep. The `elif` and `else` portions are also optional.

`newgrp [`*`groupname`*`]`	This changes your group name to *`groupname`*. If no name is specified, this changes it to your default group.
`set variable = value`	Sets a shell variable to `value`.
`pwd`	This prints your current working directory.
`read vars list`	This reads from the standard input into `vars`. It also assigns words read one at a time to each variable in the list, and assigns any remaining words to the last `var` in the list. If more variables exist than words, the extra variables are not assigned values.
`readonly variable`	This tells the shell that the variable cannot be reassigned a value. The variable is irreversible for the duration of the shell.
`return [n]`	This is similar to the `exit` statement except that it terminates a function and a return code of `n`. If `n` is omitted, the exit code of the last command in the function is returned.

continues

Table A.6. continued

`shift [n]`	This shifts the command-line arguments to the left *n* times. After this call, the value of `$0` is lost and is overwritten by `$1`. `$1` is overwritten by `$2`, and so on.
`test condition` or `[ condition ]`	This is used to return the test of a `condition` for `if` statements. See Day 9 and Table A.7 for more information.
`times`	This returns the times used by all the processes.
`trap command signals`	This processes a command when a signal is received. To reset a trap, use trap `""` signals. See Day 11 for more information.
`type command`	This tells you about the type of command, shell script, or binary (and so on).
`umask octal`	This sets the default creation mask to the octal value.
`unset variable`	Resets the value of the shell `variable` to NULL.
`ulimit blocks`	This sets the maximum size of the file to blocks for all subprocesses. This is a safety feature to prevent disk pollution from runaway processes.
`wait n`	This causes the shell to suspend it's execution for *n* seconds.

`until`
`do`
`done`
	Executes all the commands between `do` and `done` until the condition is tested true.

`while condition`
`do`
`commands`
`[...]`
`done`
	Executes all the commands between do and done until the condition is not tested true.

Table A.7. Escape characters for the `echo` statement.

Character	Function
`\b`	Backspace
`\c`	No newline
`\f`	Page break (form feed)
`\n`	Newline
`\r`	Carriage return
`\t`	Tab
`\\`	A forward slash, `\`
`\nnn`	Octal value of ASCII character

Table A.8. Test conditions.

Operator	True if
`-b file`	Block device
`-c file`	Character device
`-d file`	Directory
`-f file`	Ordinary file
`-g file`	Sticky bit set, always resides in memory
`-p file`	Named pipe
`-r file`	Read-only by this shell
`-t file`	File descriptor for standard output
`-u file`	The file has root privileges
`-w file`	Writeable by this shell
`-x file`	Executable

continues

Table A.8. continued

String operations

Operator	True if
`string`	String is not null or not defined
`-n string`	String is not null and has a length greater than 0
`-z string`	String is null or has a length equal to 0
`str1 = str2`	`str1` is identical to `str2`
`str1 != str2`	`str1` is not identical to `str2`

Integer operations

Operator	True if
`int1 -eq int2`	`int1` is equal to `int2`
`int1 -ne int2`	`int1` is not equal to `int2`
`int1 -lt int2`	`int1` is less than `int2`
`int1 -le int2`	`int1` is less than or equal to `int2`
`int1 -gt int2`	`int1` is greater than `int2`
`int1 -ge int2`	`int1` is greater than or equal to `int2`

Boolean operations

Operator	True if
`! exp`	`exp` expression is negated
`exp1 -a exp2`	If `exp1` and `exp2` are both true, this is true; otherwise, it is false.
`exp1 -o exp2`	If either `exp1` or `exp2` is true, this is true; otherwise, it is false.

B

Some Selected Scripts

B Some Selected Scripts

This appendix gives a collection of some of the shell scripts in this book for you. These are listed here as a quick reference for you to review.

Listings B.1 through B.9 show examples from the perspective of how each script's individual statements fit together.

Listing B.1. Processing shell arguments.

```
#!/bin/sh
#
# This shell script will print all the arguments
# passed to it one at a time
#
echo "$# arguments in all"
ctr=0
for i in $*
do
   ctr=`expr $ctr + 1`
   echo $ctr " " $i
done
```

Listing B.2. Checking argument extents.

```
#!/bin/sh
#
# This shell script will print all the arguments
# passed to it one at a time
#
echo $# arguments
echo arg1=:$10:
echo arg2=:$0:
echo arg3=:$1:
echo All of them are $*
```

Listing B.3. Comparing two arguments.

```
#!/bin/sh
#
# This shell script compares two arguments passed in at
# the command line. It's another way to use the else
# statement.
#
arg1=$1
arg2=$2
```

```
if [ $# -ne 2 ]
then
     echo "$0: You must supply two integers" >&2
     exit 1
fi

if [ $arg1 -eq $arg2 ]
then
     echo "arg1 equals arg2"
elif [ $arg1 -lt $arg2 ]
then
     echo "$arg1 is less than $arg2"
else
     echo "$arg1 is greater than $arg2"
fi
```

Input Output

Listing B.4. The todo list generator.

```
#!/bin/sh
# ####################################################################
#         Kamran Husain khusain@delphi.com
#
# todo: A task list manager for personal use only.
#
# Use at your own risk, copy and modify freely, just credit the
# author with the idea. No warranty of any sort is implied.
#
# ####################################################################

# ####################################################################
#    Set your required defaults.
# ####################################################################
EDITOR=${EDITOR-vi}
MORE=${MORE-less}

# ####################################################################
#    Check if the user specified a filename to work with
# ####################################################################
datafile=${1-$HOME/items}

# ####################################################################
# For debug: uncomment these lines
# echo $datafile
# echo $EDITOR
# echo $MORE
# ####################################################################

# ####################################################################
#
# Create the file if it does not exist.
#
```

continues

Listing B.4. continued

```
# ##########################################################################
if [ ! -f $datafile ]
then
     echo "Creating the items file"
     touch $HOME/items
fi

# ##########################################################################
#    Now process the commands in a while loop.
#         First present the menu
# ##########################################################################
while :
do
echo "

     TODO MANAGER
     ------------

     Change [F]ile
     [A]dd Item
     sort items by [D]ate
     sort items by [P]riority
     [E]dit the list
     [L]ist sorted items
     E[X]it

     Enter Selection: (F, A, D, P, E, L, X ):"

read response

# ##########################################################################
# Parse the response
# ##########################################################################

case $response in

     f|F) echo "File functions here"
          ;;
     a|A) echo "Add functions here"


     #
     #  Ask the user about the item.
     #
          echo -e "Enter task priority: [5] \c"
          read priority
          echo -e "Enter status [p d i]: [p]\c"
          read tstat
          echo -e "Enter due date [YYYYMMDD]: [19940101]\c"
          echo -e "Enter Task:"
          read tasktodo
```

```
     # #######################################
     # Now write the data to end of the file
     # #######################################
echo ${priority:=5}  ${tstat:=p} ${duedate:=19940101} $tasktodo >> $datafile


          ;;
     d¦D) echo "Sort by Date"
          sort +2 -3 $datafile ¦ $MORE
          ;;
     p¦P) echo "Todo list by priority `date`"
          sort -r $datafile ¦ $MORE
          ;;
     e¦E) echo "Edit the list"
          $EDITOR $datafile
          ;;
     l¦L) echo "Listing the TODO list as of `date`"
          $MORE $datafile
          ;;
     x¦X) echo "Bye"
          exit 0
          ;;

     *)
          echo "Please Enter a selection shown in [ ] ";
          ;;
     esac
done
############### end of shell script ################
```

Input Output

Listing B.5. Line number generating an awk file.

```
{
printf "%5d %s\n", NR, $0;
}
```

Input Output

Listing B.6. NF and NR testing in awk.

```
#
# Sample file to show NR, NF and tests.
# Print number of lines in the file.
awk 'END { print NR; } ' nl.awk
# Print only the tenth line
awk ' NR == 10 ' nl.awk
# Print last field in each line
awk ' { print $NF; } ' scores
# Print lines with more than four fields
```

continues

Listing B.6. continued

```
awk ' NF > 4 ' nl.awk
# Print lines in which last field is >4
awl ' $NF > 4 ' nl.awk
# Print lines with blank second field
awk ' { $2 == ""; print ; } ' scores
# Swap first two fields of each line and print them
awk ' { print $2, $1} ; ' scores
# Print # of fields in each line, followed by the line
awk ' { print NF, $0} ; ' scores
#
```

Input Output

Listing B.7. Integer operations in awk.

```
BEGIN {
     i  = 10; j  = 2;
     printf " \n set values, i = %d, j = %d \n", i, j;
     printf " i++ = %d \n", i++;
     printf " i-- = %d \n", i--;

     printf " \n set values, i = %d, j = %d \n", i, j;
     printf " --i = %d \n", --i;
     printf " ++i = %d \n", ++i;

     i  = 10; j  = 2;
     printf " \n Reset values, i = %d, j = %d \n", i, j;

     i += j;
     printf" i += j gives %d \n", i;

     i -= j;
     printf" i -= j gives %d \n", i;

     i *= j;
     printf" i *= j gives %d \n", i;

     i /= j;
     printf" i /= j gives %d \n", i;

     i %= j;
     printf" i %= j gives %d \n", i;

     i  = 10; j  = 2;
     printf " \n reset values, i = %d, j = %d \n", i, j;

     i  = i ^ j;
     printf" i ^= j gives %d \n", i;

}
```

Listing B.8. Reverse the arguments to an awk file.

```
{
     i = 1;
     while (i < NF) {
          printf "%s ", $(NF - i);
          i++;
     }
     printf "\n";
}
```

Listing B.9. Show the `printf` statement in action.

```
#
#    This is an example of a stand-alone awk program
#    which does not require an input file since it
#    does everything in between the BEGIN and END
#    statements.
#
#


BEGIN {
     # ---------------------------------------------------
     # This awk program calculates the estimated savings from
     # making extra principal payments on a conventional loan.
     # ---------------------------------------------------
     # Modify these parameters  for your loan then run
     #    awk -f amort.awk
     # ---------------------------------------------------
     rt =   8.625;           # Annual Interest Rate
     points = 1.00;          # including LOP
     loanAmt = 110000.00;    # Base Loan balance
     rolledCost = 2500.00;   # Roll in any closing costs
     yr = 30.0;              # Years to finance for
     # ---------------------------------------------------
     #    End of modifiable parameters
     # ---------------------------------------------------

     if (cmdRoll != 0) loanAmt += cmdRoll;
     if (cmdRate != 0) rt = cmdRate;
     if (cmdPts  >= 0) points = cmdPts;


     #
     #
     regac = 0;      # accumulated principal - regular
     mcsac = 0;      # accumulated principal - accelerated
     loanAmt += rolledCost;     # roll in amount
```

continues

Listing B.9. continued

```
pointAmt = loanAmt * points * 0.01;  # Add the points
regpr =  loanAmt + pointAmt;     # start with principal
mcspr = regpr;     # same for accelerated principal
npaymts = yr * 12; # total payments over loan

#
# Calculate the monthly payment based on canned formula
# store result in regmo.
#
exp1 = (1 + rt/1200.00)^(yr * 12.0);
regmo = (rt/1200.00)
regmo *= exp1;
regmo *= regpr
regmo /= (exp1 - 1);

#
# Make 1/12 payment extra per month. So mcsmo is
# the accelerated payments.
#
mcsmo = regmo * 13 / 12.0;
mcsmo = regmo + 100.00;

#
#
printf "\n                        Mortgage Acceleration Analysis";
printf "\n  Period of loan  = 30 years";
printf "\n  Interest        = %5.3f APR **** with %5.3f points", rt, points ;
printf "\n  Loan Amount     = $%9.2f (rolled cost $%8.2f)", loanAmt, rolledCost;
printf "\n  Money for points= $%9.2f", pointAmt;
printf "\n  AMOUNT FINANCED = $%9.2f", regpr;
printf "\n";
printf "\n  Mo. Payment(PI) = $%6.2f", regmo;
printf "    With Extra Principal (PI) = $%6.2f", mcsmo;
printf "\n  Difference in Mo. Payment(PI) = $%6.2f", mcsmo - regmo;
# printf "\n  Savings over current Mo. pmt  = $%6.2f",  1052.00 - regmo;
printf "\n";
printf "\n       Regular   %2d years    vs.    Prepayment    ",yr;
printf "\n Yr  Principal    Interest       Principal     Interest";

rt = rt/1200;
yr = 0;
# ------------------------------------------------------------
# For all payments.
# ------------------------------------------------------------
   for (i = 1; i <= npaymts ; i++)
{
intr = rt * regpr;
regac += intr ;
regpr += intr ;
regpr -= regmo;

#
# ------------------------------------------------------------
# If principal still exists, print it's value out
```

```
    # ------------------------------------------------------------
    #
    if (mcspr > 0)
      {
      intr = rt * mcspr;
      mcsac += intr ;
      mcspr += intr ;
      mcspr -= mcsmo;
      }
      if (i %12 == 0)
      {
      yr++;
      if ((mcspr < 0) && (done == 0))
         {
         done = 1;
         early = yr;
         }
    # ------------------------------------------------------------
    # Uncomment the next four lines for a more detailed output
    # ------------------------------------------------------------
      #   printf "\n %4d   $%9.2f   $%8.2f     $%9.2f   $%8.2f",
      #       yr, regpr, regac, mcspr,mcsac;
      #   else
      # printf "\n %4d   $%9.2f   $%8.2f", yr, regpr, regac;
      }

    if (((yr % 5) == 0)  && ((i %12 ) == 0))
        printf  "\n %2d $%9.2f   $%9.2f     $%9.2f   $%9.2f",
         yr, regpr, regac, mcspr,mcsac;
    }
    # ------------------------------------------------------------
    # Print out the savings
    # ------------------------------------------------------------
    printf "\n                                         =============";
    printf "\n Total Interest Paid Regular Payments  = $%9.2f", regac ;
    printf "\n Total Interest Paid Extra Payments    = $%9.2f", mcsac ;
    printf "\n Total Savings via Extra Principal     - $%9.2f", regac - mcsac ;
    print "\n Early Pay off in ",early, " years";

}
```

C

Editing Commands

You will find these commands helpful when using the `vi` or `emacs` editors for writing shell scripts, or when editing your Korn shell command history.

vi Editing Commands

`vi` has two modes of operation:

- Command mode
- Insert mode

In the command mode, you can issue commands to move the cursor around the screen. In the insert mode, you insert text into the document. By default, you are in the command mode when you invoke the `vi` editor.

In order to get into the insert mode, type in **`i`** at the place you want to insert it into and start typing. When you are finished typing, press the Esc key to get back into the command mode.

If you are already in command mode, typing Esc will cause `vi` to beep back at you.

> **Tip:** When in doubt about your mode, press the Esc key.

Table C.1. `vi` editor commands.

Input Mode Commands	
`ESC`	Switches to command mode
`ERASE`	Deletes the previous character or goes to the start of a line, depending on your terminal settings
`KILL`	Clears the input line
`Ctrlv`	Escapes next key
`\`	Escapes ERASE/KILL
`EOF`	Exits the shell

Cursor Movement Commands

`0`	Moves to beginning of line
`^`	Moves to first nonwhite character
`n¦`	Moves to column n
`n-`	Same as k
`n+`	Same as j
`nb`	Moves left one word
`nB`	Moves left one word
`e`	Moves to the end of a word
`E`	Moves to the end of a word
`G`	Moves to the top of history
`nh`	Moves left one character
`nj`	Moves to the next command
`nk`	Moves to the previous command
`nl`	Moves right one character
`nw`	Moves right one word
`nW`	Moves right one word

Miscellaneous Commands

`Y`	Yanks through the end of line
`yy`	Yanks the entire line
`p`	Puts yanked text after cursor
`P`	Inserts yanked text before cursor
`u`	Undoes last modification
`U`	Undoes all changes to the current line

continues

Table C.1. continued

Search Commands	
`nfc`	Moves forward to next `c`
`nFc`	Moves backward to previous `c`
`ntc`	Moves forward to before `c`
`nTc`	Moves backward to after `c`
`n;`	Repeats last `f`, `F`, `t`, or `T`
`n,`	Does ; in the reverse direction
`/string`	Searches backward for string
`/^string`	Matches only at the start of a line
`?string`	Searches forward for string
`?^string`	Matches only at the start of a line
`n`	Repeats last `/` or `?`
`N`	Repeats `/` or `?` in reverse direction
Text Change Commands	
`n-`	Inserts last word of previous line
`na`	Appends after the cursor
`A`	Appends at the end of a line
`ncmotion`	Changes through motion
`C`	Deletes the rest of a line
`ndmotion`	Deletes through motion
`dd`	Deletes the entire line
`D`	Deletes to the end of a line
`ni`	Inserts before the cursor
`I`	Inserts before a line
`nrc`	Replaces current character with C
`R`	Overtypes

`S`	Deletes the entire line
`nx`	Deletes a character
`nX`	Deletes previous characters

Modifying Text

`dw`	Deletes the current word
`dd`	Deletes the current line
`x`	Deletes a character at your location
`rc`	Replaces the character at your cursor with the next character c
`cw`	Replaces the word at your cursor with whatever you type until the next ESC character
`D`	Deletes all characters from the cursor to the end of a line

Inserting Text

`i`	Puts you in the insert mode before the current character
`a`	Puts you in the insert mode after the current character
`I`	Puts you in the insert mode at the start of a line
`A`	Puts you in the insert mode at the end of a line
`o`	Opens a new line in insert mode below this one
`O`	Opens a new line in insert mode above this one
`u`	Undoes the last operation

Moving Around

Ctrl+F	Moves forward one screen
Ctrl+B	Moves back one screen
Ctrl+D	Moves down half a screen
Ctrl+U	Moves up half a screen
H	Moves to the top of a screen
L	Moves to the bottom of a screen

Emacs Editing Commands

Table C.2. Emacs edit commands.

Cursor Movement Commands	
Esc+a	Moves to the start of a line
Ctrl+b	Moves left one character
Esc+b	Moves left one word
Ctrl+c	Moves forward to the next character c
Esc+e	Moves to the end of a line
Ctrl+f	Moves right one character
Esc+f	Moves right one word
Text Editing Commands	
ERASE	Backspaces one character
KILL	Deletes an entire line
Ctrl+d	Deletes a character
Esc+d	Deletes words
Esc+h	Deletes words backwards
Esc+Ctrl+d	Same as above
Esc+Ctrl+?	Same as above
Ctrl+k	Deletes to the end of line
Ctrl+w	Deletes to mark
History File Commands	
Esc+<	Fetches oldest history line
Esc+>	Fetches newest history line
Ctrl+n	Fetches next line
Ctrl+o	Operates

Ctrl+p	Fetches the previous line
Ctrl+r+^+string (Return)	Searches backward for string

Control Operation

\	Escapes next character
EOF	Exits the shell
Esc+Esc	Completes a pathname
Esc+=	Lists matching filenames
Esc+*	Expands matching filenames
Esc+.	Inserts last word of the previous line
Esc+_	Same as Esc
Esc+n	Repeats next command n times
Ctrl+c	Makes a word uppercase
Esc+c	Makes a character uppercase
Ctrl+j	(Newline) Executes the current line
Ctrl+l	Redraws the current line
Esc+l	Makes a word lowercase
Ctrl+m	(Return) Executes the current line
Ctrl+u	Repeats the next command four times
Ctrl+v	Displays ksh version information
Esc+letter	Expands alias `_letter`

Cut and Paste Commands

Esc+Spacebar	Marks the cursor position
Esc+p	Yanks from cursor to mark
Ctrl+t	Transposes the current and next characters
Ctrl+x+Ctrl+x	Exchanges the cursor and mark characters
Ctrl+y	Puts yanked text into a temporary cut buffer

Glossary

Some common UNIX commands are shown in Table C.3. These commands can be used in many combinations for very powerful results.

Table C.3. Glossary of common UNIX commands.

`Tat`	Schedules execution of commands at a later time. For example, `at -f script` will read the commands to be executed from the script.
`batch`	Submits a job for immediate execution.
`cat`	Takes input from the keyboard into a file— for example, `cat > file1 (^D quits reading).`
`cal`	Prints the calendar. For example, `cal 12 94` prints the calendar for the month of December 94; `cal 12 1994.`
`calendar`	Creates a `todo` list in the home directory.
`cd`	Changes the directory to where the file is located. For example, `cd '`*`dirname`*`\'path file\''` changes the directory to some location that is stored in a file, such as `cd 'cat destin'.`
`chmod`	Turns the execution bit on. For example, `chmod +x file.`
`chown`	Sets the ownership of the file to yourself, such as `chown $LOGNAME file.`
`cp`	Copies one file to another. For example, use `cp file1 file2` to copy file 1 to file 2. For recursive copying, use `cp -r dir1 dir2`, which copies the whole of directory 1 to directory 2.
`cu`	Used to call another UNIX system. For example, use `cu -ctype phone #` or `cu -acua0 9991432.`
`cut`	Selects fields from an input line. For example, `cut -c1-5 file1` cuts columns 1 through 5 on all the rows in file1.
`dd`	Used to do a complete file copy. For example, `dd if=file1 of =file2` copies file 1 to file 2. Read the man pages for `dd` if you read and write actual sectors to disk, or do conversions between ASCII and EBCDIC.
`du`	Used to summarize disk usage. For example, `du -s /*` gives the total size for all directories.

`echo`	Used to print the value of a shell variable. For example, `echo $PATH` prints the value of `PATH`.
`expr`	Evaluates an expression. For example, `expr 5 + 12` adds the numbers 5 and 12.
`file`	Gives the type of a file. For example, `file * ¦ fgrep tmp` finds all files of type `tmp`.
`find`	Used to find files. For example, to find all the files in the system use `find / -print`.
`finger`	Used to identify users. For example, to find out the names of all the users who are currently logged on, use `finger 'who ¦ cut -d' ' -f1'`.
`grep`	Used to find text in a file. For example, `find . -name -print ¦ grep 'something' > file1` tries to find the argument string in the output of the find command and then puts the result in `file1`.
`head`	Displays the first lines of a file. For example, `head filename` prints the default 10 lines of the file.
`id`	Prints the user name and group. For example, `id -a` reports all groups including the current user.
`kill`	Used to kill a process. For example, `kill -9 $!` kills the last background task.
`less`	A better version of `more` (for example, `less` *`filename`*). You have the ability to scroll up and down in the `less` program using some `vi` commands (`j`, `k`, Ctrl+F, and Ctrl+b), but you can only scroll down with `more`.
`line`	Copies one line from standard input to standard output. For example, `line='line < /dev/tty'` gets a line from the terminal.
`login`	Starts a login session. For example, `login name` is used to log in under a user name.
`ls`	Gives a list of files. For example, `ls -l` lists the long listing format of a directory.
`mail`	Used to send, receive, or forward mail. For example, `echo "Hi! there" ¦ mail roger` mails the text in the `echo` command to the user roger.

continues

Table C.3. continued

`more`	Displays the text file one page at a time. For example, use `more` *`filename`*.
`mkdir`	Used to make a directory. For example, `mkdir new` creates a directory called `new`.
`passwd`	Changes a login password. For example, `passwd: roger` lets you change the password for roger to anything desired at the root level.
`pr`	Used to format files for printing. For example, pr `'find . -name "*.txt" -print'` prints files from the list of all `txt` files.
`ps`	Reports the status of a process. For example, `ps agx` lists all processes in the system.
`pwd`	Used to get the current working directory. For example, `pwd` tells you where you are in the directory structure.
`rm`	Removes files. For example, `rm -r mydir` recursively removes everything in the directory `mydir`.
`su`	Changes to another user. For example, `su kamran` logs in the user `kamran`. To get to root, type **`su`** at the prompt.
`tail`	Prints the last few lines of a file. For example, `tail -2 myfile` is used to look at the last two lines of `myfile`.
`tee`	Used to pipe a command. For example, `dir ¦ tee capture` captures the directory listing both to the screen and to the capture file.
`touch`	Sets file access and modification times.
`wc`	Counts the words in a file. For example, `wc file` gives the number of lines, words, and characters in the file.
`who`	Identifies who is using the system. For example, `who -u` gives the list of all users currently logged in.

D

Answers

Here are the answers to selected quizzes and exercises in the book.

Day 1

Quiz Answers

1. The sequence of events that happen when you log in to UNIX are as follows:

   When you type in your login name and password, UNIX checks its list of authorized users and their respective passwords, and other information about accounts in a file.

   If UNIX finds an item in which the login name and the password matches, it allows you to log into the system. UNIX encrypts the password you type in and compares it with the list of encrypted passwords it keeps on disk. The UNIX standard password scheme makes it very difficult to go from an encrypted password back to the original string. So it's faster and easier just to compare the encrypted results of the typed password and the system copy.

   UNIX then does some housekeeping by initializing your environment and starting up a shell for your login session. The shell then provides a prompt and waits for your commands. Your environment consists of your current directory (see Day 2) and other variables (see Day 3) as long as you are logged onto UNIX. Now you can interact with UNIX while you are logged into UNIX via a shell program.

2. Someone can read your password over your shoulder as you type! It's important that no one else knows your password so that only you can log into your account.

3. This `/etc/passwd` file contains the passwords in an encrypted form in order to prevent others from reading it and finding out other users' passwords.

4. A sequence of commands is known as a program. A program can be compiled binary code or a shell script. Compiled code is the output generated from a program and is in a binary format. Binary format is intended to be read by machines only and is thus not readable by a text editor such as `vi`. Text files are those files that can be read by people and thus can be edited by a text editor such as `vi`. When a command or a program is in the running stages in the UNIX environment, it is known as a process.

5. The `ls -al` command prints out all the files in the directory. On a file, it simply lists the files. Both outputs are detailed listings.

6. You need to place quotes around `file;`. Use

```
$ ls "file;" chapter.
```

Exercise Answers

The exercises from Day 1 are simply for your practice. Their answers are not listed here.

Day 2

Quiz Answers

1. Filenames are generally composed of lower- or uppercase letters or numbers. UNIX differentiates between lower- and uppercase letters; so to UNIX, `prog1` and `Prog1` are two different files. Some limited punctuation marks are allowed, such as `.` or `_`, but these should be reserved for special files. Don't use an asterisk (`*`), question mark (`?`), greater-than symbol (`>`), less-than symbol (`<`), ampersand (`&`), or a vertical bar (`¦`) in a filename. These symbols represent different things to the command interpreter.

2. Some UNIX file systems allow filenames to be as long as you want, and some limit them to 14 characters or less.

3. The collection of the directories in UNIX is referred to as its directory tree. The tree is called a hierarchical file system because of its multilevel structure, similar to that of the root system of a tree.

4. A path is the route you would take to go from the root of the UNIX directory tree, to the file or directory you want to specify.

5. A full pathname begins with a `/`, followed by the sequence of directories from the root to get to the target file or directory. A relative pathname does not begin with a `/` and assumes a starting location of the current working directory. Therefore, it starts from the current directory and moves downward.

6. There are three types of permissions that you can grant to a file:

   Read, which gives permission to read a file

   Write, which gives permission to write into a file

   Execute, which gives permission to execute a file that contains executable code

   The scope of these read, write, and exercise permissions is based on the type of user:

   User, where permission is granted to the owner

   Group, where permission is granted to a group of users to which the owner belongs

   Other, where permission is granted to all other users

7. You count the number of characters, words, and lines in each file using the `wc` command. With the `diff` command, you compare the contents of files line by line.

8. The `file` command is useful for checking whether or not a file contains ASCII text. The `more`, `less`, `head`, and `tail` commands are sections of text files.

Exercise Answers

1. The `-C` option prints the output in columnar format. The difference between the `-a` and `-l` options is that `-a` prints the hidden files and `-l` gives a lengthy listing.

2. `ls -x` gives a column-by-column listing, and `ls -C` gives a row-by-row listing.

3. Take the tail of one and the head of another. For example:

   ```
   head +20 oldfile ¦ tail -10 newfile
   ```

   creates a file that has lines 10 through 20 only from oldfile.

4. 0744

5.

`644`	`x x _ x _ _ x _ _`	You can read/write it; others can only read it.
`711`	`x x x _ _ x _ _ x`	You read, write, and execute this; others can't.
`777`	`x x x x x x x x x`	This file is completely open.
`505`	`x _ x _ _ _ x _ x`	Your group cannot use this file.

`444 x _ _ x _ _ x _ _`	This is read only by everybody.
`400 x _ _ _ _ _ _ _ _ _`	Only a root can read this file.

Day 3

Quiz Answers

1. The shell enables the user to define variables and assign values to them. You can assign values to variables using the syntax:

   ```
   variable=value
   ```

   These values are used by UNIX to set up your session and also can be used for a variety of purposes.

2. When choosing variable names, you have to follow some rules. You cannot use any puncuation characters. So, a variable name of `t.n.t.` is not a valid name. If you have to separate words, use the underscore character; for example, `t_n_t`.

3. Shell variables are useful in a lot of ways. Two common ways are as placeholders for pathnames or as options to common commands.

4. The shell has no concept of data values. All values are strings as far as the shell is concerned. The value of `1`, `one`, and `1.23` are all stored in variables as strings. There is no concept of shell variables having any type of value other than strings.

5. Use the `${}` appendage construct. For example, if `a=CAT`, then

   ```
   $ b=${a}acomb
   ```

   sets the value of `catacomb` to `b`.

6. The environment variables refer to those shell variables that UNIX sets for you when you log in. Local variables are those that exist for a short time during a shell script, and that are not valid or reset to NULL after they are used up.

Exercise Answers

1. You should get an error message: `1234=value not found.`

2. Hint: Use the single quotes character, another variable

   ```
   $ value=""
   ```

3. You should see the same output as `$ls*`.
4. The `$*` was expanded to `*`.
5.
```
$ med="Medical "
$ echo $medHISTORY
$
$ echo ${med}HISTORY
Medical History
$ echo "Dow "${med}"College"
Dow Medical College
```
6. `$ echo  \ " My \$.02\ "`

Day 4

Quiz Answers

1. `$ ls ??*`
2. `$ ls *[._]*`
3. `$ ls *[0-9]*`
4. `$ touch "a*b"`

   and

   `$ touch 'a$b'`
5. `ls *`

   and

   `ls * ¦ more`

Exercise Answers

1. `$ echo *` lists all the files in your directory.

   `$ echo ?` lists all the one-character filenames.

   `$ echo ??` lists all the two-character filenames.

2. In the `$ echo "*"` command, the asterisk is expanded within double quotes.

3. `$ echo "This is a \"double quote\" and this is a \'single quote\'"`

4. `$ cat > "bad file"`

5.

`$ ls *`	Lists all the files in your current directory, and all subdirectories
`$ ls .`	Lists all the files in your current directory
`$ ls -X`	Should not do anything
`$ ls -x`	Sorts the output horizontally in a multicolumn format
`$ ls -al`	Gives a long listing of all files in your current directory, including hidden files (with a period as the first character in its name)
`$ -F`	Puts a forward slash (/) after each filename if it's a directory, and an asterisk (*) after each

Day 5

Quiz Answers

1. `x*` matches filenames beginning with `x`.

   `x*z` matches filenames starting with `x` and ending with `z`.

   `x\{1,5\}` matches `x` repeated 1 to 5 times.

   `[0-9]` matches a single digit.

   `[0-9]+` matches one or more digits.

   `[0-9]*` matches zero or more digits.

   `[Uu]nix` matches `Unix` or `unix`.

   `[Dd][eE][mM][Oo]` matches `Demo`, `DEmO`, `dEmO`, and so on.

   `c?t` matches `cat`, `cot`, `cbt`, and all words with one letter between `c` and `t`.

2. `^\([a-d]\)$` matches (a), (b), (c), or (d) on a line.

   `[0-9]{3,5}` matches three to five digits in a row.

   `[0-9]\{3,5\}` matches three to five digits in a row.

   `[A-Za-z_][A-Za-z_0-9]*` matches a shell variable declaration.

3. How would you count the number of lines with the word *magnet* in all the files that have the extension `*.txt`?

   ```
   $ grep magnet *.txt ¦ wc
   ```

4. `# wc *.txt`

5. How would you count the number of empty lines in a file?

   ```
   $ egrep "^$" filename ¦ wc
   ```

Exercise Answers

1. The regular expressions for the patterns are as follows:

   `" *tion"` for all words ending in *tion.*

   `" f*e "` for all words that begin with `f` and end with `e`.

   Five-letter words beginning with `q`:

   ```
   " q[a-z][a-z][a-z][a-z] "
   ```

   Four-letter words ending in `m`:

   ```
   " [a-z][a-z][a-z]m"
   ```

2. Match blank lines by using:

   ```
   "^$"
   ```

3. Use the following:

   ```
   [a-zA-Z_][ [a-zA-Z0-9_]*
   ```

4. You have to use two commands, and the results should be equal:

   ```
   fgrep "{" file ¦ wc -l
   ```

   ```
   fgrep "}" file ¦ wc -l
   ```

5. Use the following:

   ```
   $ who ¦ grep root
   ```

Day 6

Quiz Answers

1. `cal`, `dc`, `bc`, and `calendar` are some of the desktop utilities for calculators in UNIX for your shell. Look in the `/bin` and `/usr/bin` directories.
2. Use the date command and its options to get the current time on the UNIX system.
3. The difference is that local variables are not exported to subshells.
4. A subshell is another shell invoked on top of your shell. A shell script is executed by a subshell.
5. The difference between the two is that `()` executes its commands in a subshell and `{ ;}` executes its commands at the same level as your current shell.
6. `{ ls -s ¦ sort -n ¦ lpr }` is missing a semicolon at the end.

Exercise Answers

1. Modify the command like this:

```
3  3 * 3.141 * 3.141 3 *  -
```

(Note: The answers to exercises 2 and 3 are not provided here. Use these exercises for your practice only.)

4. `Area = (pi * r * 2 * ht) +  (pi * r * r * 2 )`

   is reduced to

```
Area = pi r 2 ht * * * pi r r 2 * * * +
```

5. Changing your `HOME` directory should not affect any of your executables except those that rely on `HOME` being set properly.

   Try these commands to see if the `cd` command uses the `HOME` variable:

```
$ myhome = $HOME
$ HOME = /etc
$ pwd
/home/kamran
```

```
$ cd
$ pwd
/etc

$ HOME = $oldhome
$ cd
$ pwd
/home/kamran
```

Now you can see how the value `HOME` affected `cd` commands' output. Try different commands such as `mail` and `pwd` to see how your system works.

Day 7

Quiz Answers

1. See the following:

`and`, `help`, and `bye`	Each is too common; they could exist as simple text in your document.
`NO_MORE_DATA`	Okay
`END_OF_DATA_HERE`	Okay
`GONZO_WAS_FRAMED`	Okay

(The last three, `NO_MORE_DATA`, `END_OF_DATA_HERE`, and `GONZO_WAS_FRAMED`, are unlikely to appear in text files, so they are better to use than `and`, `help`, and `bye`.)

2. `command 1>&2` will redirect the standard output to standard error.

3. Send output by using the following:

```
cal 1994 ¦ tee ¦ lp
```

4. Sort numbers by using `sort -n`.

5. Make a general purpose shell script. See Day 8.

Exercise Answers

1. The following commands will work:

```
$  < file1

$  nl < file

$  cat file ¦ nl

$  cat < file ¦ wc
```

2. Send more than one file by using:

```
$ (cat ch*)¦ lp
```

3. Send a one-page header by using:

```
$ (cat header; cat longfile) ¦ lp
```

4. The `ls -l` command displays a long listing of filename, owner, group, time of modification, and size in bytes. It may show information (based on your system's `ls` command defaults).

   The `ls -s` command shows the size of files in kilobytes.

5. Provide the numbered listing by using:

```
ls ¦ sort ¦ nl ¦ grep "17"
```

6. `sh` will work, implying that the path is not necessary.

   `who` will not work, implying this is a shorthand for executing a shell on this file only.

7. The `tar` command expects the filenames as arguments, not as input.

Day 8

Quiz Answers

1. Change the permissions (`+x`) on the shell script first, and then use one of the following:

   - `shellScript`
   - `sh shellScript`
   - `. shellScript`

You do not have to set the +x for the last two commands.

2. Create the script and then set the execute permissions.
3. Use the shift arguments.
4. You should suppress filename expansion when you compare special characters in strings. For example, if you want to echo the asterisk, use:

   ```
   $ echo '*'
   ```

   and not:

   ```
   $ echo *
   ```

   since the latter command will expand the asterisk.
5. You get an error.
6. The negative shift, `''`, will not expand the `$1`, and the comment in the first line is incorrect.
7. Modify the shell script by using `who ¦ grep "^$1 "`

   The space after the `1` forces the name to be a separate word, the `^` forces it to be the start of a line (to eliminate the `tty` in the terminal).

Exercise Answers

1. The shell script would be as follows:

   ```
   (banner $LOGNAME; cat $1) ¦ lp
   ```

2. The shell script would be as follows:

   ```
   echo $5
   echo $4
   echo $3
   echo $2
   echo $1
   ```

3. The shell script would be as follows:

   ```
   for i in 1 2 3 4 5 6 7 8 9 10
   do
   echo $i
   done
   ```

4. The shell script would be as follows:

```
#!/bin/sh
cat $1 >> $2
wc -l $2
```

Day 9

Quiz Answers

1. The `for` runs for a predetermined time. The `while` loop runs until a condition is no longer true. The `until` loop runs until a condition becomes true.
2. Send a `for` loop to the background by using:

```
for i in 1 2 3 4 5 6 7 8 9 10
do
echo $i
done &
```

   What about its output to `/dev/null`?

```
for i in 1 2 3 4 5 6 7 8 9 10
do
echo $i
done > /dev/null
```

3. If you want to compare shell variables that have blanks on either side of them, use quotes to set them up. For example:

```
$ a=" 1 "
$ b=" 2 "
$ if [ $a = $b ]
> then
> echo same
> else
> echo not same
> fi
same
```

To check for empty strings, try this command sequence:

```
$ a=""
$ b=" "
$ if [ $a" " = $b" " ]
> then
> echo same
> else
> echo not same
> fi
not same
```

4. Sometimes, long listings scroll by too quickly or have too many names to look for. Suppose you wanted to look for the name `group` in a listing of all the files in your `/etc` directory and its subdirectories. You would use this:

```
$ ls -R ¦ grep "group"
```

(The `-R` option lists all the subdirectories recursively.)

Another way to look for a specific file in a directory tree is to use the `find` command:

```
$ find . -name group -print
```

Exercise Answers

1.
```
for i in 1 2 3
do
     for j in 1 2 3
     do
          for k in 1 2 3
          do
          ....(your script here)...
          done

     done
done
```

2.
```
if [ ! timesNine ]
then
     break 2
fi
```

3. Yes. Do the following:

```
while [ .. ] ; do ; commands ; done
```

4.
```
# ! /bin/sh
# To periodically count the # of users on your system
# Usage: finduser [time in seconds]
mtime = GO
  if [ $# -eq 1 ] then
     mtime=$1
fi
while :
do     sleep $mtime
       echo "There are" `who -u | wc` "users"

done
```

5.
```
#!/bin/sh
#
#  Test if this is a valid shell variable name.
#
if [ $# -ne 1 ]
then
     echo "Usage: $0 variable"
     exit 1
fi

for var
do
     case $var in
          [0-9] | [0-9][0-9]*) echo "$var is a number";;
          [a-zA-Z_][a-zA-Z_0-9]*) echo "$var is a variable";;
          *) echo " I do not think $var is valid";;
     esac
done
```

Day 10

Quiz Answers

1. All user input to a `read` command is assigned to a shell variable `REPLY`. Use the man page of man `sh` to determine what the name of the variable is on your machine.
2. Nothing. Since `feet` was already set, it could not be reset.
3. The script exits with an error message of `FILE NOT FOUND` if `datafile` is not defined at this point.
4. This echoes the command to invoke either the `EDITOR` or `/usr/bin/vi` on the file specified in `$datafile`; or if `$datafile` is not set on the file called `todolist` if `defaultFile` is not null.

Exercise Answers

1.
```
for i in 'ls *'
do
     if [ -x $i]
     then
          echo "$i is executable"
     fi
done
```

   To make this into a shell script, accept its argument list to the `ls` command from the command line:

```
$ listOfFiles="$*"
```

   at the command prompt, and modify the `for` loop in the script file to read:

```
for i in 'ls $listOfFiles'
...
```

   (Note: The answers to exercises 2 and 3 are not listed here. They are for your practice only.)

4. Use the `+POS1` and `-POS2` options to the `sort` command:

```
sort + 2 - 3
```

5. Use the grep -v option to search for and print items that do not match a specification.

6. Add the menu option:

```
[L]ine print data file.
```

Add the case statement:

```
L¦l) echo "Printing $datafile."
    ------------------------------------
    ;;
```

Day 11

Quiz Answers

1. You have to have a means of stopping a process in UNIX. Signal 9 is the sure method of stopping a runaway process.

2. Pipe the output from the first sed script to the input of the next sed script. For example, this sequence of commands filters the output through three mutually exclusive filters:

```
sed -f script1 file ¦ sed -f script2 ¦ sed -f script3 > ofile
```

Exercise Answers

1. The script would be as follows:

```
[ a\ ]
```

2.
```
#!/bin/sh

year='echo $1 ¦ cut -c1-4'
month='echo $1 ¦ cut -c5-6'
zday='echo $1 ¦ cut -c7-8'

echo $zday
echo $month
echo $year
```

3. Add the calculator option in the display section:

```
[c]alculator
...
```

Add the case statement:

```
c¦c) dc
  ;;
```

4. Use calx as a starting point and then create the option as you did for Exercise 3.

Day 12

Quiz Answers

1. For simple string replacements, use sed. It's designed for that purpose. For more operations than string substitution—for example, sending the output to many files at once—use awk.
2. You are using print instead of printf. The % formatters apply in the printf statements only. The print statement does not recognize them.
3. `$1 > 10 && $3 == "dog"`
4. The default program of `{print $0 }` is substituted for missing actions. The `{ print }` program is equivalent of the `{ print $0 }` program.

Exercise Answers

1.
```
if [ $# -lt 1 ]
          then
          do
               echo "Enter filename : "
               read filename
               if [ $filename -eq "" ]
               then
                   exit 0
               fi
               awk -f nl.awk $filename
               while :
```

```
          else
..............for i
              do
                  awk -f nl.awk $filename
              done
          fi
```

Note that there may be many different solutions for this exercise. Learn what you can from this one, and invent your own method for solving this problem.

2. `regmo = ((rt/1200.0) * exp1 * regpr)/(exp1 - 1) ;`

   The main reason for not writing this statement as one line was to make the steps easy to understand and read. Use your own style and preferences to judge whether a statement should be broken into separate segments.

   Often, especially with complicated statements, it's easy to spot bugs and typos if the code segments are kept short and simple. Performance is generally not a factor unless you are doing fairly sophisticated operations, in which case your reader will be able to follow along. Just keep your code simple so that when you read it a year later, you will still be able to understand what you did. This, of course, is my own humble opinion after experiencing several hours of frustration while looking at my own code written not less than a few years ago, and not fully comprehending what it was supposed to do and how it was supposed to work.

3. Check if `field` in the colon-delimited file is blank.

4. ```
   IFS=':'
   { print $5; }
   ```

Day 13

Quiz Answers

1. The difference between the `[[ ]]` test and the `(( ))` test is that in the `[[ ]]` test, you must provide a white space in between the `[[` and the variables. In the `(())`test, you do not.

   Also, the comparison operator in the `[[ ]]` is an =, whereas in the `((..))`, it is the == operator.
   ```

Finally, you do not have to specify dollar signs ($) in the `((..))`test, but you do in the `[[ ]]` test.

2. `/???/?.?m` matches all files that are under the root directory in a directory with a three letter name, and which have a basename containing one character followed by a '.', followed by another single character.

   `*/*.[chyl]m` matches all '.c', '.h', '.y', and '.l' files in a subdirectory of the current directory.

   `~linux/*.c` matches all `*.c` files in the home directory of user '`linux`'.

3. The return $variable statement returns the value of the variable as the functions return value. For example:

```
function sqr()
     {
     (( s= $1 * $1))
     return $s
     }
```

The `return $variable` statement returns the value of the variable as the function's return value. For example:

```
function sqr()
{
(( s= $1 * $1))
return $s
}
....
s=10
x = sqr
```

4. The `$*` expands all the parameters into one long double quoted string, `"$1 $2 ..."`. The `$@` expands to `"$1", $2", ....`

Exercise Answers

1.
```
#
#
#
for i = 0 1 2 3 4 5 6 7 8 9
do
    (( j = 9 - i ))
```

```
    array[i]=$(array[j])
done
```

2. (The answer to this exercise is not provided here. This exercise is for your practice only.)

3. The output is as follows:

```
typeset x y
x=10
y=3

((z=x + y))
print "$x plus $y = $z"
10 plus 3 = 13
((z=x - y))
print "x minus y = $z"
10 minus 3 = 7
((z = x / y))
print "$x divided by y = $z"
10 divided by 3 = 3
((z = x * y))
print "x times $y = $z"
10 times 3 = 30
```

The preceding example shows how the mathematical operations work in the Korn shell.

(Note: The answers to exercises 3 and 4 are not provided here. Those exercises are for your practice only.)

Day 14

Quiz Answers

1. `mesg n` will turn the annoying messages off, and `mesg y` will allow users to write to your terminal again.

2. `"UNIX command" | getline var`

   will set the return value to `var` from the UNIX command.

3. Run crontab without the -e option. Then delete all the lines from the file, save it, and exit. On some UNIX machines, crontab -r will remove the file too.

Exercise Answers

1. For these scripts, use the crontab command to schedule these commands every week. Use the following command entries:

```
0 17 * * 1,2,3,4,5 gohome
```

```
0 2 * * 6 backmeup
```

2. Use the following at command to execute the mail message command four days from today at 1:00 p.m.:

```
$ at 1 pm now + 4 days
```

3. Use "date %D %M %Y" ¦ getline today to read the date into a variable called today in the awk program.

Index

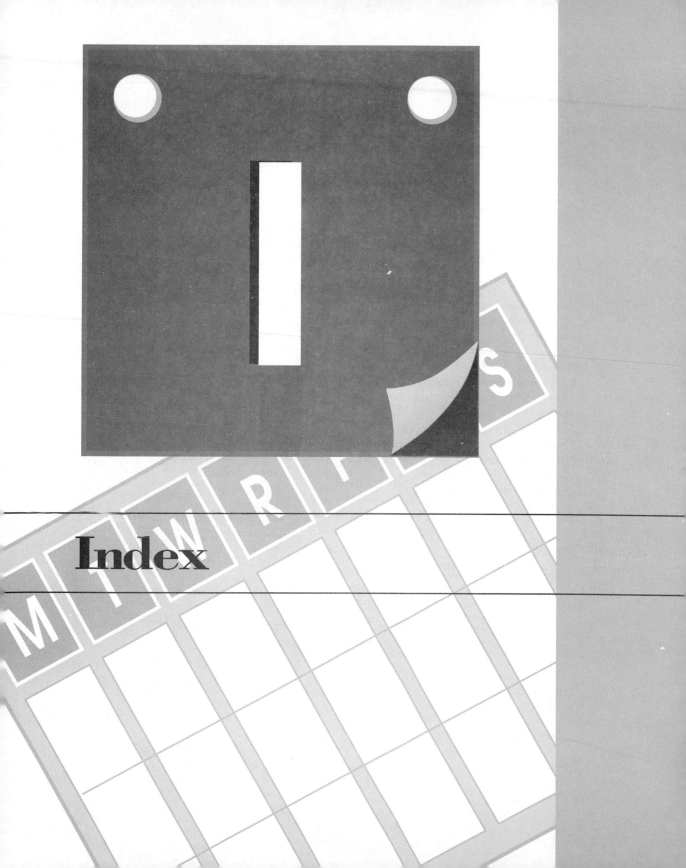

Symbols

A

B

C

D

E

F

G

H

L

M

N

O

Q

R

S

X–Z

Book ISBN 0-672-30583-6